The Indescribable God

The Indescribable God

Divine Otherness in Christian Theology

BARRY D. SMITH

☙PICKWICK *Publications* • Eugene, Oregon

THE INDESCRIBABLE GOD
Divine Otherness in Christian Theology

Copyright © 2012 Barry D. Smith. All rights reserved. Except for brief quotations in critical publications or reviews, no part of this book may be reproduced in any manner without prior written permission from the publisher. Write: Permissions, Wipf and Stock Publishers, 199 W. 8th Ave., Suite 3, Eugene, OR 97401.

Pickwick Publications
An Imprint of Wipf and Stock Publishers
199 W. 8th Ave., Suite 3
Eugene, OR 97401

www.wipfandstock.com

ISBN 13: 978-1-62032-104-1

Cataloging-in-Publication data:

Smith, Barry D., 1957 Dec 4–

The indescribable God: divine otherness in Christian theology / Barry D. Smith.

xviii + 168 p. ; 23 cm.

ISBN 13: 978-1-62032-104-1

1. Negative theology—Christianity—History of doctrines. 2. God (Christianity)—History of doctrines. 3. Fathers of the church. 4. Mysticism. I. Title.

BT148 S658 2012

Manufactured in the U.S.A.

Contents

List of Abbreviations | vii
Introduction | xiii

1 Biblical Data on God's Otherness | 1
Hebrew Bible
New Testament
Conclusion

2 God's Essence or Nature as Unknowable | 19
Hellenistic Origin of Concept
God's Essence as Unknowable in Christian Theology
Conclusion

3 God as Nameless and Not in A Genus | 56
God as Nameless
God as Not in a Genus
Conclusion

4 God as The One Who Is | 78
The Original Meaning of Exod 3:14–15
God as the One Who Is in Hellenistic Judaism
God as the One Who Is in Christian Theology
Conclusion

5 God as The Good | 100
God as Good in the Old Testament
Platonism and the Good
Synthesis of Hellenism and the Scriptures
God as the Good in Christian Theology
Conclusion

6 God as Infinite | 121
Scriptural Basis of God's Infinity
Hellenistic Origin of Concept of Infinity
God as Infinite in Christian Theology
Conclusion

7 God as Invisible | 141
The Use of the Term Invisible in Hellenism
God as Invisible in Christian Theology
Conclusion

8 Other Possibilities of Expressing The Otherness of God | 161
The Tao
Brahman
Emptiness in Mahayana Buddhism
Conclusion

Abbreviations

Alcinous, *Didask.*   *Didaskalikos (Handbook of Platonism)*
Ambrose, *De fide*   *De fide ad Gratianum Augustum (Exposition of the Christian Faith)*

Anselm

Monol.   *Monologium*
Prosl.   *Proslogium*

Aristotle

Anal. post.   *Posterior Analytics*
Categ.   *Categories*
Meta.   *Metaphysics*
Phys.   *Physics*

Athanasius

Adv. gent.   *Oratio contra gentes (Against the Nations)*
Ar.   *Orationes contra Arianos (Orations against the Arians)*
De syn.   *De synodis Arimini in Italia et Seleuciae (On the Synods of Ariminum and Seleucia)*
Decr.   *De decretis Nicaenae synodi (On the Council of Nicaea)*
Ep. Afr.   *Epistula ad Afros (Letter to the Bishops of Africa)*

Abbreviations

Augustine

Civ. Dei	*De civitate Dei* (On the City of God)
De Trin.	*De trinitate* (On the Trinity)
Doct. chr.	*De doctrina Christiana* (On Christian Doctrine)
En. ps.	*Enarrationes in Psalmos* (Expositions on the Psalms)
Fide et symb.	*De fide et symbolo* (Of Faith and the Creed)
Io. ev. tr.	*Tractatus in evangelium Iohannis* (Homilies on John)
Ser.	*Sermones* (Sermons)
Barth, *CD*	*Church Dogmatics*

Basil of Caesarea

Adv. Eunom.	*Adversus Eunomium* (Against Eunomius)
De Spiritu	*De Spiritu Sancto* (On the Holy Spirit)
Ep.	*Epistolae* (Letters)
Hex.	*In hexaemeron* (Six Days of Creation)

Boethius *De Hebd.* — *De Hebdomadibus*

Bonaventure

Comm. sent.	*Commentaria in quatuor libros sententiarum* (Commentary on the Four Books of Sentences)
Itin. men.	*Itinerarium mentis in Deum* (Journey of the Mind into God)
Calvin, *Inst.*	*The Institutes of the Christian Religion*

Clement of Alexandria

Paedag.	*Paedagogus* (Tutor)
Strom.	*Stromata* (Miscellanies)
Cyprian, *De idol. vanit.*	*De idolorum vanitate* (On the Vanity of Idols)

Cyril of Alexandria

De Trin.	*De Sancta Trinitate (On the Holy Trinity)*
Comm. in evang. Ioan.	*Commentarius in evangelium Ioannis (Commentary on Gospel of John)*
Cyril of Jerusalem, *Cat. lect.*	Catechetical Lecture

Ephraim of Nisibis

CH	*Hymns against Heresies*
HdF	*Three Hymns concerning the Faith*

Eusebius

H.E.	*Historia ecclesiastica (Church History)*
Praep. ev.	*Praeparatio evangelica (Preparation for the Gospel)*
Gregory of Nazianzus, *Or.*	Oration

Gregory of Nyssa

Abl.	*Ad Ablabium. Quod non sint tres dei (On Not Three Gods)*
Anim. et res.	*De anima et resurrectione (On the Soul and the Resurrection)*
Or. cat.	*Oratio catechetica magna (The Great Catechism)*
Con. Eunom.	*Contra Eunomium (Against Eunomius)*
In beat.	*De beatitudinibus (Homilies on the Beatitudes)*
In cant.	*In canticum canticorum (Song of Songs)*
In eccl.	*In ecclesiasten homiliae (Homilies on Ecclesiastes)*
Maced.	*Adversus Macedonianos de Spiritu Sancto (On the Holy Spirit. Against the Followers of Macedonius)*
Vit. Mos.	*Vita Mosis (Life of Moses)*

Abbreviations

Gregory Palamas

Cap. phy.	*Capita physica (Chapters Physical)*
Triads	*Triads in Defense of the Holy Hesychasts*
Herm., *Mand.*	*Shepherd of Hermas, Mandate*
Hilary, *De Trin.*	*De Trinitate (On the Trinity)*

Irenaeus

Adv. haer.	*Adversus haereses (Against Heresies)*
Demonstr.	*Demonstration of the Apostolic Preaching*
Jerome, *C. Eph.*	*Commentariorum in epistolam beati Pauli ad Ephesios (Commentary of Ephesians)*
John Chrysostom, *De incomp.*	*De incomprehensibili Dei natura (On the Incomprehensible Nature of God)*
John Calvin *Inst.*	*The Institutes of the Christian Religion*

John Duns Scotus

DPP	*Tractatus de primo principio (Treatise on the First Principle)*
Ord.	*Ordinatio or Opus Oxoniense (Oxford Lectures)*
John of Damascus, *O.F.*	*An Exact Exposition of the Orthodox Faith*

Justin Martyr

1 Apol.	*First Apology*
2 Apol.	*Second Apology*

Lactantius

D.I.	*Divinarum institutionum (Divine Institutes)*
Ira Dei	*De ira Dei (On the Anger of God)*

Maximus Confessor

Cent. gnost.	*Centuria gnostica (Chapters on Knowledge)*
Myst.	*Mystagogy*
Minucius Felix, *Oct.*	*Octavius*

Origen

Con. Cels.	*Contra Celsum (Against Celsus)*
Prin.	*De principiis (On First Principles)*
Peter Lombard, *Sent.*	*Sententiae (Sentences)*

Philo

Abr.	*De Abrahamo (On the Life of Abraham)*
Conf.	*De confusion linguarum (On the Confusion of Tongues)*
Det.	*Quod deterius potiori insidari soleat (That the Worse Attacks the Better)*
Deus	*Quod Deus sit immutabilis (That God is Unchangeable)*
Her.	*Quis rerum divinarum heres sit (Who is the Heir?)*
Leg.	*Legum allegoriae (Allegorical Interpretation)*
Legat.	*Legatio ad Gaium (On the Embassy to Gaius)*
Mos.	*De vita Mosis (On the Life of Moses)*
Mut.	*De mutatione nominum (On the Change of Names)*
Opif.	*De opficio mundi (On the Creation of the World)*
Post.	*De posteritate Caini (On the Posterity of Cain)*
Praem.	*De praemiis et poenis (On Rewards and Punishments)*
Prelim. Studies	*Preliminary Studies*
Sacr.	*De sacrificiis Abelis et Caini (On the Sacrifices of Cain and Abel)*
Somn.	*De somniis (On Dreams)*

Abbreviations

Spec.	*De specialibus legibus* (On the Special Laws)
Virt.	*De virtutibus* (On the Virtues)

Plato

Phaed.	*Phaedrus*
Rep.	*Republic*
Plotinus, *Enn.*	*Enneads*
Proclus, *Instit. theol.*	*Institutia theologica* (Elements of Theology)

Pseudo-Dionysius

Ep.	*Epistulae* (Letters)
De div. nom.	*De divinis nominibus* (On Divine Names)
Mys. th.	*De mystica theologia* (Mystical Theology)
Sib. Or.	*Sibylline Oracles*

Tertullian

Adv. Marc.	*Adversus Marcionem* (Against Marcion)
Adv. Prax.	*Adversus Praxeam* (Against Praxis)
Adv. Valen.	*Adversus Valentinianos* (Against the Valentinians)
Apol.	*Apologeticus pro christianis* (Apology for the Christians)

Theodoret of Cyrus

De incarn.	*De incarnatione Domini* (On the Incarnation of the Lord)
De Sanct. Trin.	*De Sancta Trinitate* (On the Holy Trinity)

Thomas Aquinas

SCG	*Summa contra gentiles*
Sent.	*Scriptum super libros sententiarum (Commentary on the Sentences)*
ST	*Summa theologiae*

Introduction

THE CHRISTIAN SCRIPTURES MAKE many different assertions about God that collectively can be placed under the rubric of the otherness of God: God is *other than* all created things and for that reason is incomprehensible. To understand a thing is to identify it as something; but God is beyond all human experience and for this reason cannot be identified as anything. The early church assumes Scripture's teaching about God's otherness and with the assistance of Greek philosophy further refines it with its own set of apophatic conceptual tools. The purpose of this study is to investigate how Christian theologians have expressed the biblical concept of the otherness of God; as such it is both theological and historical in nature. It becomes clear after this investigation that the rejection of ontotheology long precedes postmodernism. It should be noted that often there is little awareness of the difference between what the Scriptures affirm and its further development by Christian theologians.

Seven ways of expressing the otherness of God by Christian theologians can be identified. These concepts sometimes occur together in the same literary context and need to be disentangled. First, Christian theologians express the biblical teaching about the otherness of God by asserting that the essence or nature of God is either unknowable or that God does not have an essence or nature, unlike created things. Second, God's otherness is expressed by saying that God is nameless; in this case, the name of God is used as a synonym for God's essence or nature. God is nameless either in the sense that God's name is unknowable or that God does not have a name. A variation of this is to assert that to know God's names in the sense of the divine attributes is not to know the essence or nature of God. Third, God's otherness is expressed by asserting that God is not in a genus, which implies that God cannot be defined. Fourth, Christian theologians interpret God's self-identification as "the one who is" (ὁ ὤν) in LXX Exod 3:14 as an expression of God's otherness. God's self-revelation to Moses is said to mean first that, unlike all things, God is eternal and necessary and second, because of this, God is other than all created things. That God cannot be defined explains why simply the bare fact that God exists is revealed as God's name: the one who is. Fifth, beginning from the fact that in Scripture God is said to be good, Christian theologians further identify God with Plato's idea of the Good, which is beyond essence in the sense of being ontologically before all the good things that participate in it. God as the Platonic Good is other than all things dependent upon God for their existence and so is incomprehensible. Sixth, God's otherness is expressed by affirming that God is infinite in the sense of not being finite: God is not a substance. As infinite God cannot be defined. Finally, the otherness of God is expressed by saying that God is invisible. To say that God is invisible means not only that God is not a possible sensible object but by extension is not a possible intelligible object. God as invisible is incomprehensible either because God is not knowable in terms of human experience or because God is indefinable in principle.

In the last chapter of this investigation, three additional ways of expressing the biblical teaching of the otherness of God are briefly considered, drawn from philosophical traditions other than the Greek philosophy used by early Christian theologians. The early church's theological method of using non-biblical concepts to clarify biblical revelation is extended beyond the use of Greek philosophy. The concepts of the Tao from Taoism, Brahman from the Vedantic tradition, and emptiness (*sunyata*) from Mahayana Buddhism could profitably be used by Christian theologians in order to clarify and refine further the biblical teaching of the otherness of God.

The focus of this investigation is on primary sources. The aim is to allow Christian theologians to speak for themselves on the theme of the otherness of God, rather than to provide fodder for personal theological reflection. It is important and valuable to know how each individual theologian expresses himself on the topic of the otherness of God. In addition, this approach to the topic provides the reader with the benefit of historical perspective, which is useful as a remedy against theological presentism. Obviously no claim is made in this investigation to being exhaustive, which arguably is impossible. Instead what is presented is intended more to be representative, with priority being given to the first known expression of a position, which means that greater emphasis will be placed on the church

Introduction

fathers. Also no attempt is made in this monograph to include a critical discussion of secondary sources; given the number of Christian theologians considered from different historical periods, this would be a Herculean task and would detract from its purpose. Besides it would make this monograph cluttered and virtually unreadable. To include some secondary sources but exclude others would be inconsistent and unfair.

1

Biblical Data on the Otherness of God

In different ways the Bible expresses the idea that, in spite of his self-revelation to Israel, God always remains incomprehensible to human beings. This is because God is other than all created things and so can never be known in terms of them, as like anything. In some cases, anthropomorphic concepts are used to express this idea. The early church takes over the biblical doctrine of God's otherness, and, influenced by Greek philosophical thought, formulates a more precise and refined expression of it. Some of the texts discussed below are cited by Christian theologians in support of their view, but some are passed over.

HEBREW BIBLE

God as Holy

God as other than all things and thereby incomprehensible is expressed by asserting that God is *holy*. In the Hebrew Bible, the basic meaning of holiness is separateness (Lev 20:26).[1] Holiness is predicated of God in this non-moral sense to mean God's separateness from all things, or God's otherness.[2] In other words, holiness is that in virtue of which God is God and

---

1. The term did not originally refer to moral rectitude. The opposite of the holy is the common or profane (Lev 10:10; Ezek 22:26).

2. The same meaning occurs in this sense in Luke 1:49, "For the Mighty One has

different from what is not God.³ Because there is no such abstract term in Hebrew, the term holiness in this sense is the functional equivalent of deity,⁴ what it is to be God.

It is often affirmed that holiness belongs to YHWH⁵ and YHWH is sometimes described by the predicate nominative "holy."⁶ Also the name of YHWH⁷ is said to be holy, which is really another way of saying that YHWH is holy, since YHWH's name is the equivalent of YHWH.⁸ In Isa 6:3 the trisagion ("holy, holy, holy") addressed to YHWH by the seraphim implies that YHWH is exclusively holy, since threefold repetition is the strongest form of the superlative in Hebrew. A designation for YHWH, especially common in Isaiah, is "the holy one of Israel." This phrase denotes that God as separate from, or other than, all created things, has nonetheless freely chosen to be in a covenant relationship with the nation of Israel.⁹ In Hab 3:3, God (אֱלוֹהַ) and holy one (קָדוֹשׁ) are used synonymously in synthetic parallelism—"*God* comes from Teman, and [the] *holy one* from Mount Paran"—indicating that holiness is a synonym for deity. This

---

done great things for me—holy is his name"; Rev 3:7, "These are the words of him who is holy and true"; and Rev 4:8, "Holy, holy, holy is the Lord God Almighty, who was, and is, and is to come."

3. As H. Berkhof explains, holiness not a moral attribute that can be coordinated with other attributes, but "is rather something that is co-extensive with, and applicable to, everything that can be predicated of God" (*Systematic Theology*. 4th ed. [Grand Rapids, Mich.: Eerdmans, 1941], 73).

4. Greek, θειότης; Latin, *divinitas*.

5. קָדוֹשׁ (Exod 15:11; 2 Chr 31:18; Pss 60:6; 68:17; 89:35; 93:5; 108:7; Ezek 28:22; Amos 4:2).

6. קָדוֹשׁ (Lev 19:2; 20:26; Josh 24:19; Job 6:10; Pss 22:3; 77:13 (YHWH's way); 98:1 (holy arm); 99:3, 5, 9; Prov 30:3; Isa 5:1; 6:3; 40:25; 43:15; 49:47; 52:10 (holy arm); Hos 11:12; Hab 3:3).

7. Out of reverence for the divine otherness, Jews from the Second Temple period onwards have refused to speak the divine name, YHWH, out loud. In its place they speak the word, "Adonai," meaning "Lord." Thus יהוה (YHWH) is never written in Hebrew with its vowels (instead, the vowels of Adonai are inserted). We maintain that reverence for the holy name and the divine transcendence it connotes by rendering it without its vowels.

8. שֵׁם קָדוֹשׁ (Lev 20:3; 22:2, 32; 1 Chr 16:10, 35; 29:16; Pss 33:21; 103:1; 105:3; 106:47; 145:21; Isa 57:15; Ezek 20:39; 36:20, 21, 22; 39:7, 25; 43:7, 8; Amos 2:7).

9. קְדוֹשׁ יִשְׂרָאֵל (2 Kgs 19:22; Pss 71:22; 78:41; 89:18; Isa 1:4; 5:19, 24; 10:20; 12:6; 17:7; 29:19; 29:23 (of Jacob); 30:11, 12, 15; 31:1; 37:23; 41:14, 16, 20; 43:3, 14; 45:11; 47:4; 48:17; 49:7; 54:5; 55:5; 60:9, 14; Jer 50:29; 51:5; Ezek 39:7 (in Israel). See Holy One in Job 6:10; Prov 9:10; 30:3; Hab 1:12; 3:3).

equation explains why, when he swears by his holiness, God is really swearing by himself.[10] In these passages for YHWH to be holy is to be separate from and other than all things.

In several cases, YHWH is said anthropomorphically to dwell inaccessibly in a high and *holy* locality, sometimes identified as heaven.[11] In these contexts, the spatial metaphor of divine transcendence is used to describe God's holiness in the sense of separateness from creation, or otherness: God as holy exists above and beyond the created realm. One way in which YHWH is separate from and other than all things is that he alone is from everlasting: "Are you not from everlasting, YHWH, my God, my holy one?" (Hab 1:12). To be from everlasting (מקדם) is what separates God from his creation and makes him holy. The same point is made in Isa 57:15, where YHWH is described as one "who lives forever, whose name is holy" (שכן עד קדוש שמו).[12]

---

10. דבר / שבע בקדשי (Pss 89:35; 108:7; Amos 4:2) (see Amos 6:8; Gen 22:16).

11. Deut 26:15: "Look down from your holy habitation, from heaven" (השקיפה ממעון קדשך מן־השמים); Ps 68:5 "Is God in his holy habitation" (אלהים במעון קדשו); Ps 102:19 "For he [YHWH] looked down from his holy height; from heaven YHWH gazed upon the earth" (כי־השקיף ממרום קדשו יהוה משמים אל־ארץ הביט); Isa 57:15: "I dwell on a high and holy place" (מרום וקדוש אשכון); Isa 63:15: "Look down from heaven and see from your holy and glorious dwelling place" (הבט משמים וראה מזבל קדשך ותפארתך); Jer 25:30: "And gives his voice from his holy habitation" (וממעון קדשו יתן קולו); Zech 2:13: "For he is aroused from his holy habitation" (כי נעור ממעון קדשו); 2 Chr 30:27: "Their prayer came to his holy habitation, to heaven" (ותבוא תפלתם למעון קדשו לשמים)

12. Even though they tend not to express God's otherness in terms of God's holiness, Christian theologians still sometimes recognize the biblical understanding of holiness as separateness, or otherness. Justin Martyr contrasts the true God with the false gods, the demonic idols of the nations; influenced by biblical idiom, he writes, "Glory and praise are before his face, strength and glorying are in the place of his holiness (ἐν τόπῳ ἁγιάσματος αὐτοῦ)" (1 *Apol.* 41). He portrays God as dwelling in a holy locality, symbolizing his separateness, or otherness, in particular his true deity in contrast to demons merely posing as gods. Athanasius, arguing against the claim that pagan gods are true gods, affirms that the God whom Christians worship is the true God. Echoing the biblical meaning of God's holiness, he characterizes this God as "most holy and above all created existence" (πανάγιος καὶ ὑπερέκεινα πάσης γενητῆς οὐσίας) (*Adv gent.* 40.1–2). These two terms are coordinate in meaning, so that to be above all created existence is entailed in being most holy. By virtue of being most holy, God is other than all created things. Basil of Caesarea, in dependence on Scripture, calls God the holy one (ὁ ἅγιος), often in benedictions in his letters; he also uses the term the holy God (ὁ ἅγιος θεός) and the holy Trinity (ἡ ἁγία Τριάς). Basil views holiness as a quality belonging by nature to the triune God (like goodness). For this reason, he refers to "the holy and uncreated essence of God" (τὴν οὐσίαν τοῦ θεοῦ τὴν ἁγίαν καὶ ἄκτιστον) (*Ep.* 8.3).

The Indescribable God

God as holy is said to be completely unlike human beings, with the implication that God is incomprehensible in terms of human experience. YHWH announces to the prophet Hosea that he will never abandon Israel, in spite of the nation's disobedience. Unlike what a human being would do, YHWH will deal mercifully with the nation: "I will not execute my fierce anger; I will not destroy Ephraim again for I am God and not man, the holy one among you" (Hos 11:9) (see also 11:12 "faithful holy one").[13] The clause "I am God and not man" (אל אנכי לא־איש) is in apposition to "(I am) the holy one among you" (בקרבך קדוש). It is clear that in this passage for YHWH to be holy is be unlike a human being.[14] If God were like a human being, then God would have abandoned Israel long ago; but since he is holy, God maintains an enduring love for the nation. Likewise, when they proclaim, "Who is able to stand before YHWH, this holy God?" (יהוה האלהים הקדוש), the men of Beth-shemesh are using YHWH and "holy God" in apposition, confessing that YHWH as holy is incomparable in power (1 Sam 6:20). When it is said that "God speaks in his holiness" (אלהים דבר בקדשו), what is meant is that God speaks as God, and

---

Nevertheless, he also asserts that the angels receive holiness derivatively from the Holy Spirit (*Ep.* 159; *De Spiritu* 16 [38]). Gregory of Nyssa, influenced by Ps 99:4–5, associates God's holiness with his otherness and consequent incomprehensibility. He writes, "Still when one shall have reached the highest limit of human faculties . . . even then one must believe it is far below the glory that belongs to him, according to the words in the Psalms, that 'after exalting the Lord our God, even then you scarcely worship the footstool beneath his feet': and the cause of this dignity being so incomprehensible is nothing else than that he is holy (ἢ ὅτι ἅγιός ἐστιν)" (*Maced.*). In this context, rare in his works, for God to be holy results in being beyond human comprehension. Likewise, Gregory equates God's holiness and essence and affirms that both are without limit and so are ineffable (*In eccl.* 7.415). In this context, holiness is a synonym for the limitless essence of God. In order to prove that God is the highest good, Aquinas quotes 1 Sam 2:2 "Hence what is written in 1 Samuel (2:2): 'There is none holy as the Lord is'" (*SCG* 1.41.6). In this case he brings the non-biblical idea of the highest good into relation with the biblical understanding of holiness as separateness, or otherness: holiness as a biblical synonym for God as the highest good. In addition, second-century Gnostics used the term holy to refer to the otherness of the divine. Irenaeus explains, "And the names of the first Tetrad, which are understood to be *most holy*, and not capable of being expressed in words, are known by the son alone, while the father also knows what they are" (*Adv. haer.* 1.15). This may have tainted the usage for some subsequent theologians.

13. קדושים is an intensive plural of majesty that has a single adjective; see Prov 9:10; Josh 24:19.

14. Samuel explains to Saul that "the glory of Israel," Israel's God, is not like a human being that he would lie or change his mind (1 Sam 15:29).

so what he says is not uncertain, as when human beings speak (Pss 60:6; 108:7).

Along the same lines, YHWH announces through the prophet Ezekiel that he will prove himself or his name to be holy in the sight of the nations by bringing the people back to the land (Ezek 20:41; 28:25; 36:23). The idea is that the restoration of the nation is so difficult that no human being could accomplish it, only God. To bring the nation back is to demonstrate by means of his inimitable works that God is holy: God is not a human being but immeasurably greater. Likewise YHWH shows himself as holy in his judgment. Having holiness means that, unlike human beings, God has the right and power to bring judgment on Sidon: "Then they will know that I am YHWH when I execute judgments in her, and I will manifest my holiness in her" (Ezek 28:22). Similarly, in Isa 5:16, it is said, "But YHWH of hosts will be exalted in judgment, and the holy God will show himself holy in righteousness." The two statements are in synthetic parallelism, so that to be exalted in judgment (יגבה . . . במשפט) is synonymous with showing himself holy in righteousness (נקדש בצדקה). In other words, when he judges or brings righteousness, YHWH is exalted over creation and shows himself to be holy, or to be God and not a human being. In Ps 111:9, the psalmist attributes holiness and awesomeness to YHWH: "Holy and awesome (נורא) is his name." The implication is that to be one is necessarily to be the other.

Not only is YHWH unlike human beings, but as holy stands in contrast to the gods of the nations; the implication is that, although they exist, the other gods are nothing like YHWH, but are immeasurably inferior to him. In the Song at the Red Sea, Moses asks rhetorically "Who is like you among the gods, O YHWH, who is like you majestic in holiness, awesome in praises, working wonders?" God demonstrates his superiority to the gods by his works, in particular by his destruction of the powerful Egyptian army: "I will sing to YHWH, for he is highly exalted; the horse and its rider he has hurled into the sea" (Exod 15:11). In this context, holiness is that in virtue of which God is superior to the other gods and therefore praiseworthy. In Ps 77:13 the psalmist confesses that YHWH's way is holy: "Your way, O God, is in holiness" (אלהים בקדש דרכך); in this passage, YHWH's "way" is what YHWH is, in this case, holy, unlike the mode of being of anything else, including the other gods, which is why the author asks rhetorically: "Which god is great as God?" (מי־אל גדול כאלהים). The point is that only the way of YHWH is holy because YHWH's mode of being as

The Indescribable God

God is other than that of the other gods. Along the same lines, Hannah prays, "There is no one holy like YHWH; indeed, there is no one besides you" (1 Sam 2:2). This statement indicates that to be holy is to be absolutely unique and inimitable, even in comparison to other gods. YHWH is other than the gods of the nations.

Other Ways of Expressing God's Otherness in the Old Testament

YHWH as Obscured by a Cloud

In the Hebrew Bible, YHWH appears in or as a cloud, which functions to symbolize his otherness, insofar as a cloud conceals what is within it, rendering it obscure to onlookers. In general, the presence of YHWH is often associated with the appearance of a cloud.[15] In a cloud YHWH led Israel and protected the nation during the exodus: "YHWH was going before them in a pillar of cloud (בעמוד ענן) by day.[16] In response to the Israelites' grumbling, the glory of YHWH appears in the cloud (כבוד יהוה נראה בענן) (Exod 16:7, 10). Whereas the glory of YHWH is equated with the cloud, YHWH himself, however, remains enshrouded and obscured by it; the glory of YHWH is his self-manifestation to human beings, but is not to be identified with YHWH himself. Before the giving of the Law, YHWH reveals himself to the Israelites in a thick cloud (בעב הענן), which is actually a revelation that a revelation of himself is impossible, since a cloud is indistinct, concealing what is within it (Exod 20:21). Similarly, the Israelites may have heard YHWH's voice from the cloud but he himself remains hidden (Exod 19:9; see 24:16). In the New Testament, on the Mount of Transfiguration, the disciples heard God speak from a cloud: "Then a cloud formed, overshadowing them, and a voice came out of the cloud, 'This is my beloved son, listen to him'" (Mark 9:7).

Not surprisingly, the glory of YHWH, YHWH's special presence, manifests itself as a cloud in the tabernacle and Temple.[17] After the cloud, identified as the glory of YHWH, fills the Temple, Solomon says that YHWH dwells in the darkness (לשכן בערפל), presumably referring to

---

15. Exod 33:9–10; 34:5 Num 11:25; 12:5, 10; Deut 5:22; Ps 99:7.

16. Exod 13:21–22; see 14:19–20, 24; 40:35–37; Num 9:21–22; 10:11–12, 34; 14:14; Deut 1:33; Neh 9:12, 19; Ps 78:14; 105:9.

17. Exod 40:34–35; see Num 9:15–21; Num 16:42; 1 Kgs 8:10–11; 2 Chr 5:13–14; Ezek 10:3–4.

the darkness of the cloud that has filled the Temple.¹⁸ The idea is that, as dwelling in the tabernacle and Temple, YHWH is obscured by the cloud; nevertheless, the cloud itself is a partial revelation of YHWH and so is identical to his glory. So while YHWH does indeed dwell in the tabernacle and Temple, his otherness remains, in contrast to every other ancient Near Eastern temple where an idol representing the god and mediating its presence was placed in the *adytum*.

Cannot See YHWH

The incident when Moses is allowed to see only YHWH's back as he passed by and not his face may be interpreted as an anthropomorphic depiction of God's otherness and incomprehensibility (Exod 33:18–23). In response to his request to see his glory in Exod 33:18, YHWH tells Moses that he is forbidden to look at his face: "You cannot see my face, for no man can see me and live" (Exod 33:20).¹⁹ In this context, glory (כבד) and face (פנה) are synonymously parallel terms, each denoting what God is in himself, as opposed to God's self-revelation. So not being allowed to see YHWH's "face" can be interpreted as symbolizing the impossibility of knowing God. In other words, it is not a prohibition punishable by death, but a statement of impossibility.²⁰ Likewise, the fact that Moses is only allowed to see God's "back" (אחר) can be interpreted as symbolizing God's otherness, insofar as a person is known by his face and not his back, a non-distinguishing feature of an individual (Exod 33:23).²¹

YHWH's otherness is also implied in Deut 4:12: "Then YHWH spoke to you from the midst of the fire; you heard the sound of words, but you saw no visible form—only a voice."²² The word used for "form" (תמונה)

---

18. 1 Kgs 8:12 and 2 Chr 6:1; see Lev 16:2; Deut 31:15

19. See Exod 33:23: "My face shall not be seen."

20. Seemingly at odds with this statement is the one found a few verses earlier: "Thus YHWH used to speak to Moses face to face, just as a man speaks to his friend" (33:11). Rather than attributing this apparent discrepancy to the use of different sources, it is better to interpret "my face" (פני) in Exod 33:20 to mean something different from the use of "face" in the phrase "face-to-face" (פנים־אל־פנים), which is an idiom meaning with intimacy or unusual familiarity, parallel to "just as a man speaks to his friend."

21. In *1 Enoch* 14:21 it is said that no angel can see the face of God, who is in the holy of holies in heaven.

22. In the Hebrew Bible, however, there are numerous theophanies in which God is anthropomorphically visible to human beings (Gen 32:30; Exod 24:10–11; 33:20–23;

refers to a visible likeness; it is used in Exod 20:4 as a synonym for an idol (פסל), which the Israelites are forbidden to make. The statement that the Israelites saw no form of YHWH can be taken to mean that YHWH is not knowable to human beings as a sensible object. But, in addition, to see no form of YHWH may also imply that YHWH is incomprehensible even as an intelligible object.[23]

The "Ways," "Way," and "Thoughts and Ways" of YHWH

Moses asks to be allowed to know YHWH's "way" with the result that he would know YHWH. He says, "Let me know your way that I may know you" (Exod 33:13).[24] Knowing YHWH's way (דרך) is the semantic equivalent of knowing YHWH. Then in Exod 33:18 Moses makes a similar request, asking this time, however, not to know YHWH's way but to see YHWH's glory: "And I say, show me your glory."[25] In response to this request, YHWH explains that no one can see his face and live: "You cannot see my face, for no man can see me and live" (33:20).[26] In this context, to see YHWH's face (פנה) is the same as to see his glory (כבד), and both of these are synonymous with knowing YHWH's way. If any of these were possible for a human being, then the result would be to know YHWH. The term "ways" or "way" when used as something that belongs to YHWH has other meanings, in particular YHWH's intentions or works[27] as well as YHWH's ethical requirements for human beings.[28] But different from

---

Judg 6:22–23; 13:20–23; Isa 6:5). Early Jewish and Christian theologians interpret these as revelatory accommodations, since otherwise God could be portrayed as a sensible object (idol).

23. Detracting from this conclusion is what is said about Moses in Num 12:8, who is contrasted with other prophets to whom YHWH speaks in visions and dreams: "And he beholds the form (תמונה) of YHWH." It is arguable that "form" in Num 12:8 refers to a unique Mosaic theophany without requiring the conclusion that Moses knows YHWH as he is *in himself*. Similarly, David's statement in Ps 17:15, "As for me, I shall behold your face in righteousness; I will be satisfied with your likeness (תמונתך) when I awake" could refer to a similar beatific vision.

24. הודעני נא את־דרכך ואדעך

25. ויאמר הראני נא את־כבדך. See Ps 138:5 for YHWH's ways and glory in synthetic parallelism.

26. לא תוכל לראת את־פני כי לא־יראני האדם וחי

27. For "way" or "ways" as God's intentions and works, see Pss 18:30; 67:2[3]; 90:16; 103:7; 138:5; Deut 32:4; 2 Sam 22:31; Dan 4:37.

28. For "way" or "ways" as God's ethical requirements for human beings, see Exod

these usages, in Exod 33:13 the term "way" refers to what YHWH is, the knowing of which would be equivalent to knowing YHWH. While it is true that knowing YHWH's historical intentions for Israel would in a sense be to know YHWH, nevertheless in this passage what Moses seeks is knowledge of *YHWH himself*, not simply knowledge of his intentions. This explains the equation of YHWH's "way" with YHWH's "glory" and "face." In conclusion, to know YHWH's way is to know YHWH as he really is, as opposed to YHWH as he appears to the Israelites in his saving work; human beings, however, including even Moses, are denied access to the former, and must be content with the latter.

In Ps 77, in a time of distress, the psalmist wistfully recalls YHWH's past saving works. He writes, "I shall remember the deeds of YHWH; surely I will remember your wonders of old. I will meditate on all your work and muse on your deeds" (77:11–12). Then he confesses, "Your way, O God, is in holiness" (אלהים בקדש דרכך) (77:13). In this context, YHWH's way is equivalent to what YHWH is. The psalmist is confessing that what YHWH is, which only partially manifests itself in what YHWH does, is inaccessible to him, with the result that YHWH is incomprehensible; the implication is that YHWH is other than all the things of human experience. The psalmist then adds that, insofar as his "way" is holy, YHWH is greater than all the other gods: "Which god is great like God?"[29] YHWH's unparalleled redemptive works remembered by the psalmist derive from his "way," which is other than that of any of the gods.[30]

In Isa 55:8–9, YHWH reveals through the prophet Isaiah that his "thoughts" and his "ways" are not like those of human beings: "'For my thoughts are not your thoughts, nor are your ways my ways,' declares YHWH. 'For as the heavens are higher than the earth, so are my ways higher than your ways and my thoughts than your thoughts.'" YHWH's "thoughts" and "ways" are as much greater than those of human beings as the heavens are higher than the earth.[31] The comparison is intended to be

---

32:8; Deut 11:28; Pss 25:4, 8–9; 27:11; 51:13; 81:13; 86:11; 95:10; 119:3, 27, 33, 37; Isa 2:3; 58:2; Jer 32:39; 42:3; Hos 14:9; Mic 4:2. Often these ethical requirements are explicitly identified with the Law: Exod 18:20; 32:8; Deut 5:33; 8:6; 9:12; 10:12; 11:22; 19:9; 26:17; 28:9; 30:16; Josh 22:5; Pss 18:21; Isa 42:24; Jer 7:23.

29. מי־אל גדול כאלהים

30. See Exod 15:11: "Who is like you among the gods, O YHWH? Who is like you, majestic in holiness, awesome in praises, working wonders?"

31. See Hab 3:6: "He [YHWH] stood and surveyed the earth; he looked and startled the nations. Yes, the perpetual mountains were shattered, the ancient hills collapsed. His

superlative, since there is nothing more removed from each other than the heavens and the earth. The meaning of the concepts of YHWH's "thoughts" (מחשבות) and "ways" (דרכב) in Isa 55:8–9 are determined by Isa 55:7, in which YHWH exhorts through the prophet, "Let the wicked forsake his way and the unrighteous man his thoughts." There is an implicit contrast between YHWH's "thoughts" and "ways" and the "way" and "thoughts" of human beings, in this case the wicked. (Why YHWH has "ways," whereas the wicked has a "way" is not clear, but there does not seem to be any difference of meaning.) Since the terms "wicked" and "unrighteous" are in synonymous parallelism, one should interpret "way" and "thoughts" as synonymous terms. Together they express the central purposes and beliefs of a person. So likewise YHWH's thoughts and ways are his central beliefs and purposes. In general, as expressed by the comparison of the heavens and the earth, the difference between YHWH and human beings in regard to their respective thoughts and way(s) is absolute.[32] What YHWH believes and purposes is completely different from what human beings do. What is implied is that YHWH himself is other than human beings and so is incomprehensible.

God as Incomparable

There are several passages in the Hebrew Bible in which YHWH is said to be incomparable to other gods, with the result that he cannot be classified as one of them. This stress on YHWH's uniqueness is understandable in light of the fact that in the Bible other gods are sometimes described in terms similar to YHWH; the purpose is to correct the mistaken conclusion that YHWH is one of the gods. So it is emphasized that there are no similarities between YHWH and other gods. YHWH is also said to be incomparable to every other type of being, not just the other gods. Being incomparable to all beings is a way of expressing YHWH's otherness, which explains his incomprehensibility.

---

ways are everlasting" (הליכות עולם לו).

32. One particular difference between YHWH and human beings in this comparison is that, unlike fickle, powerless human beings, YHWH accomplishes his purposes, which is expressed as his personified word going out from him into the earth and accomplishing his will before returning to him (Isa 55:10).

Exod 15:11

In the Song at the Red Sea, Moses celebrates YHWH's victory over Pharaoh's army. Not only does he conclude that YHWH is greater than the gods, who cannot do such spectacular works, but also that YHWH is *incomparable*. He asks rhetorically, "Who is like you among the gods, O YHWH?" (מִי־כָמֹכָה בָּאֵלִם יְהוָה). Who is like you, majestic in holiness, fearful in praises, working wonders?" The expected answer is that no god is comparable to YHWH. Moses refers to YHWH's majesty resulting from his holiness (נֶאְדָּר בַּקֹּדֶשׁ), by which he means YHWH's majesty resulting from his incomparability.[33] As incomparable YHWH is other than all the gods and incomprehensible in terms of them. God's incomparability is demonstrated by the destruction of Pharaoh's army.[34] It is an argument from sufficient reason: only one is who unlike all other gods can produce such an incomparable effect (i.e., "work wonders" (עֹשֵׂה פֶלֶא)) such as this. For this reason human beings are fearfully to praise him, which is the only appropriate response to such incomparable greatness.

---

33. Similarly, in Deut 3:24, Moses prays, "O Adonai YHWH, you have begun to show your servant your greatness and your strong hand; for what god is there in heaven or on earth who can do such works and mighty acts as yours?" Based on YHWH's unprecedented acts in Israel's recent history, the conclusion invariably follows that YHWH alone is God, for no other so-called god has done what YHWH has done (Exod 7:4; 13:9, 14; 14:31; 18:11; 34:10; Deut 4:32–36; 9:29; 10:21; 11:2–3; 20:1; 32:31; Josh 2:10–11; 3:10; 4:23–24; 2 Sam 7:23; Ps 86:8; see Isa 64:4). For this reason, YHWH is described as supreme God among gods: "For YHWH your God is the God of gods and the Lord of lords, the great, the mighty and awesome God" (Deut 10:17). What is meant is that YHWH alone is truly divine and that the other gods are not in the same class as YHWH. The same line of argumentation occurs outside of the historical context of the Exodus. The narrative of Elijah's contest with the 450 prophets of Baal and 400 prophets of Asherah on Mount Carmel is intended to prove the unreality of the other gods (1 Kgs 18:17–40). Similarly, in response to his healing, Naaman confesses that YHWH alone is God: "Now I know that there is no God in all the world except in Israel" (2 Kgs 5:15) (see also 1 Kgs 20:23, 28; 2 Chr 2:5). Isaiah argues for YHWH's uniqueness based upon his power to deliver, in contrast to any other god that Israel may recognize (Isa 43:11–13; 64:4; see Hos 13:4).

34. In imitation of biblical expression, the author of the Qumran *War Scroll* confesses, "Who is like you God of Israel in the heavens or on earth who does great deeds as your deeds and marvels like your acts of power" (1QM 10.8). God proves his incomparability by his incomparable acts.

The Indescribable God

Exod 8:10; 9:14

YHWH displays his incomparability by his acts, in particular by his ability to bring upon the Egyptians the plague of frogs and then to remove them from the land. Moses tells Pharaoh to decide when the frogs would leave in order that he would know that their mass extermination was not a coincidence: "Then he said, 'Tomorrow.' So he said, 'May it be according to your word, in order that you may know that there is no one like YHWH, our God'" (כי־אין כיהוה אלהנו) (Exod 8:10). Later, in Exod 9:14, YHWH sends Moses to tell Pharaoh that there will be a plague of hail, the result of which will be to demonstrate YHWH's incomparability: "For this time I will send all my plagues on you and your servants and your people, in order that you may know that there is no one like me in all the earth" (בעבור תדע כי אין כמני בכל־הארץ). The idea is that to do such a thing is impossible for the Egyptian gods or any other being, so that the only conclusion possible is that YHWH is incomparable, which makes him other than all beings. This further implies that YHWH's acts are not like the acts of others and are "acts" only in an equivocal sense. Likewise, the use of the pronoun "me" in both assertions is an accommodation because YHWH as incomparable should not be referred to by using common pronouns since this implies that he is comparable to personal beings.

Ps 89:6–8

A hymnic description of the incomparability of YHWH is found in Ps 89:6–8 [7–9]. Angels, variously designated as those "in the skies," "the sons of God,"[35] the "council of the holy ones" and those who are "around" YHWH are said to be nothing like YHWH. The psalmist asks rhetorically, "Who . . . is comparable to YHWH, who is like YHWH?"[36] and "YHWH . . . who is like you?" (יהוה . . . כמוך). This explains why YHWH is greatly feared (נערץ) by the angels (89:7a) and appears as awesome (רבה) to them (89:7b). There is an implicit argument from minor to major in Ps 89:6–8: if angels are nothing like YHWH how much less are human beings. In fact, however, both angels and human are equally unlike YHWH because the difference between YHWH and created beings is absolute, thereby admitting no gradations. This makes YHWH incomprehensible.

---

35. See Ps 29:1 בני אלים.
36. מי בשחק יערך ליהוה ידמה ליהוה

2 Sam 7:22

After hearing the promise that he would be the founder of a dynasty, David confesses to YHWH, "There is none like you, and there is no God besides you" (כי־אין כמוך ואין אלהים זולתך). Evidence of YHWH's incomparability is his redemption of Israel and making the Israelites into his people, which is a reference to the exodus and conquest of the Promised Land (2 Sam 7:23). The assumption is that no known being could do what YHWH did, so that YHWH is incomparable. It is another argument from sufficient reason: the cause of a unique effect must be similarly unique. So any similarity between YHWH and the gods of the nations is deceptive. Because of its unique God, Israel as a people is unique among the nations.

Isa 40

As a polemic against idolatry, the prophet Isaiah asks rhetorically in synonymous parallelism, "To whom then will you liken God (אל־מי תדמיון אל), or what likeness will you compare with him (מה־דמות תערכו־לו)?" (Isa 40:18–19). The expected answer is that God cannot be likened to anything, that nothing can be said to be in the likeness of God. (The use of the future tense in Hebrew is the equivalent of "to be able.") Since God cannot be compared to anything, the futility of the practice of idolatry becomes obvious. In this context, however, "likeness" means more than external appearance or physical form, but includes also the general idea of what YHWH is, what later theologians call God's essence or nature (see its use in Gen 1:27). Somewhat later, YHWH asks through the prophet, "To whom then will you liken me that I would be his equal?" (ואל־מי תדמיוני ואשוה) (40:25). Again the expected answer is that *no one* is equal to YHWH. To be equal to YHWH is to be the same as him or at least similar enough to him to be comparable. But YHWH is other than everything so that nothing can be comparable or equal to him, which further implies that God is incomprehensible. Since he is incomparable, the use of the pronoun "me" should be understood as being used of YHWH equivocally: YHWH is not a person in the same sense that human beings, who use personal pronouns, are. As a corollary, Isaiah says that there is no searching out YHWH's understanding (אין חקר לתבונתו) (40:28), which follows from YHWH's incomparability.

The Indescribable God

Ps 145:3

In an acrostic psalm extolling the greatness of YHWH, the psalmist proclaims not only that YHWH is great but that there is no searching out of YHWH's greatness (ותלדגלו אין חקר). The reason for this is not stated, but implicitly it is because YHWH is incomparable: nothing considered great in human experience can be said to be like the full extent of YHWH's greatness. In Ps 145:4–7, the psalmist continues and provides evidence for YHWH's greatness from Israel's history: "Men shall speak of the power of your awesome acts, and I will tell of your greatness" (145:6). Such great acts, however, do not exhaust YHWH's greatness, since it is beyond searching out.

God as not Flesh, but Spirit

Through the prophet Isaiah, YHWH criticizes the Israelites for relying upon Egypt for military support when the nation should rely upon YHWH exclusively. In order to make the point of his superiority over the Egyptians, YHWH is set in contrast to what is not YHWH: "Now the Egyptians are human beings and not God, and their horses are flesh and not spirit" (Isa 31:3). The prophet uses two synthetically parallel, contrasting sets of terms to differentiate between YHWH and what is not YHWH: human beings and not God (אדם ולא־אל) and horses as flesh and not spirit (בשר ולא־רוח). The intention is to understand human beings and horses as flesh together in contrast to God as spirit.[37] It should be noted that the term "flesh" should not primarily be interpreted as meaning bodily, but created; the connotations of the term are finitude and weakness (see Gen 6:3; 2 Chr 32:8; Pss 56:4, 11; 78:39; Jer 17:5). This means that not only are horses fleshly but all created things are also. So God as spirit is the opposite of all created things. The term spirit (רוח) does not denote positively the nature of God as incorporeal, as if God were some type of ethereal being, but negatively denotes that YHWH is completely other than all created things: nothing is spirit but YHWH. For this reason אל and not אלהים is used, since the latter can sometimes be used of created beings, angelic and human. The

---

37. See Zech 4:6, "This is the word of YHWH to Zerubbabel saying, 'Not by might nor by power, but by my spirit,' says YHWH of hosts." In this passage, YHWH is not spirit but has a spirit (רוחי).

Biblical Data on the Otherness of God

conclusion follows that God as spirit is other than all created things, or flesh, and for that reason is incomprehensible.

Zophar's Apophatic Statement (Job 11:7)

Zophar, one of Job's so-called comforters, in response to Job's protestations of his undeserved suffering, asks him rhetorically whether he can find out what can be investigated about God (הַחֵקֶר אֱלוֹהַּ). The term חֵקֶר denotes an object of investigation; in this instance, it is God (אֱלוֹהַּ).[38] In other words, Zophar asks Job whether he knows enough about God to understand God's wisdom and providential dealings with him.[39] He also asks whether Job can find the limits of the Almighty (תַּכְלִית שַׁדַּי), by which is meant the full extent of the reality of God.[40] The limits of God are said to be beyond the four realms of the universe known to human beings: heaven, Sheol (underworld), earth, and sea (Job 11:8). Zophar's intention is to convince Job that the reason for his guilt that has led to his suffering is beyond his own understanding and found only in the unfathomable wisdom of God. On the assumption of the reliability of Zophar as a theologian, God's otherness is established.

Sirach 43:27–33

Jesus ben Sirach in the fourth stanza (Sir 43:27–33) of a poem extolling the works of God in creation affirms the otherness of God by asserting that the greatness of God always exceeds that of his works. Concluding his enumeration of God's great works ("more than this we will not add"), he asserts about God that "He is the all" (הוּא הַכֹּל), by which is meant that all things have their origin in God and cannot be explained without God (Sir 43:27).[41] He then says that God is greater than his works. He writes, "Let us praise him all the more since we cannot search him out, and he is greater than all his works" (וְהוּא גָדוֹל מִכֹּל מַעֲשָׂיו) (Sira 43:28). The implication is that to know creation exhaustively would still fall short of knowing the creator, since God's greatness is never completely manifested in his works.

---

38. See Job 5:9; 8:8; 9:10; 34:24; 36:26; Isa 40:28; Ps 145:3.
39. See the use of חֵקֶר in Job 38:16: "recesses of the deep" (חֵקֶר תְּהוֹם).
40. See Job 26:10; 28:3.
41. As opposed to a more pantheistic interpretation

The Indescribable God

Ben Sirach advises that a Jew praise God as much as is possible even though there are always more praiseworthy facts about God that remain unknown (Sir 43:30). In the Greek translation of his work, Ben Sirach asks rhetorically, "For who has seen him and can describe him? Or who can praise him as he is?" (Sir 43:31).[42] No one has seen God, by which is meant no one knows God as God actually is. For this reason no one can describe what God is. When they praise God, Jews should always be aware that what they are saying about God falls short of the divine reality, which implies that God is incomprehensible and other than all things.

NEW TESTAMENT

No One Has Seen the Father (John 6:46)

Jesus explains, "Not that anyone has seen the Father, except the one who is from God; he has seen the Father" (John 6:46). His meaning is not so much that God is not a possible sensible object, but that God cannot be seen in the sense of being understood by anyone other than the Son. In this context, since it is the most important of the five senses, sight functions as a metaphor for understanding: to see is to understand. Being unable to see God is an expression of the otherness and incomprehensibility of God. The reason that the Son knows God is because he has come from God (ὢν παρὰ τοῦ θεοῦ), which is not true of anyone else. Jesus makes the same point using different words: "You have neither heard his voice at any time nor seen his form (εἶδος)" (John 5:37). This may be intertextually allusive of Deut 4:12; if so then εἶδος is the equivalent of תְּמוּנָה. Unlike the generation of the exodus, Jesus' audience has not heard God's voice, but like it they have never seen the form of God. Jesus' point is that no one has ever seen God in the sense of understanding the form of God, what God is; the implication is that to see the form of God is impossible for human beings. This makes God other than all things.

At the end of his prologue, the author of the Fourth Gospel echoes this view, "No one has seen God at any time" (John 1:18). John also makes the same point in one of his letters: "No one has ever seen God" (1 John 4:12). Again, more is meant than that God is not a possible sensible object, to be seen by physical eyes; rather, the meaning is that no one has a complete understanding of God. Jesus as the only-begotten of God (or Son) alone is

---

42. τίς ἑόρακεν αὐτὸν καὶ ἐκδιηγήσεται; καὶ τίς μεγαλυνεῖ αὐτὸν καθώς ἐστιν.

said to have a complete knowledge of God; this is because he is from the bosom of the Father, which is a metaphor describing Jesus' unique relationship to God: unlike all others, Jesus is from the very presence of God (John 1:18; see Luke 16:22–23).

Dwelling in Unapproachable Light (1 Tim 6:16)

In 1 Tim 6.16, Paul asserts that God "dwells in unapproachable light." This explains why no one has seen or can see God, by which is meant that no one has comprehended or can comprehend God. By saying that God dwells in light, Paul is not thinking that God is somewhere (i.e., in a light-filled place); rather, insofar as God is nowhere in particular, his meaning is that God himself is light, which is to say that the mode of God's existence is light-like (see the parallel in 1 John 1:5: "God is light, and in him there is no darkness at all"). God is sometimes associated with light in the Old Testament. In Ps 104:2, YHWH is described as covering himself "with light as with a cloak" in a theophanic self-manifestation; it is as if God puts on a garment of light when he appears to human beings. In both cases, the manifestation of YHWH to human beings is light-like. Likewise, the prophet Habakkuk describes the theophanic appearance of YHWH at Mount Sinai as blazing sunlight: "His radiance is like light; he has rays flashing from his hand" (Hab 3:4). This is consistent with Exod 24:17, which describes YHWH's appearance to the Israelites as a fire: "And to the eyes of the sons of Israel the appearance of the glory of YHWH was like a consuming fire on the mountain top." A common idiom in the Old Testament is the light of YHWH's face.[43]

Paul's statement that God metaphorically dwells in the light, or is light, probably means that God is the source of all things. The metaphor of God as light derives from human experience of the effects of the sun's light, which, apart from much inferior moonlight, was the only real source of light in the ancient world. Sunlight is energy and gives life; without the sun's light nothing living would exist on the earth. So God's life-giving power is like the light of the sun, insofar as God gives existence to all things. Paul

---

43. In Ps 4:6; 44:3 there is a reference to "the light of your face," which is symbolic of God's lovingkindness, or saving intention. Related to this is the idea of YHWH making his face to shine upon human beings (Num 6:25; Pss 31:16; 67:1; 80; 119:135). In these cases, the manifestation of YHWH's favor to human beings is expressed as being light-like.

qualifies his statement that God is light by asserting that this light in which God dwells is unapproachable (ἀπρόσιτον), which is a metaphorical way of describing God as incomprehensible: what cannot be approached cannot ever be seen. The point is that God as the source of all things is not like any of things that derive from him. In other words, God is *other than* all things and so is incomprehensible.[44]

CONCLUSION

In the Hebrew Bible, YHWH or God is asserted to be other than all things; he is like neither human beings nor the other gods. God's otherness is expressed by asserting that he is holy, by which is meant separate from all things. It is also expressed by depicting him as appearing in or as a cloud and by saying that God cannot be seen. In addition, the "ways," "way," and "thoughts and ways" of God are inaccessible to human beings. God is said to be incomparable to both human beings and the other gods, and to be spirit and not flesh. The Book of Job and Wisdom of Ben Sirach each assert the otherness of God, and the New Testament reiterates it in different ways.

---

44. Appropriately, Josephus and Philo use the term "unapproachable" (ἀπρόσιτος) to describe Mount Sinai at the time of the giving of Law (*Ant.* 3.76; *Mos.* II.70).

2

God's Essence or Nature as Unknowable

CHRISTIAN THEOLOGIANS EXPRESS THE biblical teaching about the otherness of God by asserting that, unlike created things, the essence or nature of God is unknowable. On the assumption that, if he were like anything, God would be knowable, God is said to be other than all things. This extension of scriptural teaching ówes its possibility to Greek philosophy.

HELLENISTIC ORIGIN OF CONCEPT

The conceptual framework in which something can be said to have an essence or nature is mostly foreign to the Bible.[1] Rather it is characteristic of Greek philosophy to analyze a thing in terms of its essence or nature, distinguishing it from its non-essential or accidental qualities. For some Greek philosophers, however, this type of analysis is inapplicable to God. As a way of expressing Plato's view that "the father and maker of this universe is past finding out" (*Tim.* 28c), later Platonists assert the inaccessibility of the

---

1. The phrase θεία φύσις ("divine nature") occurs in 2 Pet 1:4. In addition, terms equivalent in meaning to essence or nature are used in christological assertions in the New Testament. The hymn that Paul cites in Phil 2:6–11 uses the term μορφή with the meaning of essence or nature, that which defines a thing (2:6). Likewise, in the hymn quoted by Paul in Col 1:15–20 the phrase εἰκὼν τοῦ θεοῦ τοῦ ἀοράτου ("image of the invisible God") occurs; its meaning is that Christ derives from and shares the essence or nature of God (1:15). Finally, the author of Hebrews uses the term ὑπόστασις to mean the nature or essence of something, in particular God (Heb 1:3).

The Indescribable God

essence or nature of God to human beings. Apuleius, for example, summarizes Plato's teaching about God as follows, "Whom he calls the heavenly, the ineffable, the unnamable, or as he says himself, *aoraton, adamaston*; whose nature (*cuius naturam*) is difficult to discover, and, if discovered, it cannot be proclaimed to the many" (*Plato* 1.5). For Apuleius, the semantic equivalent of Plato's statement in the *Timaeus* is that the *nature* of God is virtually unknowable to human beings.

Philo is the first known biblical exegete to appropriate the Hellenistic concept of the unknowability of God's essence or nature as a means of expressing the otherness of God. He says that God, whom he identifies as "the cause" (τὸ αἴτιον), "has not shown his nature (φύσις) to human beings, but keeps it invisible" (*Leg.* 3.206). He then adds, "Who can venture to affirm anything firmly about his [God's] essence (περὶ οὐσίας), or his character, or his constitution, or his movements?" (3.206).[2] In this passage, he uses "nature" and "essence" as synonyms. Each denotes what God is, which accordingly to Philo is unknowable. Similarly, Philo further explains that the human mind (νοῦς) would like to comprehend the ungraspable nature of God (τὴν ἀκατάληπτον θεοῦ φύσιν), but it cannot (*Det.* 89).[3] Along the same lines, he explains that, upon receiving the divine oracles, Abraham was spurred on to know the one God, but what he came to know was only the fact of God's existence and providential operations in the world, *not* God's essence (οὐσία), since knowledge of the latter was impossible (*Virt.* 215).[4] Philo rejects the Platonic claim that the sun in the visible realm is analogous to the good in the intelligible realm (*Somn.* I.73–76). In his view, nothing resembles God, not even the sun: "For as the Lawgiver tells us, 'God said, "Let light come into being,"' whereas he himself resembles none of the things that have come into being (αὐτὸς δὲ οὐδενὶ τῶν

---

2. In *Spec.* 1.20, Philo seems to contradict what he asserts in *Leg. all.* 3.206. He writes, "So that, transcending all visible essence by means of our reason, let us press forward to the honor of that everlasting and invisible being who can be comprehended and appreciated by the mind alone." In the former, unlike the latter, God's invisibility refers only to his incorporeity, not his incomprehensibility; God cannot be depicted as having a physical form but can nevertheless be understood by the mind. Philo seems to be influenced by Plato's contrast between what is "visible" to eyes with what is invisible to the eyes but nonetheless intelligible (νοητόν) (*Rep.* 6.509d; 7.524c).

3. Philo also holds that beyond the fact of God's existence, nothing else can be affirmed about God (τῶν δὲ γε χωρὶς ὑπάρξεως οὐδὲν) (*Deus* 62; see *Praem.* 39).

4. οὐχὶ τῆς οὐσίας—τοῦτο γὰρ ἀμήχανον—ἀλλὰ τῆς ὑπάρξεως αὐτοῦ καὶ προνοίας.

γεγονότων ὅμοιος)" (*Somn.* I.75; see I.184). He concludes, "In order to comprehend God we must first become God, which is impossible" (*Frag.* a 654).

Philo finds his view that knowledge of God's essence or nature is unknowable to human beings expressed in Exod 33. Reflecting upon Moses' request in Exod 33:13—"Let me know your ways that I may know you"—he states, "When the God-loving soul probes the question of the essence of the existent one (τὸ ὂν κατὰ τὴν οὐσίαν), he enters on a quest that is obscure and invisible (εἰς ἀειδῆ καὶ ἀόρατον)" (*Post.* 15). He interprets Moses' request to know God's ways and thereby to know God as a request to know the essence of God, whom he calls "the existent one" (τὸ ὄν), dependent upon Exod 3:14 (ὁ ὤν). He concludes that what Moses requests is impossible because the being of God is inaccessible to human beings: "That the being of God is not grasped by anyone" (*Post.* 15; see 13).[5] In this context, the adjectival phrase κατὰ τὸ εἶναι means something like according to what God really is, or God's essence or nature, and not merely God's bare existence. Philo adds that the fact that Moses requests that God show himself to him indicates Moses' awareness that "no created being is competent by himself to learn the being of God (τὸν κατὰ τὸ εἶναι θεὸν ἀναδιδαχθῆναι) (*Post.* 16).[6] Later in the same work, Philo reflects exegetically on Moses' request that God show himself to him (Exod 33:23) (*Post.* 169). He interprets the statement that Moses will see God's back but not his front as meaning that, while there is ample evidence of God's existence ("back"), God nonetheless remains incomprehensible to human beings ("front"). He finds this interpretation to be confirmed by Deut 32:39 "Behold. It is I" (*Post.* 167-68). According to Philo, when in the Song of Moses, God says "Behold. It is I," what is meant is that human beings are only capable of inferring that God exists. God did not say "Behold me," which would mean to understand the being of God (τὸν κατὰ τὸ εἶναι θεόν), which is a synonym for the essence or nature of God. He writes, "He does not say, 'Behold me,' for it is wholly impossible that God according to his essence should be perceived or beheld by any creature, but he says, 'Behold! it is I,' that is to say, behold my existence" (*Post.* 168). As a generalization, he states, "So as to pursue investigations into the essence or qualities of

---

5. ὅτι ἀκατάληπτος ὁ κατὰ τὸ εἶναι θεὸς παντί.

6. Philo has "show me yourself" (ἐμφάνισόν μοι σεαυτόν) rather than the LXX's "show your glory" (Δεῖξόν μοι τὴν σεαυτοῦ δόξαν). Presumably for him these are equivalent in meaning.

God (περὶ οὐσίας ἢ ποιότητος), is an absolute piece of folly" (*Post.* 168). Along the same lines, Philo interprets YHWH's statement that no one can see his face and live (Exod 33:20) to mean that it is impossible for someone "to set his gaze upon the supreme essence" (τὴν δ' ἡγεμονικὴν οὐσίαν) (*Fug.* 161–65; see *Leg.* I.51). No doubt he intends to preclude the possibility of seeing with the mind. In another work, Philo explains that Moses already knows that God exists, so that in asking to see God's glory (Exod 33:18), he is supposed to be seeking to know what God is according to his essence (κατὰ τὴν οὐσίαν) (*Spec.* I.41). This request is denied because what Moses desires is impossible to obtain: "But not only is the nature of mankind, but even the whole heaven and the whole world is unable to attain to an adequate comprehension of me" (*Spec.* I.44).

GOD'S ESSENCE OR NATURE AS UNKNOWABLE IN CHRISTIAN THEOLOGY

Synopsis

Like Philo, Christian theologians make use of the conceptual tool of the unknowability of God's essence or nature originating in Greek philosophy in order to express the otherness of God.[7] Sometimes a synonymous term for essence or nature is used. Once it becomes part of the tradition, the assertion that the essence or nature of God is unknowable becomes generally accepted until the modern period, when Hellenistic categories fall into disrepute among theologians. The view that God's essence or nature is unknowable is most vigorously argued by the Cappadocian fathers in their dispute with neo-Arians. Eunomius' claim that God's essence is ingenerateness prompts the apophatic response that becomes Christian orthodoxy. In the medieval period, Aristotelian epistemology is used for the purpose of further clarifying how and why the essence of God is unknowable.

Christian theologians assert that God's essence or nature is beyond human comprehension. Human beings are assumed to lack the cognitive resources to comprehend God and, correlatively, human language is said to

---

7. Origen remarks apologetically, "And further, we are not to imagine that a truth adorned with the graces of Grecian speech is necessarily better than the same when expressed in the more humble and unpretending language used by Jews and Christians, although indeed the language of the Jews, in which the prophets wrote the books which have come down to us, has a grace of expression peculiar to the genius of the Hebrew tongue" (*Con. Cels.* 7.59).

be a woefully inadequate tool to express the essence or nature of God. From the fact that the essence or nature of God is unknowable, the conclusion is drawn that God has nothing in common with creation, from which it follows that God is other than all things. God is not to be considered a knowable being among other knowable beings. This is God's separation from all things. On this basis God is said to be immeasurably great or immense. Sometimes an argument from minor to major is offered for the position that a knowledge of God's essence or nature is inaccessible to human beings. If what God has made cannot be understood by human beings, how much less can the essence of God be understood. A distinction is often made by Christian theologians between knowing *that* God exists and knowing the essence or nature of God: while the former is possible, the latter is not. A further distinction is made between God's essence or nature and what God does, identified as God's accidents, works, effects, energies, or some other synonymous term. The latter is knowable, while the former is inaccessible to human beings. This distinction becomes further refined and elaborated as Christian theology evolves. No divine attribute, such as ingenerateness, can be said to express the divine essence or nature. Even the name "God" is not an expression of the divine essence, but denotes only what God *does*. It should likewise not be thought that the divine essence is the totality of the predicates attributed to God, as if collectively they were the essence. Along the same lines, a difference is sometimes posited between knowing God's essence or nature and knowing things about God or about God's essence or nature.[8] The various predicates attributed to God in Scripture are explained as statements of the latter and not the former.

Although this is not as clearly developed, Christian theologians sometimes state or at least imply that the reason that the essence or nature is unknowable is because God does not actually have an essence or nature. The fact that there is nothing to know explains why the essence or nature of God is unknowable. It follows that God is unknowable in principle, which is to say indefinable. This is also expressed by saying that God is not an essence. The same point is made by saying that God is beyond essence or created existence in the sense of surpassing it. Another way of expressing this is to say that God is above essence, superessence, superbeing, or supernatural

---

8. This is contrary to Barth who seems to hold that God's essence is God's self-revelation. He writes, "He [God] can be known of and by Himself. In His essence, as it is turned to us in His activity, He is so constituted that He can be known to us" (*CD* 2/1: 65). The translation used is that of G. T. Thomson *et al.* (Edinburgh: T. & T. Clark, 1936–77).

The Indescribable God

nature.[9] It is explained that God as the source of all is not *a* being that can be circumscribed, which is to say, distinguished from other beings. In other words, the cause of all created things and their essences cannot be like any created thing. It is also explained that, because he metaphorically encloses all things, but is enclosed by nothing, God is other than all the things that are enclosed and so cannot be defined as one thing and not another. Finally, sometimes God's simplicity (the idea that God is not composed of parts) is used to explain why God is unknowable in principle: what is incomposite cannot have predicates and so God cannot be said to have an essence or nature as this would require predication. In other words, being simple precludes being definable insofar as a definition would add something to the subject (God) with the result that God would be a composite of subject and predicate. It happens that Christian theologians assert both that God does not have an essence or nature at all and that God's essence or nature is unknowable because, although it exists, it is beyond human comprehension without recognizing the difference in meaning between these two propositions and even their mutual exclusivity.

It follows that the theophanies in Scripture cannot be interpreted literally as the actual appearance of God to human beings, since this would imply that God's essence or nature is knowable.[10] John 1:18 "No man has seen him, nor can see" is interpreted to mean that God cannot actually be seen and Hos 12:11 "I have multiplied visions" is said to refer to God's theophanic accommodations to created beings. The fact that God's essence or nature is unknowable is the rationale for the adoption of the *via negativa*, the theological method of describing God only by negation, by what God is *not*. Paradoxically it is asserted that to know God is not to know God.

In some cases there is a concern to ground in Scripture the assertion that the essence or nature of God is unknowable. Of course, no passage from Scripture can be cited that explicitly states that the essence of nature of God is unknowable. Rather the exegetical goal is to demonstrate that what is being asserted is an extrapolation from Scripture and not a foreign body awkwardly interpolated into it. Some of the texts cited can reasonably be interpreted to support this position, whereas other alleged scriptural

---

9. Another way of expressing that God's essence or nature in unknowable is to assert God's transcendence (ὑπεροχή), by which is meant that God is beyond all conceptual categories. See Clement of Alexandria, *Strom.* 7.5; Irenaeus, *Adv. haer.* V. 2.3.

10. In the modern period, G. Kaufman distinguishes between the real referent for God and the available referent (*God the Problem* [Cambridge, Mass.: Harvard University Press, 1972], 82–115).

support is less convincing. As with Philo, Exod 33:20, "You cannot see my face, for no man can see me and live," is interpreted to mean that the essence or nature of God is unknowable. Likewise, Moses' entrance into the darkness in Exod 20:21, "the darkness where God was," is said to symbolize that what God is will always be incomprehensible to human beings. Another supporting scriptural text associating God with darkness is Ps 18:11 "He made darkness his hiding place." The Bible's proscription of idolatry is said to be the prohibition against any comparison of God with created things on the assumption that God has no knowable essence or nature. Jeremiah's statement that God is "the one who draws near" (Jer 23:23) is interpreted in terms of God's power and not essence, since God's essence cannot be known. Other passages from Scripture thought to assert or imply that God's essence or nature is unknowable include Exod 33:7; Judg 13:22; Job 11:7; 33:23; Ps 139:6; 145:3; Eccl 5:2. New Testament passages cited as supporting the assertion that the essence or nature of God is unknowable include 1 Tim 6:16 "whom no man has seen or can see" and John 1:18 "No man has seen him, nor can see." In both cases "to see" is interpreted to mean to understand with the mind. Another passage used is Rom 11:33 "How unsearchable are his judgments and unfathomable his ways," which is taken to imply that God is unknowable. Other New Testament passages that are said to imply that the essence or nature of God is unknowable are 1 Cor 2:9; 13:12; Phil 4:7; and 2 Cor 9:15.

Individual Christian Theologians on God's Essence or Nature as Unknowable

Irenaeus

Criticizing his Gnostic opponents for positing the existence of an unknown God beyond the creator, Irenaeus explains that the one true God is not concealed from human beings but is known to them by means of his creative effects. He writes, "He has come within reach of human knowledge . . . we should know that he who made, and formed, and breathed in them the breath of life, and nourishes us by means of the creation, establishing all things by his word, and binding them together by his wisdom" (*Adv. haer.* III.24.2). Irenaeus includes, however, an important proviso to his statement of the knowability of God. For him the one God is known *only* as his creative effects, for there is no knowledge "with regard to his greatness, or with regard to his essence (*non secundum magnitudidem, nec secundum substantiam*), for that has no man measured or handled." His point is that, although, contrary to his Gnostic opponents, it is possible to know *that* God is, no one can know *what* God is and therefore how great God really is. This is expressed by saying that God's essence, or what God is, is unknowable. Rather, one can only know God by what God has done.[11]

Clement of Alexandria

Clement of Alexandria holds that God's essence or nature is inaccessible to human beings with the result that God is incomprehensible. He makes a distinction between "saying God" (τὸν θεὸν εἰπεῖν), by which is meant stating what God is essentially, and "saying things about God" (τὰ περὶ θεὸν εἰπεῖν), which is to state what is true of God non-essentially and relationally, the equivalent of what God *does* rather than what God *is* (*Strom.* 6.17). In other words, he distinguishes between God's essence (οὐσία) and the many accidents (συμβεβηκότα) that can be attributed to God. He calls the former the truth itself, which is inaccessible to human beings, different from the latter, which he calls partial truths (τὰς ἐπὶ μέρους ἀληθείας). For him, it is impossible for philosophers to know the essence of God, which means that for human beings God will always be unknowable.

Similarly, interpreting Jer 23:23–24, "I am the God who draws near," Clement distinguishes between the unknowable essence of God and the knowable power of God. He claims that, although he "is in essence remote" (πόρρω μὲν κατ' οὐσίαν), God is the one who draws near in power (δύναμις) (*Strom.* 2.2). By power he means what God does. For Clement, it is axiomatic that human beings can never comprehend what God *is*, the essence of God: "For how is it that what is begotten can have approached the unbegotten" (τὸ ἀγέννητον) (2.2). God, as unbegotten, is absolutely unlike what is begotten. Nevertheless, human beings constantly experience the power of God in the sense of the creative and sustaining effects of God. He writes, "For the power of God is always present, in contact with us" (2.2). In this context, Clement interprets Moses' request in Exod 33:18 "Show me your glory" to mean that God cannot be known through human

---

11. See *Adv. haer.* IV.20.1 "As regards His greatness, therefore, it is not possible to know God, for it is impossible that the Father can be measured" and II.13.4 "He is, however, above these properties, and therefore indescribable."

wisdom, but only revelation (2.2).¹² Not surprisingly, he describes God as "difficult to grasp and apprehend, ever receding and withdrawing from him who pursues" (2.2).¹³

Clement states that human beings have no relation to God, by which he means that they are completely unlike God with respect to nature: "being by nature wholly estranged" (καὶ φύσει ἀπηλλοτριωμένων πανλελῶς) (*Strom.* 2.16). For this reason God is incomprehensible to human beings: God is not like anything in human experience. In spite of being unlike God with respect to nature, human beings are nevertheless objects of God's mercy, which is proof of God's goodness. (Clement assumes that like is only attracted to like, which makes God's mercy unusually great.) The only connection human beings have to God is that they are products of God's creative will.

Origen

Origen asserts that "God is unknowable and inestimable," which are synonymous expressions, each referring to God's incomprehensibility. The reason that God is incomprehensible is said to be that God's "nature (*natura*) cannot be grasped or seen by the power of any human understanding" (*Prin.* 1.1.5). Origen makes a distinction between the nature of God and the "works of divine providence" (*opera divinae providentiae*), or God's effects in creation. Whereas the former cannot be known, the latter can be known and used to formulate an inadequate idea of God, a pragmatic substitute for the unknown nature. He compares God to the sun, upon which human beings cannot look, and God's works to the rays of the sun at which human eyes can look (*Prin.* 1.1.6). He even states his agreement with Celsus who favorably quotes Plato's *Timaeus* to the effect that it is difficult to know God and even more difficult to make God known (*Tim.* 28c) (*Con. Cels.* 7.42). Origen also describes God as the one "who contains the whole of all things"

---

12. Clement interprets Paul's disclosure that he was taken into the third heaven and heard unutterable things to support the view that human language is inadequate to express what God is. He writes, "To these statements the apostle will testify: 'I know a man in Christ, caught up into the third heaven, and thence into Paradise, who heard unutterable words which it is not lawful for a man to speak,'—intimating thus the impossibility of expressing God, and indicating that what is divine is unutterable by human power" (*Strom.* 5.12).

13. δυσάλωτόν τι χρῆμα καὶ δυσθήρατον, ἐξαναχωροῦν ἀεὶ καὶ πόρρω ἀφιστάμενον τοῦ διώκοντος.

(τὸν περιέχοντα τὰ ὅλα) (*Con. Cels.* 4.92). The implication is that God is not one of the things that are contained, which may be taken to imply that God does not have an essence or nature at all, not simply that it is too great to be known.

Athanasius

Athanasius holds that the essence or nature of God is unknowable, and he seems to mean by it both that God does not actually have an essence or nature and that, although it exists, the divine essence or nature surpasses human comprehension. In some passages he makes statements that imply that God does not have an essence or nature. He asserts that God is "the one who is beyond all essence and human power of thought" (*Adv. gent.* 2.1; see *Ar.* 2.32: "the inability of human nature to comprehend God").[14] For God to be "beyond essence" means that human beings can never know what God is and thereby define God. As implied by the phrase "beyond all essence" (ὑπερέκεινα πάσης οὐσίας), Athanasius may in fact be saying that God has no essence, not simply that human beings cannot know the divine essence. Likewise, he refers to God as being beyond all created existence (ὑπερέκεινα πάσης γενητῆς οὐσίας), the implication being either that God is nothing like the essence of any created thing or that God has no essence at all since only a created thing has an essence (see *Adv. gen.* 35.1 "by nature invisible and incomprehensible, having his being beyond all created existence"). In order to preclude God as a possible object of knowledge, Athanasius describes God metaphorically as that which encloses all things rather than being a thing enclosed; as such God is self-existent, whereas all things depend on God's goodness and power for their existence. He writes, "But God is self-existent, enclosing all things, and enclosed by none" (*Decr.* 11.3).[15] Conceiving God as that which encloses all things implies that God does not actually have an essence or nature, since to have an essence or nature belongs only to what is enclosed by God.

In other passages Athanasius speaks as if God has an essence or nature that is unknowable. He refers to God as being "the invisible and ungraspable essence" (τὴν ἀόρατον αὐτοῦ καὶ ἀκατάληπτον οὐσίαν), presumably on the assumption that God has an essence (*Decr.* 22.1). In this context

---

14. ὁ ὑπερέκεινα πάσης οὐσίας καὶ ἀνθρωπίνης ἐπινοίας ὑπάρχων.

15. ὁ δὲ θεὸς ὤν ἐστι καθ' ἑαυτὸν περιέχων τὰ πάντα καὶ ὑπ' οὐδενὸς περιεχόμενος.

"invisible" and "ungraspable" are synonyms, referring to the unknowability of what God is, the essence of God. He also says that it is impossible "to comprehend what the essence of God is" (τί ποτέ ἐστιν ἡ τοῦ θεοῦ οὐσία) (22.3).[16] Any designation attributed to God can never be understood as univocally applicable because God as enclosing all things is "yet outside of all in his own nature" (*Decr.* 11.3).[17] In other words, God's nature, which Athanasius seems to assume exists, even though it is arguable that what encloses all things has no essence or nature, is so different from all things that are enclosed by God that nothing in human experience can be compared to God. In his view, God as that which encloses is different in kind from all the things that are enclosed. This then disqualifies all anthropomorphic, pagan gods from being considered as true gods (*Adv. gent.* 40.1–2). In addition, he holds that inferential and indirect evidence of the existence and even the nature of God is possible from knowledge of created things (*Adv. gent.* 35.1–3).[18]

Ephraim of Nisbis

Ephraim of Nisibis holds that the divine essence is concealed from human beings and for that reason is ineffable, which makes God incomprehensible (*CH* 48.4). Alluding to Job 33:23 "If there is an angel as interpreter for him," he writes in his *Hymns against Heresies*, "It is concealed from all in all respects. And if he willed not to set himself plainly forth unto us, there is none among the creatures that could serve as interpreter to him." To be an interpreter of God is to be in a position to explain what God is to human beings, but no created being qualifies for that role. Likewise, in his *Three Hymns concerning the Faith* Ephraim asserts that between God the

---

16. Since God is simple (incomposite), Athanasius argues that to say that the Son is "from the Father," as the Arians prefer, and "from the essence of the Father" mean the same thing (*Decr.* 22): "Therefore let no one be startled on hearing that the Son of God is from the essence of the Father; but rather let him accept the explanation of the fathers, who in more explicit but equivalent language have for 'from God' written 'of the essence.' For they considered it the same thing to say that the Word was 'from God' and 'from the essence of God.'" The advantage of the latter expression, however, is that it eliminates the possibility of Arian equivocation.

17. ἔξω δὲ τῶν πάντων πάλιν ἐστὶ κατὰ τὴν ἰδίαν φύσιν.

18. According to Athanasius, the assertion of the unknowability of God must be qualified since human beings are unique among God's creatures insofar as they alone are made according to God's own image. This enables human beings to have a partial knowledge of God (*Adv. gent.* 2.1).

creative essence and the creature there is an unbridgeable gap, so that God must always remain incomprehensible (*HdF* 1.6). He argues from minor to major that, if earthly things are impossible to understand, how much less understandable is God, who is above the earth.

Cyril of Jerusalem

Cyril of Jerusalem insists that human beings are so constituted that they can have only a partial knowledge of God. He writes, "For we explain not what God is but candidly confess that we do not know accurately that which concerns him" (*Cat. lect.* 6.2). Not to know what God is (τὸ, τί ἐστι θεὸς) and not to know accurately that which concerns God (τὸ ἀκριβὲς περὶ αὐτοῦ) are synonymous with not knowing the essence or nature of God. This explains why God is incomprehensible to human beings. Cyril concludes that human beings do not speak all they could and ought to speak about God (ὅσα δεῖ περὶ θεοῦ) because of their inherent cognitive limitations: "For of God we speak not all we ought (for that is known to him only), but so much as the capacity of human nature has received, and so much as our weakness can bear." He explains paradoxically that not to know God is actually to know God: "For in what concerns God to confess our ignorance is the best knowledge." Human knowledge of God consists in knowing that all assertions about God fall short of the divine reality.

Cyril extrapolates from Job's confession in Job 11:7 to the conclusion that it is impossible to comprehend God: "Will you find a footstep of the Lord? says Job, or have you attained unto the least things that the Almighty has made? If the least of his works are incomprehensible, shall he be comprehended who made them all?" (*Cat. lect.* 6.9).[19] If, as Job ultimately confesses, human beings cannot understand what God has created, how much less can they understand the creator? Cyril then argues similarly from minor to major from two other scriptures to the conclusion that God is incomprehensible. First, citing 1 Cor 2:9 "What the eye has not seen nor the ear heard" [Isa 64:4; 52:15], he asks, "If the things which God has prepared are incomprehensible to our thoughts, how can we comprehend with our mind himself who has prepared them?" Likewise, quoting Rom 11:33 "Oh, the depth of the riches both of the wisdom and knowledge of God. How unsearchable are his judgments and unfathomable his ways," he asks

---

19. Cyril has interpreted τὰ ἔσχατα to mean the least, not the utmost.

rhetorically, "If his judgments and his ways are incomprehensible, can he himself be comprehended?" (*Cat. lect.* 6.9).

Cyril of Alexandria

Cyril of Alexandria holds that "it is impossible to say anything about God according to essence" (ἐπὶ θεοῦ τί ἐστιν εἰπεῖν ἀδύνατον κατ' οὐσίαν) (*De Trin.* 3). It seems that the reason for the impossibility is that God is beyond essence (τὸ ὑπὲρ οὐσίαν) in the sense of not having an essence at all (*De Trin.* 3). Cyril also writes that God is beyond all beings and even beyond being itself (ὑπὲρ πάντα τὰ ὄντα καὶ ὑπὲρ αὐτὸ δὲ τὸ εἶναι ὤν) (*De Trin.* 3). His meaning is that God is not *a* being, but more than that, that God cannot even be said to *exist* since only beings exist. For this reason he calls the divine infinite and incomprehensible (ἄπειρον . . . καὶ ἀκατάληπτον). By infinite he means that God is not limited by having an essence; being infinite then explains why God is incomprehensible. Any discourse about God must be about something other than the essence of God.

Cyril also speaks as if God has an essence or nature but that it is unknowable to human beings. He refers to God as "the nature that is above all" (ἡ ἐπὶ πάντας φύσις), and explains that human beings can only speak about God inadequately (*Comm. in evang. Ioan.* II.5; 1.295). He makes the statement that the greatness of the divine nature is proclaimed by creation (τὸ μεγαλεῖον τῆς θείας . . . φύσεως) (*De Trin.* 1). In addition, he writes that while the existence of God is evident, what God is with respect to essence and nature is not (see *De Trin.* 1, 3).[20] (Cyril uses the terms "nature" and "essence" as synonyms.) His view is that, although God's existence and greatness is evident from creation, the full extent of God's greatness is unknown since God's essence and nature is unknowable. Cyril distinguishes between two ways of speaking about God: negatively, by denying that God is something, or affirmatively, by stating "the things about the nature" (τὰ περὶ τὴν φύσιν), by which he means God's attributes, or what God does (*De Trin.* 3). He stresses that whatever is said about God affirmatively is not the nature (ὅσα δὲ λέγομεν ἐπὶ θεοῦ καταφατικῶς, οὐ τὴν φύσιν) (*De Trin.* 3). In other words, in making statements about God one can either deny that God has some positive quality, such as saying that God is ingenerate, unoriginative, unchangeable, or imperishable, or affirm that

---

20. He writes, τί δέ ἐστι κατ' οὐσίαν καὶ φύσιν, ἀκατάληπτον τοῦτο παντελῶς καὶ ἄγνωστον (*De Trin.* 3).

The Indescribable God

God has the attributes of being good, righteous, wise etc., what he calls "the things about the nature." These positive qualities describe how God relates to created things: they are *about* the nature but not *expressive* of the nature. What is not possible for human beings is to state positive knowledge of the essence or nature of God.

Hilary of Poitiers

Hilary of Poitiers asserts that God has a nature (*natura*) that is impossible to understand and express with words. He writes, "This is a true statement of the mystery of that unfathomable nature (*hoc imperspicabilis naturae nomen*) which is expressed by the Name 'Father': God invisible, ineffable, infinite. Let us confess by our silence that words cannot describe him; let sense admit that it is foiled in the attempt to apprehend, and reason in the effort to define" (*De Trin.* 2.6).[21] The term "nature of God" denotes what God is. What God is, according to Hilary, is always inaccessible to human understanding. All that remains open for a human being is to abandon any attempt to define God ("express with words") and so remain silent. Likewise Hilary refers to God's nature as "unapproachable, invisible, inviolable, ineffable, and infinite" (*De Trin.* 11.4). These negative terms are roughly synonymous, each referring to the incomprehensibility of God's nature. Not surprising, Hilary holds that nothing created can be compared to God: "There can be no comparison between God and earthly things" (*comparatio enim terrenorum ad Deum nulla est*) (*De Trin.* 1.19).

Basil of Caesarea

Because of his apophatic theological emphasis, Basil of Caesarea is accused by his Arian opponents of worshipping what he does not know.[22] In his response to this charge, he argues that this is inevitable since God's essence (οὐσία) is unknowable. He writes, "I do know that he [God] exists; what his essence is, I look at as beyond intelligence" (ὑπὲρ διάνοιαν)

---

21. In reference to not being able to understand the relation between God the Father and God the Son, Hilary makes the interesting remark that, "the proper service of faith is to grasp and confess the truth that it is incompetent to comprehend its object" (*De Trin.* 2.11)

22. This was a stock accusation against those who deny that the divine essence could be known, a type of *reductio ad absurdum* argument.

God's Essence or Nature as Unknowable

(*Ep.* 234.2). He quotes John 1:18 "No man has seen God at any time" to make his case, interpreting the passage to mean that God is unknowable even as an intellectual object, being beyond intelligence. Basil differentiates between the divine attributes and the essence of God: "We say that we know the greatness of God, his power, his wisdom, his goodness, his providence over us, and the justness of his judgment; but not his very essence" (αὐτὴν τὴν οὐσίαν) (*Ep.* 234.1). According to Gregory of Nyssa, contrary to the claim of the heretics, Basil holds the view that the divine nature "transcends reason" (ἀκατανόητον) and for this reason is "the unapproachable and lofty nature" (τῆς ἀπροσπελάστου καὶ ὑψηλῆς φύσεως) (*Con. Eunom.* 2.1.138). To transcend reason means to be beyond intelligibility. The adjectives "unapproachable" and "lofty" appropriately describe how God's nature is unknowable insofar as it is beyond all possible human experience.

Behind Basil's denial that the divine attributes collectively express the essence of God is his view that God is simple: what is incomposite cannot have one or more attributes, from which it follows that God cannot be defined as "something." He considers the Arian Eunomius' view that God's essence is to be ingenerate as naïve, insofar as he does not recognize a distinction between God's energies (αἱ ἐνέργειαι), what God does, the semantic equivalent of the divine attributes, and God's essence (*Ep.* 234.3).[23] He writes, "The energies are various, and the essence simple, but we say that we know our God from his energies, but do not undertake to approach near to his essence. His energies come down to us, but his essence remains inaccessible" (ἡ δὲ οὐσία αὐτοῦ μένει ἀπρόσιτος) (*Ep.* 234.1). What knowledge of God exists for human beings, which is the basis of their worship of God, is only of the divine energies, never the essence, because God is incomprehensible. In Basil's view, God's attributes singly or collectively cannot describe the essence of God because God is one and simple (see *Adv. Eunom.* II.29). Whether Basil is aware of it or not, the assertion that God is one and simple could be interpreted as implying that God does not have an essence or nature at all, since to have one would necessitate being composite: God would be distinguishable from his essence or nature. Being simple would explain why the essence of God is unknowable: it does not exist to be known.

23. Eunomius taught the intelligibility of the divine essence: "God knows no more of his own substance, than we do; nor is this more known to him, and less to us: but whatever we know about the divine substance, that precisely is known to God; on the other hand, whatever he knows, the same also you will find without any difference in us" (Socrates, *Church History* IV.7). To be ingenerate expresses the nature of God.

The Indescribable God

Gregory of Nazianzus

Using the biblical example of Manoah, Gregory of Nazianzus argues from minor to major in order to prove that the nature of God is unknowable to human beings. He writes, "And are you not amazed at Manoah the judge . . . saying, 'We are undone, O wife, we have seen God' [Judg 13:22], speaking as though even a vision of God could not be grasped by human beings, let alone the nature of God" (μὴ ὅτι γε φύσεως) (*Or.* 28.19). By the term "nature" Gregory means what God is; his view is that God's nature is beyond human understanding. Gregory further asserts, "The divine (τὸ θεῖον) cannot be apprehended by human reason, and that all its completeness (ὅλον ὅσον) cannot be represented" (*Or.* 28.11). Echoing Aristotle, he emphasizes that the reason for this is not that God withholds such knowledge out of envy, since this would be incompatible with the divine nature as passionless and good.[24] Rather, his view is that, if it were possible for a human being to apprehend the divine, God would willingly disclose such knowledge, but it is not possible. For Gregory any comprehension of God would mean that God is circumscribed, which is contradictory since God is by definition uncircumscribed: "The divine would be altogether circumscribed (τὸ περιγραπτὸν πάντως εἶναι τὸ θεῖον), if he were even comprehensible in thought: for comprehension is one form of circumscription (ἓν γὰρ περιγραφῆς εἶδος καὶ κατάληψις)" (*Or.* 28.10).[25] To comprehend an object is to know what it is and what it is not, which is to say, to circumscribe it. God, however, is uncircumscribed, which means that no one can comprehend either what God is or what God is not. To say that God is uncircumscribed in fact may be interpreted as implying that God has no nature at all, since to be circumscribable is to be definable.

Gregory of Nyssa

Gregory of Nyssa repeatedly and with some variation in expression affirms that the essence or nature of God is unknowable; he believes that this view is supported by Scripture. He rejects Eunomius' claim that human beings have the capacity to know the essence or nature of God. This leads him to distinguish between knowing that God exists and knowing the essence of God: "Even so, with regard to the creator of the world, we know

---

24. *Meta* 982b 30–983a 3.
25. τὸ περιγραπτὸν εἶναι τὸ θεῖον.

that he exists, but of his essence (τὸν δὲ τῆς οὐσίας λόγον) we cannot deny that we are ignorant" (*Con. Eunom.* 2.1.71). For Gregory, the human capacity for knowledge is severely limited, which he calls "the poverty of our own nature" (ἡ κατὰ τὴν φύσιν ἡμῶν πτωχεία) (*Con. Eunom.* 2.1.586-87). In particular, human beings do not have the capacity to understand the nature of God. He writes, "For as the hollow of one's hand is to the whole deep, so is all the power of language in comparison with that nature which is unspeakable and ungraspable" (πρὸς τὴν ἄφραστον καὶ ἀπερίληπτον φύσιν) (*Con. Eunom.* 3.5.54). Language is inadequate to express the nature of God, for which reason God must remain incomprehensible to human beings. He explains further, "There is no faculty in human nature adequate to the full understanding of the essence of God" (*Con. Eunom.* 2.1.67).[26] Along the same lines, Gregory writes, "Now the divine nature as it is in itself (ἡ θεία φύσις αὐτή), according to its essence (κατ' οὐσίαν), transcends every act of mental comprehension, and it cannot be approached or attained by any mental speculations. Men have never discovered a faculty to comprehend the incomprehensible; nor have we ever been able to devise an approach for grasping the inconceivable" (*In beat.* 6). The terms "divine nature as it is in itself" and "essence" are synonyms, each denoting what God is in contrast to how God appears to be to human beings. The divine nature according to its essence, what God is in himself, is inaccessible to human beings, although no explanation is provided as to why this is so. Gregory finds his view expressed by Paul in Rom 11:33 "How unsearchable are his judgments and unfathomable his ways" (*In beat.* 6). Finally, Gregory calls the nature of God ineffable: "the nature of the ineffable good" (τῆς φύσεως τῶν ἀφράστων ἀγαθῶν), adapting a quotation from the apostle Paul, "that good that eye has not seen, nor ear heard" (1 Cor 2:9) (*In cant.* 8; 247).

It is no surprise that Gregory rejects Eunomius' realist theory of names, dependent in part on Plato's *Cratylus*, according to which every name corresponds to and gives direct knowledge of the essence of the thing named. Rather, for him the names, or attributes of God, do not give access to the divine essence (see *Con. Eunom.* 2.1.62-63). He finds this principle expressed in Wis 13:5 "'For,' as says the Wisdom of Solomon, 'by the greatness and beauty of the creatures analogically (ἀναλόγως) the maker of them is seen'" (*Con. Eunom.* 2.1.154). Since God is incomprehensible, the attributes assigned to God by human beings are only analogically true, *never*

---

26. οὐκ ἔστιν ἐν ἀνθρωπίνῃ φύσει δύναμις εἰς ἀκριβῆ καταβόησιν οὐσίας θεοῦ.

univocally. God may be described as *like* aspects of human experience but these should never be taken as statements about the essence or nature of God. For this reason he criticizes Eunomius, who claims that the essence of God is ingenerateness (ἀγεννησία), in which God glorified before creation and in which human beings can now glorify (ἀγάλλειν). He explains why it is impossible to glory in God by using human linguistic constructions, as Eunomius claims: "We hold, however, that to add any honor to the divine nature, which is above all honor, is more than human infirmity can do"[27] (*Con. Eunom.* 2.1.157). It is impossible to add honor to ("glory in") what is above honor in the sense of being incomprehensible. He interprets LXX Ps 16:2 (15:2) "You are my God, you have no need of my goods" to refer to the impossibility of describing the essence of God: whatever a human can say about God is the "goods" of which God has no need (*Con. Eunom.* 2.1.155). According to Gregory, the purpose of making any statement about God is paradoxically "to guide our own selves by the aid of such terms towards the comprehension of the things which are hidden" (πρὸς τὴν τῶν κρυπτῶν κατανόησιν) (*Con. Eunom.* 2.1.154–55). To know God is to know that God is hidden. Earlier in this context, he writes that the knowledge of God is actually a non-knowing: "For such knowledge it attains in part by the touch of reason, in part from its very inability to discern it, finding that it is a sort of knowledge to know that what is sought transcends knowledge" (*Con. Eunom.* 2.1.139–40). Along the same lines, Gregory explains that people wrongly assume that the name "deity" (θεότης) is like any other noun, denoting an object like the heavens or the sun (*Abl.* 42–44). He insists rather that the divine nature (ἡ θεία φύσις) is "unnamable and unspeakable" (ἀκατωνόμεστον τε καὶ ἄφραστον) (*Abl.* 42).

From what Gregory writes, Eunomius argued from John 10:9 "I am the way" that Christ allows access to an understanding of the essence of God (τοῦ θεοῦ τὴν οὐσίαν) (*Con. Eunom.* 3.8.7–10). Gregory objects that this saying has nothing to do with the essence of God, but is soteriological in intention. He quotes 1 Tim 6:16 "No man has seen him, nor can see" and Exod 33:20 "You cannot see my face, for no man can see me and live" to prove that the essence of God cannot be known and that all that can be known of God is God's effects. He writes, "But, as I am so taught by the inspired Scripture, I boldly affirm that he who is above every name has for us many names, receiving them in accordance with the variety of

---

27. ἡμεῖς δὲ προσθεῖναι μέν τινα τῇ θείᾳ φύσει τιμὴν τῇ ὑπὲρ πᾶσαν οὔσῃ τιμὴν μεῖζον ἢ κατὰ τὴν ἀσθένειαν τὴν ἀνθρωπίνην οἰόμεθα.

God's Essence or Nature as Unknowable

his gracious dealings with us" (τὰς τῶν εὐεργεσιῶν ποικιλίας). This is how God receives predicates, or names, from human beings, such as light, life, way, and so forth: they are the result of human experience of God. Yet none of these names expresses the essence of God, since God is above every name. For this reason it is important to add the disclaimer to all statements of the divine attributes that none of these describes God's essential nature. He writes,

> For by these expressions we are taught either his power, or that he admits not of deterioration, or that he is without cause and without limit, or that he is supreme above all things, or, in short, something, be it what it may, respecting him. But his very essence (αὐτὴν τὴν οὐσίαν), as not to be conceived by the human intellect or expressed in words, this it has left untouched as a thing not to be made the subject of curious enquiry, ruling that it be revered in silence, in that it forbids the investigation of things too deep for us, while it enjoins the duty of being slow to utter any word before God.
>
> (Con. Eunom. 2.1.105)

The attributes assigned to God (θεοπρεπεστέραι) are expressions of what God does, or how God is experienced by human beings.[28] These terms derive from ordinary human experience and are then re-applied analogically to God.[29] For this reason, none of these is an expression of the nature of God. It is not, however, that speech about God is meaningless. Gregory explains that whatever is said of the divine nature negatively and positively is still explanatory of the nature, even if it does not signify the nature itself (Abl. 42–44).[30]

---

28. Or "energies of power" (δυνάμεως ἐνεργείας) (Abl. 44).

29. Gregory writes, "But all the terms that are employed to lead us to the knowledge of God have comprehended in them each its own meaning, and you cannot find any word among the terms especially applied to God which is without a distinct sense" (Abl. 43).

30. Gregory makes several statements of this position: 1. "And we say that every term either invented by the custom of men, or handed down to us by the Scriptures, is indeed explanatory of our conceptions of the divine nature, but does not include the signification of that nature itself" (οὐκ αὐτῆς τῆς φύσεως περιέχειν τὴν σημασίαν) (Abl. 42–43); 2. "But in each of these terms we find a peculiar sense, fit to be understood or asserted of the divine nature, yet not expressing that which that nature is in its essence" (οὐ μὴν ἐκεῖνο σημαίνουσιν, ὅ ἐστι κατ' οὐσίαν ἡ φύσις) (Abl. 43); 3. "We find that all else which results from the significance involved in the names expressing the divine attributes either forbids us to conceive what we ought not to conceive of the divine nature,

The Indescribable God

Gregory argues from minor to major that, if human beings cannot even understand the creation, how much less can they understand the creator (*Con. Eunom.* 2.1.79–82; see 2.1.106–7; *In Eccl.* 7.415–16). He asks rhetorically, "If, then, the lower creation which comes under our organs of sense transcends human knowledge, how can he, who by his mere will made the worlds, be within the range of our apprehension? Surely this is vanity, and lying madness, as says the prophet, to think it possible to comprehend the things which are incomprehensible" (*Con. Eunom.* 2.1.79). The identity of the prophet quoted by Gregory is not clear, but given that he called this endeavor a 'futility' (ματαιότης), he may be alluding to Eccl 5:2 "For God is in heaven and you are on the earth; therefore let your words be few," which he sometimes quotes in support of his position (see *Con. Eunom.* 2.1.94–95). He is thereby adding another futile endeavor to the list already found in Ecclesiastes. It is on this basis that he criticizes any theologian who believes that he knows the nature of God, in particular Eunomius. He writes, "So pettily and so childishly laboring in vain at impossibilities do they set themselves to include the inconceivable nature of God in the few syllables of the term 'ingenerate,' and applaud their own folly, and imagine God to be such that human reasoning can include him under one single term" (*Con. Eunom.* 2.1.82). To do this is to go beyond the limits of human intelligence.[31] He applies 1 Tim 1:7 "understanding neither what they say, nor whereof they affirm" to Eunomius and others who would dare to speak about the divine essence (*Con. Eunom.* 2.1.83).

The distinction between what God is in himself and God as experienced by human beings is the basis for Gregory's distinction between God's essence (οὐσία) and God's energies (ἐνεργεῖαι): "Thus in speaking of God, when there is a question about his essence, then is the time to keep silent. When, however, it is a question of his energy, a knowledge of which can come down to us, that is the time to speak of his omnipotence by telling of his works and explaining his deeds, and to use words in this respect" (*In eccl.* 7.415). While the essence of God is inaccessible, the energies of God, what God does, are not. Along the same lines, he writes, "For God is not an expression, neither has he his essence in voice or utterance . . . But

---

or teaches us that which we ought to conceive of it, but does not include an explanation of the nature itself" (αὐτῆς δὲ τῆς φύσεως ἑρμηνείαν οὐ περιέχοντα) (*Abl.* 44). In the second statement he uses the interesting phrase "nature according to essence" (κατ' οὐσίαν ἡ φύσις).

31. See Athanasius' discussion of the use of the term ingenerate of God (*Decr.* 28–32). One of his complaints is the non-biblical origin of the term.

he is named . . . not what he is essentially (for the nature of him who is is unspeakable [ἄφραστος γὰρ ἡ φύσις τοῦ ὄντος]), but he receives his appellations from what are believed to be his energies in regard to our life" (*Con. Eunom.* 2.1.149). For Gregory, the attributes predicated of God do not express God's essence but rather God's energies, or effects, as experienced by human beings. This point he expresses succinctly by saying that "essence is prior to energies" (προϋγέστηκε τῶν ἐνεργειῶν ἡ οὐσία) (*Con. Eunom.* 2.1.150). He re-applies the expression in Phil 4:7 "which passes all understanding," originally ascribed to God's peace, to the divine essence (*Con. Eunom.* 2.1.154). Based on its alleged etymological derivation from θεάεσθαι ("to view, behold"), even the name "God" (09 θεός) does not denote the divine essence but describes the energy of God of "overlooking and surveying all things, and seeing through the things that are hidden" (*Con. Eunom.* 2.1.149–50; see *Abl.* 44).

In *Life of Moses*, Gregory makes several statements about the impossibility of knowing the essence or nature of God inspired by events in Moses' life. Anticipating what he writes in part two, Gregory explains that, when he entered into the dark cloud (Exod 20:21), Moses received the "divine ordinances," one of which was "having the proper notions about the divine nature."[32] In other words, part of a human being's ethical duty is to think about the divine nature truthfully, which is actually, according to Gregory, not to think about it at all: "It transcends all cognitive thought and representation and cannot be likened to anything that is known" (*Vit. Mos.* I.47). Although one may legitimately affirm the bare existence of God, no attributes with respect to quality, quantity, origin and mode can be predicated of God.

In part two of *Life of Moses*, Gregory discourses at length on the incomprehensibility of the divine nature.[33] Exegeting Exod 20:21, he interprets the fact that Moses is said to enter the darkness and see God to refer to a vision of God constituted paradoxically by not seeing: "This is a seeing that consists in not seeing" (καὶ ἐν τούτῳ τὸ ἰδεῖν ἐν τῷ μὴ ἰδεῖν) (*Vit. Mos.* II.163). The darkness into which Moses entered symbolizes the incomprehensibility of God, and Moses' entrance into the darkness represents a type of negative knowledge, knowing what God is not (see *De an. et res.*). He writes, "Because that which is sought transcends all knowledge, being separated on all sides by non-graspability (ἀκαταληψία) as by a

---

32. τὸ τὰς πρεπούσας ὑπολήψεις περὶ τῆς θείας φύσεως ἔχειν.
33. *Vit. Mos.* II.162–66 based on Exod 20:21; II. 221–22, 231–39 based on Exod 33.

kind of darkness" (*Vit. Mos.* II.163; see *In cant.* 11.323). (He also uses the metaphor of entrance into inner sanctuary [ἄδυτον] to express this non-knowing of God [*Vit. Mos.* II.164].) In his view, this second theophany was an advance over the first, the theophany of the burning bush, symbolized by light, because Moses now realizes that true contemplation of the divine nature consists in non-contemplation (τὸ ἀθεώρητον), symbolized by darkness (*Vit. Mos.* II.162). Moses penetrates into what Gregory calls the "luminous darkness" (λαμπρὸς γνόφος), an oxymoronic term. What Moses "saw" was the negation of all created things. In other words, Moses learns that "with respect to its nature what is divine is beyond all knowledge and graspability";[34] a view that Gregory finds expressed in LXX Ps 17:12 (18:11), "He made darkness his hiding place" (καὶ ἔθετο σκότος ἀποκρυφὴν αὐτοῦ) (*Vit. Mos.* II.164; see *In cant.* 6.181). Gregory quotes John 1:18 "No one has ever seen God" as confirmation of his view; by not seeing God he means not understanding the nature of God. Since John 1:18 has "no one" (οὐδεὶς) rather than "no man," he concludes that no intelligent creature can know the divine nature, not just human beings. Similarly, Gregory interprets the commandment prohibiting idolatry (Exod 20:2) to include making any positive assertion about God: "The divine word at the beginning forbids that the divine be likened to any of the things known by men, since every concept that comes from some comprehensible image by an approximate understanding and by guessing at the divine nature constitutes an idol of God and does not proclaim God" (*Vit. Mos.* II.165).[35] For him, idolatry includes, not only making physical likenesses of God, but also making positive affirmations about the divine nature: "None of those things known by human comprehension is to be ascribed to him" (*Vit. Mos.* II.166).

Exod 33:18–23 also gives Gregory occasion to reflect upon the unknowability of the essence or nature of God. Predictably, he rejects the literal interpretation of God's "face" and "back" in this passage (*Vit. Mos.* II.221–22). This allows him to give a unique interpretation to the statement "You cannot see my face, for man cannot see me and live" (Exod 33:20) (*Vit. Mos.* II.224–35). It does not mean that a human being who looks at God's face will be punished for this misdeed by being killed, since it makes

---

34. τῇ φύσει τὸ θεῖον ὃ πάσης γνώσεώς τε καὶ καταλήψεώς ἐστιν ἀγώτερον.

35. ὡς παντὸς νοήματος, τοῦ κατά τινα περιληπτικὴν φαντασίαν ἐν περινοίᾳ τινὶ καὶ στοχασμῷ τῆς θείας φύσεως γινομένου, εἴδωλον θεοῦ πλάσσοντος καὶ οὐ θεὸν καταγγέλλοντες.

no sense to say that "the face of life" (τὸ τῆς ζωῆς πρόσωπον) could ever be the cause of death. The qualification of God's face as "the face of life" derives from his assertion that "the divine is by nature life-giving" (ζωοποιὸν μὲν τῇ φύσει τὸ θεῖον), by which he means that God gives existence to all things.[36] So, according to Gregory, the reason why no one can look into the face of God and live is that, if one thinks that one can comprehend God, which is expressed symbolically as seeing the face of God, one does not understand the nature of the divine as transcending all characteristics and so one does not have true (spiritual) life. He writes, "He who thinks God is something to be known does not have life, because he has turned from true being to what he considers by sense perception to have being."[37] In place of God as life-giving he now affirms God as true being (ὄντως ὄν), a Platonically-inspired designation, although these no doubt are complementary designations. God as true being or life-giving stands in contrast to all created things to which existence is given and which have only apparent being, as perceived by the senses.

John Chrysostom

In a series of homilies known as *On the Incomprehensible Nature of God*, John Chrysostom takes up the cause of opposing the Anomoeans, heretics of Arian pedigree who claim that the Son and the Spirit are unlike the essence of the Father. In the first five of these homilies, he seeks to establish that the essence of God is ungraspable (ἀκατάληπτος). Like the Cappodicians, his strategy is to call into question the central tenet of this heresy, namely that the essence of God is ingenerateness (ἀγεννησία). He writes, "It is clear that God is unbegotten. But no prophet has said, no apostle has hinted, nor evangelist suggested that this is the name of his essence" (*De incomp.* 5.36). He blames the Anomoeans for their pretentious claim to a knowledge of the divine essence, what no human being possesses: "But such men, who are far removed from the virtue of the righteous man,

---

36. Yet immediately afterwards he writes, "The characteristic of the divine nature is to transcend all characteristics (ἴδιον δὲ γνώισμα τῆς θείας φύσεώς ἐστι τὸ παντὸς ὑπερκεῖσθαι γνωρίσματος)." So apparently to be life-giving is not a characteristic (γνώισμα), but is actually an expression that God has no characteristics. The argument seems to be that the nature of what gives life or existence to all things is not like any of those things.

37. ὡς παρατραπεὶς ἀπὸ τοῦ ὄντως ὄντος πρὸς τὸ τῇ καταληπτικῇ φαντασίᾳ νομισθὲν εἶναι.

The Indescribable God

profess to know with all exactness the highest and first of essences, the very essence of God" (*De incomp.* 3.23).[38] Based on Heb 11:6 "Anyone who comes to God must believe that he exists," he claims that all that is required of human beings is to believe *that* God exists; there is no further requirement to inquire into the divine essence (οὐσία) (*De incomp.* 5.40). In fact, Chrysostom adopts a skeptical position towards the possibility of knowing the essence of God; he holds that to do so is beyond human capability, a view that he finds expressed in Scripture. He states, "You are only a man, and bare names we call a man are enough to prove how excessive your madness is. A man is dust and ashes [Gen 18:27], flesh and blood [Sir 10:9; 17:27; Matt 16:17], grass and the flower of grass [Isa 40:6], a shadow [1 Chr 29:15; Ps 101(102):12], smoke [Ps 101(102):4], and vanity [Eccl 1:2], and whatever is weaker and more worthless than these" (*De incomp.* 2.19). To be content to be in a state of ignorance concerning God is to remain within the epistemological bounds fixed for human beings (*De incomp.* 1.21). Not even the angels can know the essence of God, so how much less, he argues, can a lowly human being do so (see *De incomp.* 1.34–36; 3.6–8, 13, 23; 4.11, 17). Practically, abandoning confidence in one's capability to investigate the essence of God will lead to being submissive to the Scriptures, the only source of knowledge of God (*De incomp.* 2.6, 8, 11). To make the claim that one knows the essence of God is both absurd and even morally perverse. Chrysostom writes, "But whenever a man is meddlesome and inquisitive about God's essence, he insults God (*De incomp.* 2.32; see 3.6).[39]

In addition, rather than simply denying that human beings and angels can know the essence of God, Chrysostom denies that God even has an essence. According to him, God has no essence because God has no limits on his being by which a definition of God would be possible. He asks, "His greatness has no limit, and do you put his essence with the limits of a definition?" (*De incomp.* 1.26; see 4.17).[40] This implies that God has no essence at all insofar as only that which has limits can be said to be definable. This view is in tension with his assertions that the essence of God is unknowable.

Chrysostom marshals several key scriptural passages as stating or implying that the essence of God is unknowable. Like many of his theological forbearers, he interprets John 1:18 "No one has ever seen God" to mean

---

38. οἱ δὲ τοσοῦτον τῆς ἀρετῆς ἀφεστηκότες τοῦ δικαίου αὐτὴν ὑπισχνοῦνται τὴν οὐσίαν εἰδέναι μετὰ ἀκριβείας ἁπάσης, τὴν ἀνωτάτω καὶ πρώτην.

39. ὑβρίζει δὲ ὁ τὴν οὐσίαν αὐτοῦ περιεργαζόμενος.

40. ἡ μεγαλωσύνη αὐτοῦ οὐκ ἔχει πέρας, καὶ τὴν οὐσίαν αὐτοῦ περιγράφεις.

God's Essence or Nature as Unknowable

that "No one knows God in his essence with complete exactness" (*De incomp.* 4.22).[41] He also cites 1 Cor 13:12 "My knowledge is imperfect now; then I shall know even as I was known" as implying that no one knows the essence of God. He writes, "Paul said this because on the one hand he knows that God exists, whereas, on the other, he does not know what God is in his essence" (*De incomp.* 1.33).[42] Based on 1 Tim 6:15-16 "dwells in unapproachable light," he argues that God is unapproachable, which is a stronger statement than saying that God is incomprehensible; something is incomprehensible when someone seeks after it but fails to comprehend it. This is different from being unapproachable: "We call that thing unapproachable which from the start cannot be searched out or investigated" (*De incomp.* 3.11-12; see 3.24; 4.8).[43] To be unapproachable is to be in principle incomprehensible, which may be interpreted as implying that God is actually without an essence. The other scriptural passages cited to support his position include 1 Cor 13:9 (1.31); Ps 138(139):6, 8, 14 (1.24); Rom 11:33 (1.29); Eph 3:8 (4.14); Exod 33:20 (4.20).

The problem of using Scripture to support an apophatic theological perspective is that there are numerous instances of God's appearance to human beings or angels, which Chrysostom's opponents no doubt pointed out. He explains the phenomenon of the theophany as a "condescension" (συγκατάθασις), which is a revelation accommodated to the particular nature of the recipient. What the seraphim saw in Isa 6:1-2 was not the "pure essence itself" (αὐτὴν ἀκραιφνῆ τὴν οὐσίαν) but a condescension. Likewise, when Isaiah says "I saw the Lord on a throne, lofty and exalted" (Isa 6:1), the reader should not understand this to mean that he saw the essence of God, but only a condescension, for after all God does not actually sit on anything since God is incorporeal (*De incomp.* 3.14-17). Ezekiel's vision of God (Ezek 1) was also a condescension because he saw only "the appearance of the likeness of the glory of the Lord" (Ezek 1:28) (3.27). Later Chrysostom contrasts several statements in Scripture in which it is stated that someone has seen God (Isa 6:1; Dan 7:9; 1 Kgs 22:19; Amos 9:1) with John 1:18 "No one has seen God" (*De incomp.* 4.17-19). He reconciles Scripture with itself by asserting that what people saw was not the essence of God, but God's condescensions to human limitations; he thereby

---

41. τὸν θεὸν οὐδεὶς ἔγνω οὐσιώδς μετὰ ἀκριβείας ἁπάσης.

42. ἀλλ᾽ ἐπειδὴ ὅτι μὲν ἔστι θεὸς οἶδε, τὸ δὲ τί τὴν οὐσίαν ἐστὶν, ἀγνοεῖ.

43. ἀπρόσιτον δὲ ἐκεῖνο λέγεται, ὃ μήτ ετὴν ἀρχὴν ζητηθῆναι δυνατόν, μηδὲ ἐρευνηθῆναι.

gives hermeneutical priority to John 1:18. He explains that, since "God is simple," not being "composed of parts," and therefore "without figure and form"—which he accepts as an established fact not requiring proof—it follows that no one could have seen the form of God. What is simple could not have predicates, which is what a statement of essence would be. Whether he is aware of this or not, what Chrysostom writes implies that the reason God cannot be seen is that God has no essence at all, even though other of his statements assume the opposite. Besides, he argues, each visionary saw something different, which can only mean no one saw the essence of God for otherwise they would all have seen the same thing. Chrysostom quotes as a proof text for his position LXX Hos 12:11, "I have multiplied visions," which he interprets as follows, "What God was saying was: 'I did not show my very essence but I came down in condescension and accommodated myself to the weakness of their eyes.'"[44]

Theodoret of Cyrus

In refuting Apollinariarism, Theodoret of Cyrus reflects upon the ineffable essence of God. Exegeting Phil 2:3–8, he identifies the form of God (μορφὴ τοῦ θεοῦ) with the essence of God (οὐσία τοῦ θεοῦ) and the form of a servant with the essence of human beings. For him, the divine (τὸ θεῖον), which is a synonym for the essence of God, in addition to being simple, is ἀμόρφωτον ("formless"), ἀνείδεον ("idealess") and ἀσχημάτιστον ("shapeless"), all of which are synonyms denoting that God has no essence at all (*De. incarn.* 10). For this reason, he explains in another work that human beings do not know the nature or essence of God because God does not have one; rather whatever is asserted about God only relates to God's energies (αἱ ἐνέργειαι) (*De Sanct. Trin.* 16).

Pseudo-Dionysius

Pseudo-Dionysius holds that God is "above every essence and knowledge" (ὑπὲρ πᾶσαν οὐσίαν καὶ γνῶσιν) (*Mys. th.* I.1) and "highly established above mind and essence" (ὑπὲρ νοῦν καὶ οὐσίαν) (*Ep.* I). What he means by saying that God is above essence is that God does not have an essence, which further means that God cannot be said to be a particular thing. God

---

44. οὐκ αὐτὴν τὴν οὐσίαν ἔδειξα τὴν ἐμήν, ἀλλὰ συγκατέθην, φησί, πρὸς τὴν τῶν ὁρώντων ἀσθένειαν.

is not a being that can be defined in relation to other beings. Pseudo-Dionyius uses the neo-logism "superessential" (ὑπερούσιος) to describe God as without essence. The same thing is meant by calling God the supernatural (τὸ ὑπερφυές) (*De div. nom.* XI.6). Whatever can be said about God is not univocally true, since God is above all predicates. Along the same lines, he describes God as "above the principle of deity" (ὑπὲρ θεαρχίαν), which means that God is more than the God that human beings understand God to be, namely a being with a knowable essence (*Ep.* II).

Pseudo-Dionysius explains that the various attributes predicated of God (τὰ θεῖα), even those that are revealed in Scripture, are known to human beings only "by the participations alone" (ταῖς μετοχαῖς μόναις), which is a Platonically-inspired idiom virtually synonymous with what other Christian theologians understand as God's "energies" (*De div. nom.* II.7). While Scripture and human experience may reveal God to be certain ways relatively, which are then expressible as "participations" in God, God in himself is above these and every attribute. Pseudo-Dionysius explains that what these participations, or attributes, really are, what they are in God, is beyond all human understanding: "And themselves, such as they are in their own source and abode, are above mind and all essence and knowledge" (*De div. nom.* II.7).[45] He holds that God can never be an object of knowledge: "Never, then, is it true to say, that we know God—not from his own nature for that is unknown, and surpasses all reason and mind" (*De div. nom.* VII.3).[46] In this passage, "nature" (φύσις) denotes what God is, or the reality of God. Since God is inaccessible to human intelligence, no human being can claim to know God. Given that Pseudo-Dionysius refers to God as superessential and supernatural, it seems that the reason that God cannot be known from his own nature is that God does not have a nature. Human reason operates discursively by distinguishing one thing from another on the basis of their respective natures; but God is above all such distinctions and so cannot be known.

Paradoxically, according to Pseudo-Dionysius, to know God is not to know God, what he calls being in the state of *agnosia* (ἀγνωσία). He finds this symbolically expressed in Moses' entrance into the darkness on Mount Sinai (Exod 20:21): "And [Moses] enters into the darkness of the *agnosia*, a

---

45. αὐτὰ δὲ, ὁποῖά ποτε ἔστι κατὰ τὴν οἰκείαν ἀρχὴν καὶ ἵδρυσιν ὑπὲρ νοῦν ἔστι καὶ πᾶσαν οὐσίαν καὶ γνῶσιν.

46. μήποτε οὖν ἀληθὲς εἰπεῖν, ὅτι θεὸν γινώσκομεν οὐκ ἐκ τῆς αὐτοῦ φύσεως, ἄγνωστον γὰρ τοῦτο καὶ πάντα λόγον καὶ νοῦν ὑπεραῖρον.

The Indescribable God

darkness veritably mystic, within which he closes all perceptions of knowledge and enters into the altogether impalpable and invisible, being wholly of him who is beyond all" (*Mys. th.* I.3). The darkness where God was that Moses entered symbolizes the state of the suspension of all cognitive activity, known as *agnosia*; this is the only access to God who is "beyond all." Pseudo-Dionysius also identifies the "divine darkness" (ὁ θεῖος γνόφος) in Exod 20:21 with the "unapproachable light" in 1 Tim 6:6, and he finds his view of *agnosia* likewise expressed in Ps 139:6 ("Such knowledge is too wonderful for me; it is too high, I cannot attain to it"), Rom 11:33 ("Oh, the depth of the riches both of the wisdom and knowledge of God . . ."), 2 Cor 9:15 ("Thanks be to God for his indescribable gift"), and Phil 4:7 ("And the peace of God, which surpasses all comprehension") (*Ep.* V).

Maximus the Confessor

Under the influence of Pseudo-Dionysius, Maximus Confessor denies that God is an essence (οὐσία), by which is meant a definable being among other definable beings (*Cent. gnost.* 1.4).[47] Rather, he explains that God "is a principle of being who is creative of essence and beyond essence" (οὐσιοποιός καὶ ὑπερούσιος ὀντότης). To be a principle of being (ὀντότης) and creative of essence (οὐσιοποιός) seem to be synonyms, meaning that God is the source of all essences, but is not an essence himself. For God to be beyond essence (ὑπερούσιος) is to be indefinable. The assumption is that whatever is an essence is limited, so that by virtue of its limit it is what it is: "Every essence implies in itself its own limit (πᾶσα οὐσία τὸν ἑαυτῆς ὅρον ἑαυτῇ συνεισάγουσα) (*Cent. gnost.* 1.3). He expresses the same idea by asserting that God "transcends the essence of all that can be thought or said" (*Cent. gnost.* 1.50).[48] His point is that God is not a thing whose essence can be stated and so be defined. Similarly, Maximus asserts that God is ground (ἵδρυσις), and, drawing upon Aristotelianism, says that God is creative of potentiality but beyond potentiality (καὶ δυναμοποιός καὶ ὑπερδύναμος). A created thing has potentiality by virtue of being an essence; since God is not an essence, God is beyond potentiality, although creative of potentiality.[49] This is why God can be said

---

47. Translation of *Chapters on Knowledge* from Maximus Confessor, *Maximus Confessor: Selected Writings*, translated by George C. Berthold (Mahwah, NJ: Paulist, 1985).

48. ὑπὲρ οὐσίαν γὰρ πάντων τῶν τε νοουμένων καὶ λεγομένων ἐξῄρηται.

49. See *Cent. gnost.* 1.3 "Every essence . . . is a principle of motion (δύναμις κινήσεως)."

to be "ground," in the sense of being the foundation of all things, which is a synonym for "principle of being." As beyond essence, God is incomprehensible and inaccessible to human beings (*Cent. gnost.* 1.1). It also follows that God is "unique in nature" (μόνος κατὰ φύσιν), implying that nothing is like God (*Cent. gnost.* 1.6).

In order to distinguish God from what is not-God, God is said metaphorically to be that which encloses all things: "He encloses in himself in every way the whole of what being is" (*Cent. gnost.* 1.6).[50] To be that which encloses again implies that God does not have an essence and so is not one thing among other things. Maximus also expresses this by saying that God is "beyond being itself" (ὡς καὶ αὐτοῦ τοῦ εἶναι κυρίως ὑπέρτερος): God cannot even be said to exist in the same way that created things exist. In his work *Mystagogy*, Maximus sets God in opposition to all created beings and for that reason refers to God as superbeing: "The affirmation of superbeing must be the negation of beings, and the affirmation of beings must be the negation of superbeing."[51] It follows that God can never be described in terms of created beings, which means that God is incomprehensible. According to Maximus, while the knowledge of God's essence is inaccessible to both angels and human beings, God is, however, known through the divine energies (ἐνεργεία) (*Cent. gnost.* 2.76). The energies of God are what God does, which are expressed as the divine attributes. But the energies collectively are not what God is, because God is superessence or superbeing.

Maximus connects God's superessentiality with God's simplicity. Although somewhat confusing, he seems to argue that God cannot be an essence, by which is meant to have an essence, because a distinction would be made between God as a thinker and God's essence as an object of thought. But God's simplicity precludes positing such a duality between thinker and thought. He writes, "He is entirely above essence and entirely above thought, since he is an invisible monad, simple and without parts" (*Cent. gnost.* 1.82).[52] Maximus interprets Exod 33:7 "Now Moses used to take the tent and pitch it outside the camp . . . and he called it the tent of meeting" allegorically to refer to God's lack of intelligibility, the impossibil-

---

50. ὅλον τὸ κυρίως εἶναι κατὰ πάντα τρόπον ἑαυτῷ περικλείων.

51. θέσιν εἶναι τοῦ ὑπερόντος τὴν τῶν ὄντων ἀφαίρεσιν· καὶ τὴν τῶν ὄντων θέσιν, εἶναι τοῦ ὑπερόντος ἀφαίρεσιν.

52. καὶ ὑπὲρ οὐσίαν ὅλος, καὶ ὑπὲρ νόησιν ὅλος, διότι καὶ μονὰς ἀδιαίρετος καὶ ἀμερὴς καὶ ἁπλῆ.

ity of using language to describe God: "pitching the tent of thought outside the camp and then conversing with God" (*Cent. gnost.* 1.83). He substitutes "tent of thought" (σκηνὴ τῆς διανοίας) for "tent of witness" (LXX, σκηνὴ μαρτυρίου); to be outside the camp is interpreted to mean outside of human language. Likewise the Day of Atonement on which the High Priest enters the holy of holies is said to depict the one "who has gone beyond the whole nature of the intelligible and the sensible realities" (*Cent. gnost.* 1.83).[53] Not only can God not be depicted sensibly, as idolaters wrongly assume, but God cannot be depicted intelligibly and so become an object of thought. Maximus also interprets Rom 10:6–7 [Deut 30:12] ("who shall go into heaven?") to refer to the impossibility of conceiving of God: "But heaven is to be understood as God's hiddenness by nature (ἡ φυσικὴ τοῦ θεοῦ κρυφιότης) which takes him beyond everyone's grasp" (*Cent. gnost.* 2.36). God's hiddenness is another way of expressing the fact that God is not an essence, but is superessential.

John of Damascus

John of Damascus explains that God's essence (οὐσία) and nature (φύσις) are inaccessible to human beings, even though the fact of God's existence is not: "But what he [God] is in his essence and nature is absolutely incomprehensible and unknowable" (*O.F.* 1.4).[54] In this passage, God's essence and his nature are synonyms, both denoting what God is. John also speaks about God's "separation from all things" (ἐκ τῆς ἁπάντων ἀφαιρέσεως), which accounts for why it is impossible to explain the essence of God: God cannot be described in terms of created things (*O.F.* 1.4). According to him, the divine attributes of being ingenerate, without beginning, changeless and imperishable, which are usually predicated of God, should not be mistaken for a statement of the essence or nature of God. This is because these terms are only negations, indicating what God is not, not what God is. He writes, "But when we would explain what the essence of anything is, we must not speak only negatively" (*O.F.* 1.4).

In dependence on Pseudo-Dionysus, John of Damascus also speaks about God as if God does not have an essence or nature at all. He asserts that God "is above existence itself" (καὶ ὑπὲρ αὐτὸ τὸ εἶναι ὤν), by

---

53. τὴν ἅπασαν τῶν αἰσθητῶν τε καὶ νοητῶν παρελθόντα φύσιν.

54. τί δέ ἐστι κατ᾽ οὐσίαν καὶ φύσιν ἀκατάληπτον τοῦτο παντελῶς καὶ ἄγνωστον.

which he seems to mean that God cannot be said to exist in the same way that created things do. Along the same lines, he argues that, since God is above essence in the sense of not having an essence like created beings, God must also be beyond knowledge: "For if all forms of knowledge have to do with what exists, assuredly that which is above knowledge must certainly be also above essence; and, conversely, that which is above essence will also be above knowledge" (O.F. 1.4).[55] He uses Pseudo-Dionysius' term "superessential" (ὑπερούσιος) to denote the unknowability of God in principle: God is beyond essence, or definition (O.F. 1.8, 12). God's superessentiality derives from the fact that God "is the cause and beginning of all: the essence of all that exists" (1.12).[56] In other words, he conceives God not as a particular being with an essence, but as the cause of all beings and their essences. Synonymous with superessential is the term "supernatural nature" (ἡ ὑπερκειμένη φύσις). He writes, "But God . . . who gave us the faculty of knowledge, not only did not impart to us his essence, but did not even grant us the knowledge of his essence. For it is impossible for nature to understand fully the supernatural nature" (O.F. 1.12). The phrase supernatural nature implies that God has no nature.

Gregory Palamas

In the Greek Orthodox tradition, Gregory Palamas develops further the idea of the energies (ἐνεργείαι) of God. He expresses his theological views primarily in defense of hesychasm, the monastic practice of sacred quietude, the goal of which is to experience a vision of God's uncreated light, one of the energies of God.[57] His principal theological opponent, Barlaam the Calabrian, calls into question the very possibility of an experience of God's uncreated light insofar as it is assumed that no human being can experience and be united with the transcendent divine essence (*Triads* II.iii.12).[58] Gregory agrees, but argues that God is still partially

55. εἰ γὰρ τῶν ὄντων καὶ γνώσεις, τὸ ὑπὲρ γνῶσιν, πάντως καὶ ὑπὲρ οὐσίαν ἔσται· καὶ τὸ ἀνάπαλιν τὸ ὑπὲρ οὐσίαν, καὶ γνῶσιν ἔσται.

56. ὁ θεὸς πάντων ἐστιν αἰτία καὶ ἀρχή τῶν ὄντων οὐσία.

57. This light is identified with the "Taboric Light" seen by Jesus' disciples on the Mount of Transfiguration, and is equated with the Holy Spirit and his effects in a human being. The experience of the divine light is grace and brings human beings into unmediated, deifying communion with God.

58. Gregory's most complete apology for the legitimacy of hesychastic practice occurs in his *For the Defence of Those Who Practice Sacred Quietude*, or *Triads in Defence*

knowable through the divine energies, by which God interacts and enters into union with creation. In his work, Palamas vacillates between asserting that God has no essence and that God has an unknowable essence, the latter in particular when speaking about the difference between God's essence and energies.[59]

In agreement with his theological opponent, Gregory Palamas holds the view that God is inaccessible to human understanding, which, in dependence on Pseudo-Dionysius, he expresses by the term superessential (ὑπερούσιος), or a variation of this. He writes, "But you should not consider that God allows himself to be seen in his superessential essence" (ὑπερούσιος οὐσία) (*Triads* III.i.29). To have a superessential essence is, in fact, to be without an essence, which explains why the essence of God is unknowable. Along the same lines, he holds that the divine essence "transcends all affirmation and all negation" and even claims cryptically that the term "essence" itself denotes only one of the "powers" (δυνάμεις) of God (*Triads* III.ii.11).[60] An essence that transcends affirmation and negation is really no essence. Gregory explains that God is not a possible object of human understanding, which he expresses by saying that God is "above being" and "beyond all beings." He writes, "God is not a being, for we believe him to be above being" (*Triads* II.iii.17) and "Since this reality that transcends every intellectual power is impossible to comprehend, it is beyond all beings" (*Triads* II.iii.33). What he presupposes is that to understand something is to identify its essence, which is to say to define it as something. What is "above being" and "beyond all beings," synonymous with superessential, however, has no essence and therefore cannot be defined. Following Pseudo-Dionysius, he gives the name "more than God" to God in order to distinguish the unknowable essence from how God is experienced by human beings (*Triads* III.i.31).

In dependence on Pseudo-Dionysius, Gregory makes use of the *via negativa*, but understands it only as a penultimate stage, preparing for the experience of the ineffable, deifying vision sought after by hesychastic monks.[61] He explains the limitations of the apophatic methodology: "While

of the Holy Hesychasts, nine polemical treatises published in three groups of three books.

59. Translation of *Triads* from Gregory Palamas, *Gregory Palamas: The Triads*, translated by Nicholas Gendle (Mahwah, NJ: Paulist, 1983).

60. In this case "power" seems to be synonymous with "energy." The term "power" occurs in the quotation from Pseudo-Dionysis that follows, which may explain Gregory's use of the less common alternative.

61. See Pseudo-Dionysius, *Mys. th.* I.1.

it liberates the understanding from other beings, it cannot by itself effect union with transcendent things" (*Triads* I.iii.20).[62] According to Gregory, God as superessential is not only beyond knowing, but also beyond unknowing, which means that the one who negates positive affirmations about God is not further ahead intellectually than the one who makes them (*Triads* I.iii.4). The vision of the light of God is neither sense perception nor understanding, but transcends both and strictly speaking cannot be called knowledge at all since it comes after the cessation of all cognitive activity (*Triads* I.iii.17–18). The difference between apophatic theology and the vision is explained as follows: "The mind which applies itself to apophatic theology thinks of what is different from God. Thus it proceeds by means of discursive reasoning. But in the other case, there is union. In the one case, the mind negates itself together with other beings, but in the other there is union of the mind with God" (*Triads* II.iii.35).

What can be known about God is God's energies (or energy), which describe God's effects, or how human beings experience God. In other words, God's energies are God's modes of action and interaction with created beings.[63] Everything that can be said about God, even the term "God," is a statement of the divine energies (*Triads* III.ii.10). In fact, according to Gregory, without his energies God would not be known to exist, since for human beings God is God's effects. He writes, "Not from the essence is the energy known but from the energy it is known that the essence is, but not what it is" (*Cap. phy.* 141).[64] In this passage he refers to God's unknowable essence, which is distinguished from God's knowable energies. The divine energies are real distinctions, not merely conceptual ones, although their precise ontological status is unclear. He describes the relationship between God's essence and the energies as one of cause and effect: "Thus, neither the uncreated goodness, nor the eternal glory, nor the divine life nor things akin to these are simply the superessential essence of God (ἡ ὑπερούσιος

---

62. See also his statement, "But, despite this inexpressible character, negation alone does not suffice to enable the intellect to attain to superintelligible things. The ascent by negation is in fact only an apprehension of how things are distinct from God" (*Triads* I.iii.19).

63. He uses the term providence as a synonym for energy: "Thus also God, not from the essence, but from his providence, is made known . . . that he is" (Διὸ καὶ ὁ θεὸς, οὐκ ἐκ τῆς οὐσίας, ἀλλ' ἐκ τῆς προνοίας αὐτοῦ γινώσκεται . . . ὅτι ἔστι) (*Cap. Phy.* 141). Both terms refer to God's modes of interaction with created reality.

64. οὐκ ἐκ τῆς οὐσίας ἡ ἐνέργεια, ἀλλ' ἐκ τῆς ἐνεργείας ἡ οὐσία γνωρίζεται ὅτι ἔστι.

οὐσία τοῦ θεοῦ), for God transcends them all as cause (αἴτιος)" (*Triads* III.ii.7). Even though he uses the phrase "superessential essence," he seems to hold that God actually does have an essence.

Although he distinguishes God's essence from God's energies, Gregory insists that the energies are not created. Using a spatial metaphor, he says that the energies are in the one essence, but are not the divine essence: "There is only one unoriginate essence, the essence of God; none of the energies that inhere in it is an essence, so that all necessarily and always are in the divine essence" (ἔνεισιν ἀεί τῇ οὐσίᾳ τοῦ θεοῦ) (*Triads* III.ii.5). He also uses Pseudo-Dionysius's metaphor of the sun and its rays to describe the relationship between the divine essence and energies. The sun is one but its rays are many; yet the rays, though different from the sun, are inseparable from it (*Triads* III.ii.13). Gregory insists that the existence of God's uncreated energies does not render God composite (*Triads* III.i.24). It should also not be thought that the superessential essence is the totality of the energies, as if they are the different aspects of God. Rather, according to Gregory, "The superessential essence of God is thus not to be identified with the energies, even with those without beginning; from which it follows that it is not only transcendent to any energy whatsoever, but that it transcends them 'to an infinite degree and an infinite number of times,' as the divine Maximus says" (*Triads* III.ii.8).

Thomas Aquinas

Thomas Aquinas holds as foundational that the essence or substance of God is not fully knowable to human beings. Unlike his many theological predecessors, however, he uses an Aristotelian framework in order to express this view. Aquinas writes, "We say that God is knowable, however not that he is knowable so that his essence may be comprehended" (*Sent.* 3.1).[65] What can be truly asserted about God does not express the essence of God, but always falls short of it. Aquinas distinguishes between the mode of the thing known (*per modum rei cognitae*) and the mode of the knower (*per modum cognoscentis*); his intention in doing so is to make a distinction between the object in itself and the object as it appears to the knower. His view is that God is not a possible object of human knowledge because "the mode of no creature . . . reaches the height of the divine majesty."[66] In other

---

65. Non autem ita est cognoscibilis, ut essentia sua comprehendatur.
66. Modus . . . nullius creaturae attingit ad altitudinem divinae majestatis.

words, human beings are incapable of truly knowing the mode of God as object, as God knows himself, but only have a partial knowledge of God. In another work, Aquinas explains that the substance of God (*substantia Dei*) is so immense, by which is meant so unsurpassingly great, that no human being can know it. He writes, "For, by its immensity, the divine substance surpasses every form that our intellect reaches. Thus we are unable to apprehend it by knowing what it is" (*SCG* 1.14). The human intellect knows a thing when it knows its form (*forma*), but what God is surpasses every possible form for the human intellect. Aquinas concludes that the only method by which one could arrive at an imperfect knowledge of God is the way of remotion (*via negationis*), according to which all negative differences between God and created beings are enumerated.

Because he holds that God is incomprehensible, Aquinas rejects the validity of what is later called the ontological argument (*ST* 1.2.1). He agrees that the proposition, "God exists" is self-evident in itself because it is an analytical proposition—"for the predicate is the same as the subject"; in other words, for God to be God is for God to exist: "Because God is his own existence (*Deus enim est suum esse*)."[67] But this does not commit him to accepting the validity of the ontological argument since this proposition, though self-evident in itself, is not self-evident to human beings. To know that by definition God exists requires that one be able to define God, to know what God is, but that is what Aquinas denies is possible. For him, the impossibility of defining God makes all discourse about God problematic.

According to Aristotle, knowledge is demonstration (ἀπόδειξις). Demonstration requires a middle term consisting of a definition; there can be no demonstration unless something can be shown to conform to the definition set forth in the middle term and so necessarily have all that is entailed by that definition. Because of the unknowability of God, Aquinas must substitute God's effects in all demonstration concerning God (*ST* 1.2.2). He explains, "Now the names given to God are derived from his effects; consequently, in demonstrating the existence of God from his effects, we may take for the middle term the meaning of the word 'God.'"[68] God is known by his effects and so all naming of God is the naming of these effects; these effects collectively, however, are not a definition of God,

---

67. Aquinas later demonstrates from God's effects that God's essence includes God's existence (*ST* 1.3.4).

68. Nomina autem Dei imponuntur ab effectibus, ut postea ostendetur: unde, demonstrando Deum esse per effectum, accipere possumus pro medio quid significet hoc nomen Deus.

what God is. Nevertheless, they unavoidably must function as the middle term in all demonstration about God, since God's real essence is unknown. Similarly, in discussing whether God is the object of sacred doctrine, Aquinas concedes that what God is cannot be known: "We cannot know what God is."[69] He quotes John of Damascus approvingly in this regard: "It is impossible to define what God is" (*O.F.* 1.4). Nonetheless, Aquinas still allows for the possibility of a science of sacred doctrine, since God's effects (either of nature or of grace) can be substituted for God's definition, or statement of the essence of God.

Protestantism

The traditional view that the essence or nature of God is unknowable insofar as God is other than all things continues into the Protestant era. Eschewing what he calls empty speculation, John Calvin insists that the essence (*essentia*) of God cannot be penetrated by human intelligence (*Inst.* I. v.9; see "incomprehensible essence" in *Inst.* I. xi.3). Likewise, Johannes Wollebius asserts that the essence of God is incomprehensible to human beings.[70] In spite of his early modern philosophical orientation, Samuel Clarke holds the same view as many pre-modern Christian theologians. In his *Demonstration of the Being and Attributes of God and Other Writings*, he seeks to prove against contemporary "atheists," in particular Spinoza and Hobbes, that on the principle of sufficient reason it is justified to hold that from eternity there has existed "some one immutable and independent being," which is the cause of all dependent beings. Nevertheless, he asserts further that the "substance or essence" of this being is incomprehensible to human beings. He writes, "What the substance or essence of that Being, which is self-existent, or Necessarily-existing, is; we have no Idea, neither is it all possible for us to comprehend it. That there is such a Being actually Existing without us, we are sure (as I have already shown) by strict and undeniable Demonstration. Also *what* it is *not*; that is, that the Material World is *not* it, as Modern Atheists would have it, has been already Demonstrated. But *what* it *is*, I mean as to its *Substance* and Essence; this we are infinitely unable to comprehend."[71] In order to support this claim, he argues from minor to major that human beings do not know the essence of the things

69. Licet de Deo non possimus scire quid est.
70. Wollebius, *Compendium Theologiae Christianae*, lib. 1, cap. 1.
71. Clarke, *Demonstration of the Being and Attributes of God and Other Writings*, 38.

of common experience so it should come as no surprise if human beings do not know the essence of God.[72] In spite of God's incomprehensibility, however, Clarke does call God a being, and enumerates several essential attributes of this being.

CONCLUSION

The assertion that the essence or nature of God is unknowable is a means of affirming the otherness of God. Whether the meaning is that the essence or nature of God is beyond human understanding or that God has no essence or nature what is being asserted is that *God cannot be said to be like anything in human experience*. Generally there is little awareness or concern on the part of Christian theologians that the concept of essence or nature is foreign to Scripture. Implicitly the theological method used is that whatever clarifies Scripture and does not contradict it is a legitimate conceptual tool.

---

72. Ibid., 39.

3

God as Nameless and Not in a Genus

GOD AS NAMELESS

Synopsis

THE OTHERNESS OF GOD is expressed by Christian theologians by asserting that God is nameless: what is nameless is incomprehensible. There are two divergent variations of the argument that God is nameless, sometimes adopted by one and the same Christian theologian.

One the one hand, it is affirmed that God is nameless *for human beings*; in other words, although God does have one, presumably known to himself, God's name in the sense of a predicate that can be assigned to the subject "God" that would define it is unknown to human beings. Human beings can know that God exists but not God's name in sense of what God is. In such cases God's name is roughly synonymous for God's essence, nature, or form. It is sometimes explained that human language is inadequate to describe God fully. For God to be nameless in this sense is to be other than all things.

On the other hand, Christian theologians assert that God is nameless *in principle*: God cannot have a name in the sense of definition, or statement of essence or nature. Whatever cannot be defined and whatever does not have an essence or nature is other than all things that can be defined and do have essences or natures. At best God can be given many names, or descriptors, but none of these defines God; these are only the energies of God, or what God is relationally. Sometimes it is also argued that God has no need of a name because God is alone and one: names function to distinguish individuals of the same type from one another. "God" is the name of God and nothing beyond this can be said, which means that the name "God" is non-descriptive, a type of proper name. In other words, the noun "God" functions merely to signify an incomprehensible object. In fact, it is said that only generated, or created, things have names in the sense of having a form, or being identifiable as something. God as creator, ingenerate, the first principle and ontologically before all things has no name by which to distinguish him from generate or created things. God's simplicity is also appealed to as the reason that God as a subject can have no name as a defining predicate. If God could be named then God would be composite. From the fact that God can receive no predicates, it follows that no demonstration is possible with respect to God. Because God is ontologically before all things, being the all-inclusive source of them, God cannot be defined; a definition, however, is required for demonstration. It is also said that there are no limits on God and so for that reason no name is attributable to God insofar as names function to limit. This is said to be the meaning of 1 Cor 15:28: God as "the all in all." The many names, or predicates, assigned to God merely approximate to an understanding of God based on what God does, but never, even collectively, provide the form of God in the sense of the definition of God. Expressed differently, names function to circumscribe, but God is said to be uncircumscribable.

By using the concept of the name of God a connection is made to Scripture, since in the Bible God's name is often used as the equivalent of God himself. Two biblical passages in which the revelation of God's name is refused are interpreted to mean that it is not possible for human beings to know what God is. Jacob's wrestling with God, and God's subsequent refusal to give his name, answering instead with the question "Why do you ask me my name?" is interpreted to mean that God is incomprehensible or that the divine essence is unknowable (Gen 32:22–32). Likewise, the angel of YHWH's question to Manoah "Why do you ask my name, seeing it is wonderful?" is taken to mean that the name of God in the sense of the nature of God is incomprehensible or that God does not have a name (Judg 13:17–18). The statement in Cant 3:1 "I sought him on my bed at night . . . I did not find him" is allegorized to refer to the impossibility of naming God

The Indescribable God

in the sense of identifying the essence of God. Other Old Testament passages quoted by Christian theologians to prove that God is nameless and therefore unknowable include Ps 145:3 "There is no end of his greatness," Exod 6:3 "By my name, YHWH, I did not make myself known to them" and Exod 3:14 "I am the one who is." In addition, Paul's phrase "name above every name" in Phil 2:9 is re-interpreted to refer to the unknowability of God's name in the sense of God's essence. Finally John 1:18 "No man has seen God at any time" and 1 Tim 6:16 "No man has seen him, nor can see" as well as "the light around him is unapproachable" are cited as proof that God is nameless.

A variation of the position that God is nameless is the use of the plural "names of God" to refer to the attributes of God. It is asserted that, unlike created things, to know God's names in the sense of attributes is not to know the essence or nature of God, but only God's energies, or the effects of God. Even to know all of God's names, or attributes, cannot bring a human being to a knowledge of God's essence or nature, since there is an irremediable disjunction between the two. The fact that many names are used of God indicates that no name or collection of names is adequate to express the divine reality. God remains other than all things no matter how many names, or attributes, are assigned to God.

Philo of Alexandria as Predecessor

Philo of Alexandria is the first known exponent of the view that the God of the Bible is nameless. In *Mut.* 14–15, he claims that the reason that the angel of YHWH, with whom Jacob wrestled all night, refuses to tell Jacob his name is because his name is unknowable insofar as God is "the indescribable existing one" (τὸ ὂν ἄρρητον). He concludes, "If he is unnamable he is also inconceivable and ungraspable."[1] In other words, the refusal to reveal a name is an expression that God is incomprehensible. Philo states as a general principle, "But as for names, symbols of generated things, do not seek for them among imperishable natures."[2] Names are symbols that apply only to generated, or created, things, functioning to distinguish one generated thing from another; no name, in the sense of a statement of definition, is applicable to God, whose nature it is to be ingenerate and imperishable,

---

1. καὶ μὴν εἰ ἄρρητον, καὶ ἀπερινόητον καὶ ἀκατάληπτον.
2. τὰ δὲ γενητῶν σύμβολα, ὀνόματα, μὴ ζήτει παρὰ φύσεσιν ἀφθάρτοις.

which is to say, the opposite of generated things. It seems that for Philo God is nameless in principle.

Individual Christian Theologians on God as Nameless

Christian theologians likewise express the otherness of God by affirming that God is nameless. Philo, or at least the Alexandrian exegetical tradition that he represents, probably influenced the development of early Christian theology in this regard. Both divergent variations of the assertion that God is nameless are found in the works of Christian theologians, often the same theologian.

Justin Martyr

Justin Martyr asserts that no one knows the name of God: "For no one can utter the name of the ineffable God" (*1 Apol.* 61).[3] What he means is that what God is shall always remain inaccessible to human beings, which is why God is ineffable. Similarly, he writes, "But to the Father of all ... there is no name given" (*2 Apol.* 6).[4] By name again he means what God is, or a definition of God. In both cases, Justin seems to assume that God has a name but that it cannot be known. He makes other statements, however, that suggest that God is nameless in principle: God does not have a name at all. He argues that the name "God" is not a name, but merely denotes the awareness implanted in human beings by God of an incomprehensible source of all named things. In the case of God, it is possible to know that God exists but have no knowledge of what God is: the word "God" functions merely to signify a nameless, or incomprehensible, object. He writes, "As also the appellation 'God' is not a name, but an opinion implanted in the nature of men of a thing that can hardly be explained" (*2 Apol.* 6).[5] The use of the term "opinion" (δόξα) for what is denoted by the term "God" probably has its origin in Platonism; it has the negative connotation of being inadequate to the object that it purports to signify. The reason that no name can be attributed to God is that God is ingenerate (ἀγέννητος) (*2 Apol.* 6). Justin means by this that God is the creator and source of all things, and so cannot

3. ὄνομα γὰρ τῷ ἀρρήτῳ θεῷ οὐδεὶς ἔχει εἰπεῖν.
4. ὄνομα δὲ τῷ πάντων Πατρὶ θετὸν ... οὐκ ἔστιν.
5. ὃν τρόπον καὶ τὸ θεὸς προσαγόρευμα οὐκ ὄνομά ἐστιν, ἀλλὰ πράγματος δυσεξηγήτου ἔμφυτος τῇ φύσει τῶν ἀνθρώπων δόξα.

be said to be like any created thing. He explains, "For by whatever name he be called, he has as his elder the person who gives him the name" (2 *Apol.* 6). God creates all things and names them, which is to say gives them essences or natures, so that each thing is what it is and not other things. To be named, or to have an essence or nature, is by definition to be created. God, however, being ingenerate, or uncreated, has no name since there is no one to give God a name. In other words, God as the all-inclusive source of all named things is not like any or all of them. The implication is that God has no name because God is the creator of all essences or natures: only created things have names.

Justin also speaks about the names of God. According to him, all the many names attributed to God in Scripture do not singly or collectively penetrate to what God is and so define God, but only describe God in relation to us, or what God does. He writes, "But these words Father, and God, and Creator, and Lord, and Master, are not names, but appellations derived from his good deeds and works" (2 *Apol.* 6).[6] The names that are attributed to God in Scripture are not true names in the sense of being statements of what God *is*; rather they derive from God's actions. In this context, by "names" Justin means divine attributes. He is making a distinction between what God is and how God is as experienced by human beings.

Clement of Alexandria

Clement of Alexandria holds that God is nameless in principle. He confesses that, insofar as God is the first principle, the cause of all things (ἀρχὴ παντὸς), all discourse about God is most difficult to handle (δυσμεταχείριστοτατος) (*Strom.* 5.12). He expresses this by saying that the first principle is "without form or name" (ἀσχημάτιστον, καὶ ἀνωνόμαστον). These two terms, "form" and "name," are synonymous, so that what has no name has no form in the sense of not being identifiable as something. Clement adds, "And if we name it, we do not do so properly. . . . We speak not as supplying his name; but for want, we use good names, in order that the mind may have these as points of support."[7] No name denoting what God is can be attributed to God; since God is ontologically before all things, being the first principle, no name is appropriate to God.

---

6. ἐκ τῶν εὐποιϊῶν καὶ τῶν ἔργων προσρήσεις.

7. κἂν ὀνομάζωμεν αὐτό ποτε οὐ κυρίως . . . οὐχ ὡς ὄνομα αὐτοῦ προφερόμενοι λέγομεν, ὑπὸ δὲ ἀπορίας ὀνόμασι καλοῖς προσχρώμεθα, ἵν᾽ ἔχῃ ἡ διάνοια.

God as Nameless and Not in a Genus

Names are simply pragmatic artifices created in order to allow the human intellect to conceive the unconceivable. He explains that predication is of two types, neither of which is applicable to God as subject: "For predicates are either from what is said of the things themselves, or from how they relate to one another" (*Strom.* 5.12).[8] A predicate could be absolute in the sense that it is said to be true of the subject itself or it could be relational in the sense that the subject is said to have a defining relation to another thing. Neither method of predication is admissible for the subject God. Drawing upon Aristotelianism, he further asserts that nothing can be learned about God by means of demonstration (ἐπιστήμη ... τῇ ἀποδεικτικῇ) because "there is nothing antecedent to the ingenerate" (τοῦ δὲ ἀγεννήτου οὐδὲν προϋπάχει). All demonstration requires premises that are what Aristotle calls "primary, immediate, better known than and before the conclusion" (*Anal. post.* 1.2; 71b). However, there can be no premise that is before God, who is ingenerate, because nothing is ontologically before God to which God can be related syllogistically. The point seems to be that God is the undifferentiated, all-inclusive source of all things and so cannot be defined, or named, and so used in a syllogism.

Clement lays down the principle that "Everything, then, which falls under a name is generated" (*Strom.* 5.13).[9] Although unexplained, it seems that Clement is asserting that all created things are named insofar as they are created to be one thing and not another. God the ingenerate, however, has no name because God is not one thing among other things, but the all-inclusive source of all things. According to Clement, all that human beings can do is give several names to God, such as the One, the Good, Mind, Absolute Being, Father, God, Creator, or Lord. None of these names, however, expresses the form of God, in the sense of the definition of God, although collectively they are "indicative of the power of the omnipotent" (ἐνδεικτεκὰ τῆς τοῦ παντοκράτοπος δυνάμεως) (*Strom.* 5.12). By using many names one can approximate to an understanding of God, but not so much by describing what God is but rather describing what God does (see *Strom.* 6.17 "not seeking to learn names").[10]

---

8. τὰ γὰρ λεγόμενα ἢ ἐκ τῶν προσόντων αὐτοῖς ῥητά ἐστιν, ἢ ἐκ τῆς πρὸς ἄλληλα σχέσεως.

9. πᾶν τοίνυν ὃ ὑπὸ ὄνομα πίπτει, γεννητόν ἐστιν.

10. See Eusebius' account of the martyrdom of Attalus: "But when Attalus was placed in the iron seat, and the fumes arose from his burning body, he said to the people in the Roman language: 'Lo! This which you do is devouring men; but we do not devour men; nor do any other wicked thing.' And being asked, what name God has, he replied, 'God

The Indescribable God

Clement interprets Exod 33:20 "No man shall see me and live," not as a prohibition, but as a statement of fact. It means that "no one during the period of life has been able to grasp God clearly" (τὸν θεὸν ἐναργῶς καταλαθέσθαι), which is why human beings need special revelation: "the Savior is sent down—a teacher and leader in the acquisition of the good" (*Strom.* 5.1).[11] He believes that Plato understood this truth about God, summarizing his view as follows: "For the God of the universe, who is above all speech, all conception, all thought (πᾶσαν φωνὴν καὶ πᾶν νόημα καὶ πᾶσαν ἔννοιαν), can never be committed to writing, being inexpressible even by his own power" (*Strom.* 5.10; see 5.14). To be above speech, conception, and thought is to be indescribable, the semantic equivalent of being nameless in principle.

Origen

Origen agrees with his opponent Celsus's view that "He [God] is not to be reached by word" (οὐδὲ λόγῳ ἐφικτός), which is synonymous with "and not by name" (οὐκ ὀνομαστὸς δέ). He writes, "If he means the word that is in us—whether the word conceived in the mind, or the word that is uttered—I, too, admit that God is not to be reached by word" (*Con. Cels.* 6.65). His agreement comes, however, with an important qualification: God *can* be reached by means of the Word. He says, "We are of opinion that God is to be reached by this Word, and is comprehended not by him only, but by any one whatever to whom he may reveal the Father" (*Con. Cels.* 6.65). In Origen's view, only a partial knowledge of God's attributes is possible: "But if you take the phrase to mean that it is possible to represent by words something of God's attributes, in order to lead the hearer by the hand, as it were, and so enable him to comprehend something of God, so far as attainable by human nature, then there is no absurdity in saying that 'He can be described by name'" (*Con. Cels.* 6.65). In short, Origen holds that human language cannot describe God fully. Whether God is nameless in principle, however, is not clear.

---

has not a name as man has'" (ὁ θεὸς ὄνομα οὐκ ἔχει ὡς ἄνθρωπος) (*H.E.* V.I.52).

11. But based on Matt 5:8 ("the pure in heart shall see God") Clement hopes that God will be eschatologically seen, "when they arrive at the final perfection" (*Strom.* 5.1). This undermines his view that God is essentially unknowable.

Minucius Felix

Minucius Felix explains that one must not ask what the name of God is because God has no name: "Neither must you ask a name for God. God is his name. We have need of names when a multitude is to be separated into individuals by the special characteristics of names; to God, who is alone, the name God is the whole" (*Oct.* 18). He takes the designation "God" to be non-descriptive, which is why he claims that the name of God is simply "God." God in fact is nameless in principle because God alone is God. He explains, "There is need of words there where a multitude is to be distinguished by the appropriate characteristics of designations; to God, who is alone, the name God is the whole" (*Oct.* 18). The purpose of a name is to distinguish one thing from other things of the same type. When there is only one of something, however, as in the case of God, no name is required. For this reason God is simply called God, which provides no knowledge of what God is. God as *sui generis* is different from all things.

Cyprian

Cyprian declines to give a name to God except the designation "God," which is non-descriptive, giving no information about God. This is because God is beyond all human conception: "This one cannot be seen, he is too bright to see; cannot be comprehended, he is too pure to grasp; cannot be estimated, he is too great to be imagined" (*De idol. vanit.* 9). To name a thing is to describe it, but, since God cannot be described, God can have no name. In fact, he seems to hold that God is nameless in principle. Borrowing from Minucius Felix, Cyprian explains that one should not seek a name for God; rather, God simply is to be called by "God," as a type of proper name: "To God, who is alone, is the whole name of God" (*Deo, qui solus est, Dei vocabulum totum est*) (*De idol. vanit.* 9). Since only God is God, there is no need of a name in the sense of a descriptor to distinguish God from things of the same type. This statement likewise suggests that for Cyprian God is nameless in principle.

Lactantius

Assuming that God has a name, Lactantius argues that God's name is nonetheless unknowable to human beings. He asserts that God "cannot

be described in words by man, or estimated by the senses" (*Ira Dei* 11).¹²
God so surpasses human intellectual capacity that, not only can God not be depicted sensibly as an idol, but also cannot be depicted linguistically using abstract terminology ("in words"). Lactantius advises human beings to know their cognitive limits. He writes, "Let him know, therefore, how foolishly he acts, who inquires into things which are indescribable. For this is to pass the limits of one's own condition, and not to understand how far it is permitted man to approach" (*D.I.* 2.9). God is indescribable by human language. Simply to know that there is one God and everything is made by God is all that a human being needs to know. Knowing "heavenly things," by which is meant what God is, is impossible insofar as a human being is an "earthly animal," which is to say a being that is cognitively limited by a body.

Lactantius also asserts that God is nameless in principle. He quotes Trismegistus approvingly to the effect that God has no name in the sense of descriptor. Probably influenced by Cyprian, he claims that the reason that God has no name is that God is alone (*solus*) and one (*unus*). He writes, "God, therefore, has no name (*nomen*), because he is alone; nor is there any need of a distinct vocabulary (*proprio vocabulo*), except in cases where a multitude of persons requires a distinguishing mark, so that you may designate each person by his own mark and appellation. But because he is always one, God's proper name is God (*proprium nomen est Deus*)" (*D.I.* 1.6; see 1.7; 2.17). Insofar as God is alone and one, nothing else is classifiable as God; from this it follows that God does not require a name by which to be distinguished from other things of the same type.

Basil of Caesarea

Basil of Caesarea argues against the Arian Eunomius that there is no name that can express the nature of God, which is why so many names, or designations, for God are used, all of which fall short of expressing the truth about God (*Adv. Eunom.* I.10). He writes, "There is no name which can adequately express all that is involved in God's nature (τὴν τοῦ θεοῦ φύσιν). We use many different words, each of which, while almost completely obscure and extremely narrow in comparison with the whole, has some meaning appropriate to our understanding." Since no name or names can be said to describe the divine nature, God remains for human beings

---

12. Tantus est, ut ab homine non possit, aut verbi anarrari, aut sensibus aestimari.

incomprehensible; what can be truly said about God provides only a partial and distorted perspective. God's name as a statement of God's nature is inaccessible to human beings.

Gregory of Nazianzus

Gregory of Nazianzus affirms that God cannot be named in the sense of defining God: "The deity is unnameable" (τὸ θεῖον ἀκατονόμαστον) (*Or.* 30.17). He then asks somewhat cryptically, "How then could they have admitted that the inexplicable and unique nature (τὴν ἄλυτον φύσιν καὶ ἰδιάζουσαν) can be explained by a dissoluble voice (λυομένῃ φωνῇ)?" God's nature is said to be inexplicable; the use of the word ἄλυτον implies that to name a thing, in the sense of explaining it, is to break it down into its component parts, presumably through a dialectical process. It is the function of language to distinguish one thing from another, which is what is meant by "dissoluble voice." The nature of God, however, is insusceptible to such a process, presumably because of its exceeding greatness.[13] In addition, God's nature is said to be unique (ἰδιάζουσαν) in the sense of being separate from and thereby unlike all things. This further explains why God cannot be named: God cannot be identified as any type of known thing. His meaning seems to be that God's name, expressive of God's nature, is inaccessible to human understanding, not that God is nameless in principle. He adds that the human mind cannot ever fully understand the essence of God, a synonym for the divine nature, and correlatively human language is inadequate to express the whole of the divine reality. He writes, "Nor has any mind entirely comprehended, or speech exhaustively contained the essence of God."[14] The most that a human being can hope for is a partial knowledge of God by means of knowing the divine attributes: "a certain faint and feeble and partial idea concerning him."

---

13. He appeals to the Jewish practice of using archaic Hebrew letters when writing the name of YHWH, in order to symbolize the incomprehensibility of God: "For they appropriated certain characters to the honor of the Deity, and would not even allow the name of anything inferior to God to be written with the same letters as that of God, because to their minds it was improper that the Deity should even to that extent admit any of his creatures to a share with himself."

14. οὔτε οὐσίαν θεοῦ παντελῶς ἢ νοῦς κεχώρηκεν, ἢ φωνὴ περιέβαλεν. He also says metaphorically, "For neither has any one yet breathed the whole air," by which he means that no has understood the whole of God.

The Indescribable God

Gregory of Nyssa

Responding to Eunomius' realist epistemology, according to which a name corresponds to an essence, Gregory of Nyssa argues that no name can express the divine essence (see *Con. Eunom.* 3.5). By name, Gregory means a descriptor expressive of essence or nature; his point is that there is no term available, like ingenerateness (ἀγεννησία), Eunomius' preference, that could provide a definition of God.[15] He writes, "We have learned no name significant of the divine nature" (*Con. Eunom.* 3.5.53–54).[16] To prove his case from Scripture, he cites the encounter between Manoah and the angel of YHWH, during which the angel refuses to disclose his name to Manoah and his wife "because it is wonderful" (Judg 13:17–18). He interprets the angel's explanation to mean that his name cannot be revealed because it is *too* wonderful (LXX θαυμαστός). In other words, the angel will not disclose it because he cannot do so since it is so wonderful as to be beyond their comprehension. Gregory writes, "By this we learn that there is one name significant of the divine nature—the wonder, namely, that arises unspeakably in our souls concerning it" (*Con. Eunom.* 3.6.4–5).[17] By using the adverb "unspeakably" (ἀρρήτως) he has transformed the wonderful name into a wonderfully unknowable name. He further claims that the only name appropriate to God is not a name, but the ineffable experience of wonder at the nameless God. Similarly, Gregory interprets the clause "I sought him on my bed at night . . . I did not find him" in Cant. 3:1 to mean that the one who seeks to know the essence (οὐσία) of God, "beginning and end, and in what his being consists" (πόθεν ἄρχεται, εἰς τί καταλήγει, ἐν τίνι τὸ εἶναι ἔχει), will not find what is sought because no such knowledge is possible (*Cant.* 6; 6.181). The next clause "I called him (by a name)" (ἐκάλουν αὐτὸν ἐξ ὀνόματος) is then interpreted to mean that the soul, represented by the bride, attempts to give God a name in the sense of identifying the divine essence, but fails to do so.

Gregory explains that, since God's nature is unknowable, no name, in the sense of attribute, can express the divine nature (ἡ θεία φύσις), which he also calls "the unspeakable and infinite nature" (ἡ ἄφροστός τε καὶ ἀόριστος φύσις) (*Con. Eunom.* 3.5.54). It is for this reason that *many*

---

15. Eunomius is not the first attribute ingenerateness to God. See Justin, *2 Apol.* 6 and Clement of Alexandria, *Strom.* 5.12.

16. ὄνομα τῆς θείας φύσεως σημαντικὸν οὐκ ἐμάθομεν.

17. διὰ τοῦτο μαθεῖν ὅτι ἕν ἐστι σημαντικὸν τῆς θείας φύσεως ὄνομα, τὸ ἀρρήτως περὶ αὐτῆς ἡμῖν θαῦμα κατὰ ψυχὴν ἐγγινόμενον.

names can be attributed to God, even though collectively they are equally inadequate to express the divine nature. What human beings know is the bare fact of God's existence, but the nature of God is unknown. Gregory quotes John 1:18 ("No man has seen God at any time"), two clauses from 1 Tim 6:16 ("No man has seen him, nor can see" and "the light around him is unapproachable" (i.e. dwells in unapproachable light)), and Ps 145:3 ("there is no end of his greatness") to support his view. The quotation from Ps 145:3 is interpreted to mean that God's greatness resulting from his essence is out of reach for human beings. Also in support of his view, he alludes to the fact that neither Abraham nor Moses was capable of knowing God's name, which is to say God's essence: "And I appeared to Abraham, Isaac, and Jacob, as God Almighty, but by my name, YHWH, I did not make myself known to them" (Exod 6:3) and "I am the one who is" (Exod 3:14) (*Con. Eunom.* 3.5.54–55). His point seems to be that God only revealed himself to Abraham as God Almighty, not by his name, and when God did reveal his name to Moses it turns out that YHWH is no name at all, but the denial of a name.

Gregory argues that since none of God's names, or attributes, is expressive of the divine essence, then Eunomius is unjustified in claiming that the essence of God is ingenerateness (*Con. Eunom.* 3.5.56–60; see *Vit. Mos.* II.176; *In beat.* 2). He writes, "Anyone, then, who undertakes to give the account of this good being, of this ingenerate being, as he is, would speak in vain, if he rehearsed the attributes contemplated in him, and were silent as to that essence that he undertakes by his words to explain. To be without generation is one of the attributes contemplated in the being, but the definition of 'being' is one thing, and that of 'being in some particular way' is another" (*Con. Eunom.* 3.5.60). All of the divine attributes are God's being in some particular way (τὸ πῶς εἶναι), but do not describe the being of God (τὸ εἶναι) in the sense of the divine essence, or definition of God. He insists that one must not confuse God's names, or attributes, with God's essence or nature, for it is possible to give names to God but still not identify God's nature. He writes, "For every name that you may use is an attribute of the being, but is not the being" (*Con. Eunom.* 3.5.59).[18] This is especially true of negative attributes such as ingenerate.

Gregory also takes the position that God is nameless *in principle*, not simply unnameable by human beings. He claims that the only designation that one can give to God is to say that God is the "name above every name,"

18. πᾶν γὰρ ὅτιπερ ἂν εἴπῃς ὄνομα περὶ τὸ ὂν ἐστιν, οὐκ ἐκεῖνό ἐστιν.

The Indescribable God

which derives from Phil 2:9, modified by Gregory to express the absolute unnameability of God (*Con. Eunom.* 1.1.683; *Abl.* 3, 1.52; *In eccl.* 7.411). By the term "name," he means, unlike Phil 2:9, predicates or attributes of God. In his view, God's simplicity precludes ever being able to state what God is essentially. He writes,

> But there is not, neither shall there be, in the church of God a teaching such as that, which can make one who is simple and in-composite (τὸν ἁπλοῦν καὶ ἀσύνθετον) not only multiform and patchwork, but also the combination of opposites. The simplicity of the true faith assumes God to be that which he is, i.e., incapable of being grasped by any term, or any idea, or any other device of our apprehension, remaining beyond the reach not only of the human but of the angelic and of all supramundane intelligence, unthinkable, unutterable, above all expression in words, having but one name that can represent his proper nature (τῆς ἰδίας … φύσεως), the single name of being "Above every name."
>
> (*Con. Eunom.* 1.1.683)

For Gregory, even to say that God has only one essential attribute, like ingenerateness, would mean that God is composite insofar as God would consist of a subject and predicate. So the only name appropriate in light of divine simplicity is the "name above every name," which is to say *no*-name. Along the same lines, he writes, "For this inability to give expression to such unutterable things . . . affords an evidence of the glory of God, teaching us as it does, in the words of the apostle, that the only name naturally appropriate to God is to believe him to be 'above every name' (Phil 2:9). That he transcends every effort of thought, and is far beyond any circumscribing by a name, constitutes a proof to man of his ineffable majesty" (*Con. Eunom.* 2.1.586–87). In this context, "the glory of God" (ἡ δόξα τοῦ θεοῦ), a functional synonym for the nature of God, is said to be ineffable (ἀφράστος), which constitutes its singular majesty (μεγαλειότης). Parallel to the term ineffable are the designations "transcends every thought" (ὑπερβαίνειν πᾶσαν διανοίας), which means that the divine nature is inconceivable and inexpressible, and being "beyond any circumscribing by a name" (ἐξώτερος τῆς ὀνοματικῆς), which means that God is indefinable and so is not one thing among other things. All these assertions are said to be implied in Paul's expression "above every name." God's nature, identical to his glory, is his ineffable majesty (ὁ ἀφράστος μεγαλειότης). In Gregory's view, the many designations attributed to God only denote

God's energies. He writes, "But he is named . . . not what he is essentially (οὐκ αὐτὸ ὅ ἐστιν) (for the nature of him who is is unspeakable), but he receives his appellations from what are believed to be his energies (ἐξ ὧν ἐνεργεῖν τι) in regard to our life" (*Con. Eunom.* 2.1.149).

Pseudo-Dionysius

Pseudo-Dionysius holds that God is both "nameless" (ἀνώνυμον) and "from every name" (ἐκ παντὸς ὀνόματος), by which he means many-named (πολυώνυμον) (*De div. nom.* I.6). For him God is nameless in principle because God does not have a defining essence or nature. Unlike some of his predecessors, Pseudo-Dionysius interprets the statement of the angel of YHWH to Manoah that he will not reveal his name to him because it is wonderful to mean he *cannot* reveal the name because there is no name to reveal. Alluding to Phil 2:9 "name above every name," he writes, "And is not this in reality the wonderful name, that which is above every name—the nameless—that fixed above every name which is named, whether in this age or in that which is to come?" God cannot be named because God is the cause of all, which is dependent upon God for its existence. This is how he interprets the meaning of Paul's statement in 1 Cor 15:28 that God is "the all in all" (τὰ πάντα ἐν πᾶσι) (*De div. nom.* I.7). What he means is that God is the limitless source and creator of all things and cannot be named or identified as one of those limited, or finite, things. He writes, "It previously embraced in itself all things existing, absolutely and without limit" (*De div. nom.* I.7).[19] God is not one thing distinguishable from other things, but that from which all things originate. As the cause of all, God is above all, ruling over all, and that on which all is dependent for its being (*De div. nom.* I.7). Nevertheless, God as "the author of all things" (τὸ πάντων αἴτιον) can be variously described by many names derived "from all created things" (ἐκ πάντων τῶν αἰτιατῶν), by which is meant insofar as God relates to all created things in various ways. However, none of these names—nor all of them collectively—describes God essentially. Rather any name predicated of God only describes God relationally, what God is *for* the things that God created, not God in himself.

---

19. πάντα δὲ ἁπλῶς καὶ ἀπεριοπίστως ἐν ἑαυτῇ τὰ ὄντα.

The Indescribable God

John of Damascus

John of Damascus asserts that God always remains nameless, by which he means that no human being can ever know what God is, the divine essence. He writes, "The Deity being ungraspable is also assuredly nameless. Therefore since we know not his essence, let us not seek for a name for his essence. For names are explanations of things" (*O.F.* 1.12).[20] As used in the passage, names are definitions, which is what the phrase "explanations of things" means. In other words, a name is a statement of essence, but no such name can be attributed to God because God's essence is unknown.

Gregory Palamas

According to Gregory Palamas, God's names, in the sense of attributes, do not describe the divine essence, not even collectively; rather they identify only the *energies* of God. God is negatively characterized as the one who is beyond being nameable: "But he who is beyond every name is not identical with what he is named; for the essence and energy of God are not identical" (*Triads* III.ii.10).[21] While the energies of God are nameable, the essence of God always remains unnameable: "But the essence of God that is beyond all names (ἡ ὑπερώνυμος οὐσία τοῦ θεοῦ) also is beyond energy" (*Triads* III.ii.10). He compares the relationship between the divine essence and the divine energies to that between a subject and its predicates. Even the name God is not God's name, but describes an energy of God insofar as God is the one who deifies human beings: "But he is called God on the basis of his deifying energy" (*Triads* III.i.31; see III.ii.10).

GOD AS NOT IN A GENUS

Synopsis

Another way used by Christian theologians to express the otherness of God is the Aristotelian-inspired assertion that God is not in a genus. Although

---

20. τὸ θεῖον ἀκατάληπτον ὄν, πάντως καὶ ἀνώνυμον ἔσται. Ἀγνοοῦντες οὖν τὴν οὐσίαν αὐτοῦ, τῆς οὐσίας αὐτοῦ μὴ ἐκζητήσωμεν ὄνομα· δηλωτικὰ γὰρ τῶν πραγμάτων ἐστὶ τὰ ὀνόματα.

21. Ταὐτὸ δὲ τῷ ὀνομαζομένῳ τὸ ὑπερώνυμον οὐκ ἔστιν· οὐ ταὐτὸ ἄρα οὐσία καὶ ἐνέργεια θεοῦ.

anticipated by earlier theologians, this concept is especially prominent in the works of medieval theologians. As formulated by Aristotle, a genus is a class of objects that share common essential characteristics; within a genus are contained species distinguished from one another by differences. Obviously, God cannot belong to a genus unless it is a genus of one. There is, however, a more important reason that God cannot be categorized generically: God is incomposite, or simple. God cannot be in a genus because whatever is in a genus is composite, consisting of a genus and species. It follows that, since God is not in a genus, God shares nothing in common with any created thing and so is other than all things. Only that which is in a genus can be said to be the same as something else in the same genus insofar as they share essential qualities. At most, what God has in common with created things is existence, but even assuming that for God to be is the same as what it means for created things to be, being cannot be considered a genus. Another reason given for the fact that God is not in a genus is that God is infinite: whatever is in a genus is limited, but God is unlimited. From the conclusion that God is not in a genus, it further follows that God cannot be defined since a genus is necessary for definition: God cannot be understood *as* something. Moreover, no univocal predication can be made of God and creatures, since between God as creator and creatures there is an unbridgeable conceptual gap.[22] This explains why idolatry is absurd.

Philo of Alexandria as Predecessor

Anticipating what will be said by Christian theologians, Philo of Alexandria explains that God, the existing one (τὸ ὄν), cannot be understood by means of concepts that derive from human experience: "They . . . do not overlay the conception of God with any of the attributes of created things" (γενέσεως οὐδὲν προσαναπλάττουσιν αὐτῷ) (*Deus imm.* 61). In

---

22. John Duns Scotus agrees with Aristotle that the discipline of metaphysics studies being as being (*ens inquantum ens*), which includes a study of infinite being. He holds that the transcendental "being" is univocally attributable to God and to created things. (Being is the simplest of all transcendental concepts and for that reason cannot be defined.) The difference between them is that God is a different *type* of being, namely, a being that has unlimitedness as its intrinsic mode of existing. (The disjunctive transcendental "infinite or finite" is co-extensive with the transcendental "being," being its first division.) Scotus advances arguments in favor of univocal predication and against the *via negativa* type of theological method, which in his view, only leads to skepticism (*Ord.* 1, d.3, p.1, q.1–2, n.10). Scotus's detractors insist that it is equivocation to say that God and created things both exist.

The Indescribable God

addition, interpreting Israel's name as meaning "seeing God," he explains that there is no true seeing of God: "Not meaning by this expression seeing what kind of being God is, for that is impossible . . . but seeing that he really does exist (*Praem.* 44).²³ The most that a human being can say truly about God is that God exists; beyond this assertion of bare existence nothing more can be said, in particular what kind of being God is. Similarly, according to Philo, God cannot be compared to anything. He writes, "But God has no likeness even to what is noblest of things" (*Gig.* 42).²⁴ It would be unworthy of God even to ascribe to him superlative attributes derived from human experience. This implies that God can never be included in a genus along with other things, even as the greatest and most exalted of great and exalted beings. Philo makes this explicit by asserting that God cannot be classified as belonging to any created genus and so cannot be understood *as* something. He writes, "There is nothing equal to him or even a little below. But everything that comes after God is found to be inferior with respect to its whole genus" (*Sacr.* 92).²⁵ To be inferior with respect to genus implies that nothing can be placed in the same genus as God, to which God then could be compared qualitatively as greater. In other words, the difference between God, the cause, and what God causes to be is absolute; God has nothing in common with created things, which is what Philo seeks to express by saying that there is "nothing equal to him or even a little below." This view of God also explains why, reflecting on the rationale behind the prohibition against idolatry (Exod 20:23), Philo asserts that God has no qualities (ἄποιος) (*Leg.* 1.51).

Individual Christian Theologians on God as Not in a Genus

Clement of Alexandria

Clement of Alexandria casserts that, because God is ontologically before all things, "the absolutely first and oldest principle" (ἡ πρώτη καὶ πρεσβυτάτη ἀρχὴ), God is not classifiable with respect to the system of things that he causes to exist. Clement asks, "For how can that be expressed which is neither genus (γένος), nor difference (διαφορά), nor species (εἶδος), nor individual, nor number; nay more, is neither an event, nor that

---

23. οὐχ οἷος ἐστιν ὁ θεός—τοῦτο γὰρ ἀμήανον . . . ἀλλ᾽ ὅτι ἔστιν.
24. ἀλλά γε ὁ θεὸς οὐδὲ τῷ ἀρίστῳ τῶν θύντων ὅμοιος.
25. ἀλλ᾽ ὅλῳ γένει καταβεβηκὸς ἅπαν τὸ μετὰ θεὸν εὑρίκεται.

to which an event happens?" (*Strom.* 5.12). What he means is that no category of thought functioning to organize the things of human experience can be applied to God. In addition, Clement makes the pantheistic-sounding statement, "On account of his greatness he is ranked as the totality, and is the father of the totality" (*Strom.* 5.12).[26] God's unique greatness consists in the fact that God is the totality and the origin of the totality. This means both that God is all things insofar as God causes all things to exist and at the same time is none of the things that he causes to exist. Consistent with this position, Clement writes that the God of the totality is "above all speech, all conception, all thought, can never be committed to writing, being inexpressible even by his own power" (*Strom.* 5.10).[27]

Thomas Aquinas

In his *Summa contra Gentiles*, Aquinas begins his reflection on the question of whether God is in a genus with his previous conclusion that, because there is no composition in God, God *is* his essence, quiddity, or nature, which means that for God to be God *is* to exist. From this he concludes that "nothing can be added to the divine being to determine it with an essential determination, as a genus is determined by its differences" (*SCG* 1.24). Nothing can be added to God because God is not composite: whatever would be added would make God composite. This conclusion then leads to the further conclusion that the incomposite God cannot be in a genus since what is in a genus "is determined to its species" (*designatur ad speciem*) (*SCG* 1.25). In other words, if God were in a genus, God would be composite since whatever is in a genus also has a species determined by its differences: "Nothing is in a genus that is not in some species of that genus" (*SCG* 1.25). Besides, if God were in a genus, that genus would be being (*ens*) since God is a necessary being, or as Aquinas put it "the quiddity of God is its own being" (*quidditas Dei est ipsum suum esse*). However, being is not a genus and so God cannot be in a genus. From this it follows that God cannot be defined. Aquinas writes, "From this it is likewise evident that God cannot be defined, for every definition is constituted from the genus and the differences"[28] (*SCG* 1.25). Also this is why no demonstration about

---

26. ἐπὶ μεγέθει γὰρ τάττεται τὸ ὅλον, καὶ ἔστι τῶν ὅλων πατήρ.

27. ὁ ὑπὲρ πᾶσαν φωνὴν καὶ πᾶν νόημα καὶ πᾶσαν ἔννοιαν, οὐκ ἄν ποτε γραφῇ παραδοθείη ἄρρητος ὢν δυνάμει τῇ αὑτοῦ.

28. Ex quo etiam patet quod Deus definiri non potest: quia omnis definitio est ex

The Indescribable God

God is possible: all demonstration presupposes the definition of what is to be demonstrated.

In his *Summa Theologiae*, Aquinas restates his argument that God cannot be in a genus. In the context of dealing with the question of God's simplicity, he asks whether it is correct to place God in a genus as a species of that genus (*ST* 1.3.5). (God cannot be an individual material exemplification of a species since God has no matter.) Because he does not know the essence or nature of God, Aquinas cannot answer *simpliciter* whether God is contained in a genus. Nevertheless, he offers three arguments against the view that God is contained in a genus, all of which ultimately derive from God as simple, or incomposite, which itself is a conclusion drawn from God as first efficient cause. First, God cannot be in a genus because God has no potentiality. The difference that constitutes the species relates to its genus as potentiality is related to actuality.[29] What this means is that all differences that constitute species are potentially in its genus. However, God cannot be in any genus as a species because this would mean that God would have potentiality: the differences that would make God a species of a genus. God has no potentiality because he is the fully actual first cause—*actus purus*. Aquinas concludes, "Hence since in God actuality is not added to potentiality, it is impossible that he should be in any genus as a species."[30]

Second, since God's essence is existence, as proven in the previous article, if God were in a genus, then God would have to be in the genus "being" (*ens*). However, being cannot be a genus, because every genus includes differences that are distinct from its generic essence (*differentias quae sunt extra essentiam generis*), but being as a genus could have no such differences and the negation of being, i.e., non-being, is not a difference. Aquinas writes, "Now no difference can exist distinct from being; for non-being cannot be a difference."[31] The genus of being to which God would belong could have no species and so God as a species of the genus could not exist. It follows that God is not in a genus.

Third, in every member of a genus existence and essence or quiddity must differ. Everything that belongs to a genus shares in the essence or

---

genere et differentiis.

29. Whether it is a correct to understand specific difference as a type of potentiality perhaps needs to be asked.

30. Unde, cum in Deo non adiungatur potentia actui, impossibile est quod sit in genere tanquam species.

31. Nulla autem differentia posset inveniri, quae esset extra ens; quia non ens non potest esse differentia.

quiddity of that genus, but each thing differs in its existence, which is not shared. In other words, each member of a genus exists as an individual being; its existence is independent of its essence. But God's essence is existence and so it follows that God cannot be in a genus as an individual belonging to a species of that genus. Aquinas concludes, "From this it is also plain that he has no genus nor difference, nor can there be any definition of him; nor, save through his effects, a demonstration of him: for a definition is from genus and difference; and the means of a demonstration is a definition."[32] If God is not in a genus as a species, then God cannot be defined because to define is to identify the genus and species of a thing by means of the differences.

John Duns Scotus

John Duns Scotus agrees that God, what he calls the "first nature," is not to be placed in a genus. The reason for this derives from God's simplicity: what is in a genus is composite insofar as its definition consists not only of the genus but also of the difference constituting its species. It follows that God as simple cannot be in a genus, since God cannot be in a species. He writes, "The whole of the nature which falls into a genus is expressed by a definition in which what the genus expresses is not entirely the same as what the difference expresses; otherwise there would be useless repetition. Such is not the case with something as simple as the first nature" (*DPP* 4.5). This makes God different from all finite, created substances, even though they all share in the transcendental of being.

Bonaventure

Bonaventure asserts that God is in no one determinate genus (*uno genere determinato*) not only because God is incomposite, or simple, but also because God is infinite. In his view, every being in a genus has a limited, constrained, and composite being (*esse limitatum et arctatum et compositum*), unlike God, who is simple and infinite (*simplex et infinitum*) (*Comm. sent.* I.8.2.4). A genus identifies the manner in which one class of things differs from another by being limited and constrained. Since God is not limited

---

32. Et ex hoc patet quod non habet genus, neque differentias; neque est definitio ipsius; neque demonstratio, nisi per effectum: quia definitio est ex genere et differentia, demonstrationis autem medium est definition.

and constrained insofar as God is infinite, it follows that God cannot be in a determinate genus. Furthermore, God cannot be in more than one genus either, since to be such requires being "composite and in a multiform manner." However, God as simple can have no such composite nature and so cannot be in more than one genus. Bonaventure adds that God cannot be conceived as being in more than one genus on account of generality (*propter generalitatem*); if this were the case, God would be a transcendental quality that is shared by many generically different things, such as the quality of oneness or being. To depict God as such would mean that God is not distinct from all other things, but rather that God is pantheistically conceived as the true but hidden reality behind the diversity of things. He writes, "But God is the one having in himself a being distinct from things" (*ens distinctum a rebus*). He concludes that God is a being unlike all other beings, since the latter are composite, unlike God. To the third objection that God is in a genus because God contains all the perfections of creatures, Bonaventure claims that every perfection and goodness is posited of God not through diversity but according to an omnimodal unity, which causes God to be outside of every genus. For this reason, God cannot be considered to be every genus collectively, as if God could be conceived as the totality of being.

Johann Gerhard

Using an Aristotelian framework, Johann Gerhard affirms that God has no genus and therefore no definition.[33] He adds that, if God had a genus, then univocal predication could be made of both God and creatures, but this would contradict the infinite distance between God as creator and the creature. In addition, Gerhard says that God cannot be defined on account of his perfection. In other words, God cannot be defined because God is pure act (*merus actus*) and highest existence (*summam entitatem*). The point is that God contains all reality in a neo-Platonic sense, so that in God are contained all genera of being in an infinite mode. This means that God is not in a genus. In fact, Gerhard agrees with John of Damascus' description of God as superessential: Deus est οὐσία ὑπερούσιος. He finds scriptural support for his view in Exod 33:20, "You cannot see my face," and 1 Cor 13:12, "For now we see in a mirror dimly." He identifies two ways in which God could be defined: essentially or causally, both of which are impossible. The first

33. *Loci Theologici*, locus secundus, cap. V.

is impossible because God has no genus and is most simple. The second is impossible because God is the cause of all but not caused by anything.

Karl Barth

In the modern period, Karl Barth makes use of the traditional concept that God is not in a genus (*Deus non est in genere*) in the service of his view of the unknowability of God without self-revelation, but, of course, without a commitment to Aristotelian philosophy. He claims that not to be in a genus means that God "cannot be classified or included in the same category with anything that He is not" and that "No higher unity is possible between them and God which can be expressed by a higher comprehensive term" (*CD* 2/1:310–11). This makes God unlike all things and so unknowable.

CONCLUSION

The otherness of God is expressed by Christian theologians by affirming that God is nameless. What is meant is either that God is nameless for human beings or that God is nameless in principle. On the former, human beings know that God exists but cannot know God's name in sense of what God is, God's essence or nature. On the latter, God is understood as being ontologically before all things and all-inclusive so that nothing can be said about God to distinguish God from created things. Whatever is nameless in either sense is incomprehensible because to name is to define. God's names, or attributes, likewise do not singly or collectively state the essence of God but only God's actions; God's relation to creation. In addition, God is said not to be in a genus. Whatever is not classifiable generically cannot be said to be anything.

4

God as the One Who Is

CHRISTIAN THEOLOGIANS INTERPRET GOD's revelation of his name to Moses in Exod 3:14 as an expression of God's otherness. They claim that the statement that God's name is "I am who I am" (אהיה אשר אהיה), "I am" (אהיה), and "he is" (יהוה) implies that God can only be said to be, and nothing more. In other words, while it is possible to affirm that God is, it is impossible to define God, which is what a real name would do. From this it follows that God is other than all things. This interpretation of Exod 3:14 was widespread until the modern period when, under the pressure of historical criticism, it was generally abandoned.[1]

THE ORIGINAL MEANING OF EXOD 3:14-15

Exod 3:14 provides the background for the explanation of the meaning of the name YHWH (hwhy) in Exod 3:15.[2] The name YHWH is probably a 3rd person singular verbal form deriving from the archaic root הוי, later היה, "to be."[3] God's name as "he is" is based on the fact that, when they

---

1. It is now the scholarly consensus that the ancient Hebrews could not have thought in such abstract terms.

2. See also Exod 15:3 Hos 12:5, 9; 13:4; Amos 9:6; Isa 42:8.

3. D. N. Freedman, "יהוה, YHWH" in G. Johannes Botterweck and Helmer Ringgren, eds. *Theological Dictionary of the Old Testament*, vol. 5 (Grand Rapids: Eerdmans, 1977) 500.

God as the One Who Is

ask who sent him, God instructs Moses to tell the Israelites that it is "I am" who sent him, which is an abbreviation of the longer, tautologous designation "I am who I am" (Exod 3:14). The designations "I am who I am" (אהיה אשר אהיה), "I am" (אהיה) and "he is" (יהוה) in Exod 3:14–15 are not proper names, but rather function to assure the Israelites that God will be present with them in accordance with the promises to the patriarchs (see Exod 6:2, 4–5; Deut 7:9; Isa 26:4). The use of the imperfect denotes continuing, unfinished action or a process of becoming, denoting God's invariable faithfulness and so immutability of purpose in history: God does not deviate from his promises and covenantal obligations to Israel. In other words, the imperfect has a dynamic and promissory thrust intended as reassurance to the Israelites of YHWH's future trustworthiness, and so the translation "I will be what I will be," "I will be," and "he shall be" would also be appropriate.[4]

GOD AS THE ONE WHO IS IN HELLENISTIC JUDAISM

The LXX translation of the Hebrew Bible opens new interpretive possibilities for Exod 3:14–15, a *sensus plenior* for God's self-identification to Moses. The Hebrew אהיה אשר אהיה is translated as ἐγώ εἰμι ὁ ὤν: "I am the one who is." The use of the gerund ὁ ὤν allows interpreters to draw certain theological implications about the nature of God from God's revealed name.[5] There are two related uses to which God's self-identification as "the one who is" (ὁ ὤν) is put. First, God's name simply as "the one who is" is said to imply God's eternity and necessity. God is named "the one who is" because, insofar as God is eternal and necessary, being can be said to belong to God in a way that it belongs to nothing else. Second, God's name as "the one who is" is used to demonstrate that God is not nameable

---

4. According to the documentary hypothesis, now almost universally accepted in some version by scholars, Exod 3:1–22 is an amalgam of the Yahwist (J) and Elohist (E) sources, although there is not complete agreement among concerning which portions of the passage belong to which source and which are redactional. Generally it is agreed that Exod 3:13–15 derives from the Elohist on the grounds that the name Elohim occurs in the text, whereas the following passage, Exod 3:16–20, is thought to derive from the so-called Yahwist since the name YHWH occurs in it. That it is possible to reconstruct the redactional history of Exod 3:1–22, however, without having access to one or more of the sources is highly questionable. Moreover, the alleged literary evidence, such as the use of divine names, literary seams, repetition, different names for the same reality and so forth is open to other, simpler explanations.

5. The LXX hinders this interpretation by translating YHWH as ὁ κύριος.

The Indescribable God

in the sense of being identifiable as something; all that can be said about God is that God exists, but nothing more. From the fact of God's eternity and necessity, it is believed to follow that God does not have a name in the sense of an essence or nature: God is not a definable being but is rather the indefinable source of all beings. This explains why God's name in Exod 3:14 is not really a name at all. Sometimes Platonic philosophy is used to explain the connection between being eternal and necessary and being indefinable.

The earliest known interpretation of LXX Exod 3:14 comes from Philo of Alexandria, who directly or indirectly influenced Christian exegesis of this passage. He interprets the revealed name "the one who is" (ὁ ὤν) to mean that God is necessary and eternal. From this he draws the further conclusion that God is not nameable. Although he does not explain it, he holds that whatever is eternal and necessary cannot be understood. Philo claims that God reveals himself to Moses by the quasi-name of "I am the one who is" (ἐγώ εἰμι ὁ ὤν) in order to lead the Israelites ultimately to the realization that no name is appropriate to God. This is because God is not a nameable being, but is rather the one to whom being truly belongs (*Mos.* 1.75). He writes, "God replied: 'First tell them that I am the one who is, that they may learn ... that no name at all can properly be used of me, to whom alone being belongs'" (ᾧ μόνῳ πρόσετι τὸ εἶναι). By saying that being (τὸ εἶναι) belongs to God alone, Philo means that God exists eternally and necessarily. This is why God cannot be named, in the sense of identifying what God is: God cannot be said to be like things dependent upon God for their existence.[6] Philo repeats this interpretation in *Mut.* 10–12, claiming that "I am the one who is" is the equivalent of "my nature is to be, not to be spoken of" (ἴσον τῷ εἶναι πέφυκα, ουο λέγεσθαι) (*Mut.* 11). To paraphrase, he is saying that, unlike created things, God exists necessarily (and eternally) and so can never be identified as a contingent thing. This means that nothing can be said about God because language can only be used to signify contingent things. Philo further states, "No name even can be properly assigned to the one who in truth is" (τῷ ὄντι πρὸς ἀλήθειαν).[7]

---

6. Philo calls God ἡ τοῦ Ὄντος ποιητικὴ δύναμις, which seems to be inspired by Exod 3:14 (*Quaest. in Gen.* 4.8).

7. Probably, in part, under the influence of his interpretation of Exod 3:14, Philo calls God "the true existing being" (τὸ πρὸς ἀλήθειαν ὄν), whom no human being can comprehend (*Abr.* 80). Similarly, he designates God as "the one who alone truly is" (μόνος γὰρ πρὸς ἀλήθειαν ὤν) (*Vit. Mos.* II.100) and simply as "the existent one" (τὸ ὄν) (*Deus* 4). Finally he refers to God as "according to being" (τῷ κατὰ τὸ εἶναι θεῷ), by which he means that God alone exists necessarily (*Conf.* 139).

God as the One Who Is

The phrase "to be in truth" is the semantic equivalent of "to whom being belongs." Since God exists necessarily (and eternally), God alone can be said truly to be, unlike all created things, which exist contingently. For this reason, according to Philo, God is different from all things, which precludes the possibility of assigning names to God in the sense of attributes (*Mut.* 10). Nevertheless God allows human beings to use the denial that God has a name—"the one who is"—as something of a makeshift name (*Mut.* 12).

In Philo's view, the fact that God's name has four letters in Hebrew is no accident. The four letters of the tetragrammaton represent the four primary numbers, one, two, three and four, which are the elements of all spatial existents: point (1), line (2), superficie (two-dimensional object) (3), and solid (three-dimensional object) (4) (*Mos.* II.115). The implication is that God is not a being among beings but is the being of beings, or that whereby all beings exist. This would explain why God cannot be named in the sense of being defined. In another work, Philo explains that "God needs no name," but has adopted a "unique name" (ἴδιον ὄνομα): "I am the one who is" (Exod 3:14). This self-designation is not really a name in the sense of predicating something of God. Joined to this unique name is the further identification of God in Exod 3:15 as "the God of Abraham, Isaac and Jacob," which Philo calls a relative name (τὸ πρός τι), as opposed to the absolute one (τὸ καθάπαξ) revealed in Exod 3:14 (*Abr.* 51). God can be known and identified by his relations to creation, in this case, to the patriarchs, but a relative name never describes what God is. Likewise, Philo writes that the true and living God, unlike the false gods of polytheism, is beyond human understanding: "There are not in God things that man can comprehend." Any discourse about God is a misuse of language. For this reason God cannot be named except to say that he alone is: "For the living God is not of the nature to be spoken of, but alone to be" (λέγεσθαι γὰρ οὐ πέφυκεν, ἀλλὰ μόνον εἶναι τὸ ὄν). This is said to be what God meant when he revealed himself as "I am the one who is" (*Somn.* 1.230–31).[8] Although in this passage he does not explain why it is so, Philo holds that beyond the assertion that God eternally and necessarily is ("to be"), which is what the divine name "I am the one who is" means, nothing can be said about God in the sense of ascribing predicates, or names, to God. Philo's

---

8. See *Post.* 15 "That the God of real being is apprehended by no one, and to see precisely this, that he is incapable of being seen" (ὅτι ἀκατάληπτος ὁ κατὰ τὸ εἶναι θεὸς παντὶ καὶ αὐτὸ τοῦτο ἰδεῖν ὅτι ἐστιν ἀόρατος).

interpretation of Exod 3:14 explains and supports his frequent reference to God as "the existent one" (τὸ ὄν).

GOD AS THE ONE WHO IS IN CHRISTIAN THEOLOGY: EARLY CHURCH FATHERS

Synopsis

The early church fathers continue Philo's exegesis of Exod 3:14–15, and in so doing they, like him, give expression to the otherness of God. First, the name that God revealed to Moses is said to express the fact that God exists in such a way that by comparison created things cannot be said to exist in the same sense. Divine existence is characterized by eternity and necessity, unlike all other types of existence. The same depiction of God is said to be found in Isa 44:6 "I am the first and I am the last." Likewise Rev 1:4 "who was, is and is to come" is sometimes interpreted as a New Testament equivalent of Exod 3:14, as is the parallel in Rev 4:8. Since it is equivocation to say that God and created things both *exist*, it becomes necessary to use qualifiers to express how God's being differs from that of created things. God's immutability and oneness are sometimes associated with God's eternity and necessity.

Second, early Christian theologians assert that, because God is eternal and necessary, God does not have a knowable essence or nature, which is the reason that God identifies himself simply as "the one who is": nothing more can be said about God. As eternal and necessary, God is the source of all things and therefore other than all created things. Sometimes it is said that God could not reveal his name, or definition, because there is none to reveal. The assumption is that only created things have names in the sense of being definable. In addition, God's eternity and necessity is correlated with God's simplicity, which provides another reason that God is named tautologously "the one who is." The fact that God is incomposite and for that reason does not have true attributes is said to be the reason that God can only be known as "the one who is." All the names, or attributes, of God in Scripture describe only God's relations to created things; this includes the second name that God reveals to Moses in Exod 3:15, "I am the God of Abraham, and the God of Isaac, and the God of Jacob." The scriptural text "An ox knows its owner, and a donkey its master's manger, but Israel does not know, my people do not understand" (Isa 1:3) is co-opted in support of this interpretation of Exod 3:14. Jesus' statement "No one knows the Father" (Matt 11:27) is likewise said to be consistent with this interpretation of Exod 3:14. The fact that God identifies himself merely as existing is also said to be consistent with the biblical prohibition of idolatry.

Sometimes the early church fathers have recourse to Platonism in interpreting Exod 3:14; this exegetical aid is used to explain how God the creator relates to created being. God as "the one who is" is identified as the ineffable good, beyond essence, in which all things participate or the good from which all good things derive their goodness. For this reason, nothing can be said to be like God, which explains why God is other than all things. Also under the influence of Platonism, it is said that God *truly* is, and as such is unlike all created things that participate in God. In addition, in order to explain the meaning of God's revealed name in Exod 3:14, the spatial metaphor of being that in which all things are contained is applied to God; the intention is to distinguish the "containing" God, who is eternal and necessary, from all "contained" things, which are temporal and created, dependent on God for their being. The same point is made by saying that God is in everything. The divine name revealed in Exod 3:14 is also said to mean that God is Being itself or that God is the self-same, based on Ps 102:24 "whose partaking is in the same." Because there is nothing contrary to Being itself except non-being, God cannot be said to be unlike or like anything.

Individual Early Church Fathers

Justin Martyr

Justin Martyr holds that the name that "YHWH" reveals to Moses at the burning bush is no name at all: "And all the Jews even now teach that the nameless God (ἀνωνόμαστον θεὸν) spoke to Moses" (*1 Apol.* 63). God can have no name because God is not a nameable thing. He then interprets Exod 3:14 in light of Isa 1:3 "An ox knows its owner, and a donkey its master's manger, but Israel does not know, my people do not understand." Contrary to its original paraenetic intention, the Isaian passage is interpreted to mean that God is inherently unnameable and so is incomprehensible. In other words, Israel's God is indefinable, which is why the Israelites do not and cannot know God. Justin joins this passage from the Old Testament with Jesus' words "No one knows the Father, but the Son; nor the

Son, but the Father, and they to whom the Son reveals him" (Matt 11:27) (*1 Apol.* 63). Jesus' point is said to be that God the Father is incomprehensible. Justin does not explain in the passage, however, why God is unnameable.

Clement of Alexandria

Clement of Alexandria connects God's self-designation as "the one who is" (ὁ ὤν) with the Decalogue's prohibition of idolatry in the second commandment: "You shall not make for yourself an idol" (Exod 20:4). He writes, "The second word intimated that men ought not to take and confer the august power of God (which is the name, for this alone were many even yet capable of learning), and transfer his title to things created and vain, which human artificers have made, among which 'the one who is' is not ranked" (καθ' ὧς ὁ ὤν οὐ τάσσεται). In his view, the bare designation "the one who is" (ὁ ὤν) is unavoidable since God is unlike all created things and is not to be ranked or classified as one of them. He then somewhat obscurely says, "For in uncreated identity the one who is is absolutely alone" (*Strom.* 6.16).[9] God, as uncreated and therefore as eternal and necessary, exists in a way that created things do not, for which reason God is unlike all things; this is what he means when he says that God exists "in uncreated identity." This is why no idol can be made to represent God. Clement conceives an idol as not simply a physical representation of God but also as a conceptual representation.[10] Similarly, commenting on John 17:21, "You, father are in me," he says, "God is one, and beyond the one and above the monad itself. Wherefore also the particle "you," having a demonstrative emphasis, points out God, who alone truly is, 'who was, and is, and is to come,' in which three divisions of time the one name 'who is'" (*Paedag.* 1.8). According to Clement, God truly is in the sense of being eternal and necessary, which is what Rev 1:4 ("who was, is and is to come") and Exod 3:14 ("who is") both affirm. This is what the emphatic use of pronoun "you" in John 17:21 is believed to imply.[11] His reference to God as the one who truly (ὄντως) is

---

9. ἐν ταὐτότητι γὰρ ἀγεννήτῳ ὁ ὤν αὐτός μόνος.

10. Clement writes that the name YHWH (Ιαού) means "the one who is and will be" (*Strom.* 5.6). For him YHWH is not a proper name but a description of God's necessary existence. Clement also identifies God's being with true being: "And what is good is that which is true, and what is true is that which finds 'true being,' and attains to it. 'The one who is,' says Moses, 'sent me'" (*Strom.* 1.25). By true being he seems to mean necessary and original being.

11. Perhaps under the influence of Exod 3:14, Clement affirms that "God, who is

depends upon Plato's depiction of the Good, with the implication that God, as the Good, is unlike all created things, being beyond essence (ἐπέκεινα τῆς οὐσίας) (*Rep.* 6.509b). Drawing upon Pythagoreanism, he also affirms that God's oneness, which presumably is inseparable from God's eternal and necessary existence, is not the oneness of the unit, nor its origin, the monad, but God's oneness is unique and incomprehensible.

Origen

Origen interprets God's self-disclosure in LXX Exod 3:14 as "I am the one who is" along Platonic lines to mean that God as eternal and necessary alone truly exists and that all things participate in God in the sense of deriving their being from God. He writes, "Now, in him who truly exists, and who said by Moses, 'I am who I am,' all things, whatever they are, participate" (*Prin.* 1.3.6). Implied is that God is unlike all of the things that participate in him and so is incomprehensible.

Athanasius

Athanasius holds that the name revealed by God to Moses is the equivalent of the Platonically-inspired statement that God truly *is* (ὄντως οὖσα), which implies God's eternity and necessity (*Ar.* 4.1; see *Ep. Afr.* 4).[12] That God truly is means that God's existence is so different from the existence of other things that God cannot be compared to anything. He writes, "When then he says, 'I am the one who is,' and 'I am the Lord God,' or when Scripture says, 'God,' we understand nothing else by it but the intimation of his ungraspable essence itself (ἀκατάληπτον αὐτοῦ οὐσίαν), and that he is (ἔστιν)" (*Decr.* 22). According to Athanasius, God is inaccessible to human beings insofar as the essence of God is ungraspable. This means that God's revealed name, "the one who is," "Lord God" (κύριος, ὁ θεός) or simply the name "God" has no conceptual content; rather it is simply a statement

---

without beginning, is the perfect beginning of the universe, and the producer of the beginning. As, then, *he is being*, he is the first principle of the area of action" (ὁ θεὸς δὲ ἄναρχος, ἀρχὴ τῶν ὅλων παντελής, ἀρχῆς ποιητικός. ᾗ μὲν οὖν ἐστιν οὐσία, ἀρχὴ τοῦ ποιητικοῦ τόπου) (*Strom.* 4.25).

12. The phrase τὸ ὄντως ὄν derives from Platonism; see *Phaed.* 246a–250c, especially 249c. See also Plotinus, *Enn.* 3.8.8, 9; 3.9.4; 5.3.5, 12, 15, 17; 5.2.1; 5.3.12; 5.5.5; 6.8.19.

that God exists and nothing more. In Platonic fashion, Athanasius traces the goodness of existent things to God as the Good, whom he identifies as "God who is," clearly dependent on LXX Exod 3:14. He writes, "But good is, while evil is not; by what is, then, I mean what is good, inasmuch as it has its pattern in God who is" (ἐκ τοῦ ὄντος θεοῦ) (*Adv. gent.* 4). No doubt, he is interpreting Exod 3:14 in light of Plato's teaching that the Good is ineffable insofar as it is "beyond essence" (ἐπέκεινα τῆς οὐσίας) (*Rep.* 6.509b). Whatever exists is good by virtue of existing, and all things derive their existence from God the Good, who is. What is implied is that God the Good is unlike all good things. Likewise, Athanasius asserts that the statements about God in Scripture, including Exod 3:14, denote "the very simple, and blessed, and ungraspable essence itself of him who is" (τοῦ ὄντος οὐσίαν) (*De syn.* 35). The reason that God is called "the one who is," which alludes to Exod 3:14, is because God's essence is unknowable: all that can be said about God is that he is. It seems that being simple also accounts for why God can only be known by the tautology "the one who is": God, as incomposite, can have no attributes.

Hilary of Poitiers

Hilary of Poitiers argues that the revealed name in Exod 3:14, "I am who am" (*ego sum, qui sum*), denotes God's eternity and necessity (*De Trin.* 1.5–6). He observes that it is the nature of God to be (*esse*): "For no property of God which the mind can grasp is more characteristic of God than existence."[13] By contrast, things that are not eternal cannot be said to exist in the same sense that God exists (*De Trin.* 1.5). Presupposing the simplicity of God, Hilary asserts that, since God's eternity cannot be separated from God, it is appropriate that God should reveal his name to Moses as "I am who am."[14] He interprets the name of God in Exod 3:14 as referring to what he calls the absolute being (*esse proprium*) of God, by which is meant eternity and necessity: God cannot be thought of as not being. He says, "For according to the words spoken to Moses, the one who is, has sent me unto you, we obtain the unambiguous conception that absolute being belongs to God" (*Deo proprium esse id quod est, non ambigens sensus est*) (*De Trin.* 12.24).[15] In addition, Hilary holds that, because God has absolute existence,

---

13. Non enim aliud proprium magis Deo, quam esse, intelligitur.
14. See *De. Trin.* 6.14: "How can we think of God, who is, being born?"
15. See *De Trin.* 12.25: "Now since it is the special characteristic of his being that his

God must remain unknowable to human beings. He writes, "The result is that the backward straining of our thoughts can never grasp anything prior to God's property of eternal existence (*semper esse*); since nothing presents itself to enable us to understand God (*ad intelligentiam Dei*), even though we go on seeking to eternity, save always the fact that God always is" (*De Trin.* 12.24). In his view, God's eternal existence, expressed by the name "I am who am" in Exod 3:14, means that the nature of God is incomprehensible.[16] Beyond existing eternally and necessarily nothing else can be predicated of God. Although he does not provide a reason, presumably it is because as eternal and necessary God cannot be understood in terms of created things.

Gregory of Nazianzus

Gregory of Nazianzus interprets God's revealed name in Exod 3:14 as expressing the essence or nature of God absolutely and not relatively (καθ' ἑαυτό, καὶ οὐκ ἄλλῳ συνδεδεμένον). In other words, it expresses what God is in himself and not a relation that God has to creation.[17] He holds that the designation "the one who is" (ὁ ὤν) is appropriately ascribed to God because, unlike all created things, being belongs to God insofar as God is eternal (*Or.* 30.18). He writes, "But being is in its proper sense peculiar to God, and belongs to him entirely (τὸ δὲ ὂν ἴδιον ὄντως θεοῦ, καὶ ὅλον), and is not limited or cut short by any before or after, for indeed in him there is no past or future." The fact that God is eternal implies that God is necessary, for only what cannot be destroyed can always exist. Along the same lines, in his *Oration on the Theophany*, Gregory interprets the revealed name in Exod 3:14 as meaning that God is eternal and includes within himself all being insofar as he is source of all things. He writes, "But he is eternal

---

Father always exists, and that he is always His Son, and since eternity is expressed in the name he that is, therefore, since he possesses absolute being, he possesses also eternal being (et in eo quod est, significatur aeternitas; per id quoque, cui quod est proprium est, proprium est et aeternum).

16. See John Chrysostom: *Homilies on St. John*, XV[2] "Would you learn also his eternity? . . . Now the expression 'I am,' is significative of being ever, and being without beginning, of being really and absolutely."

17. See Basil of Caesarea , *Adv. Eunom.* II.18. Basil of Caesarea holds the name revealed in Exod 3:14 implies that God truly is (ὄντως ὤν), is the source of life and is eternal, but his major concern in this passage is to prove that it was the son of God who spoke to Moses.

being (ὁ δὲ ὢν ἀεὶ). And this is the name that he gives to himself when giving the oracle to Moses in the mount. For comprehending in himself the whole, he contains all being" (ὅλον γὰρ ἐν ἑαυτῷ συλλαβὼν, ἔχει τὸ εἶναι) (*Or.* 38.7). Alluding to Exod 3:14, he compares God to "some great sea of essence, infinite and unlimited, transcending all intelligibility, of time and nature" (*Or.* 38.7; see also 45.3).[18] God is not one thing among other things but is the eternal and necessary source of all things, which Gregory expresses, making use of a spatial metaphor, by saying that God is that in which all beings are contained ("comprehending in himself the whole, contains all being"). This he further expresses by comparing God to the sea. Metaphorically God is the sea in which all created things are found. Unlike all the things in it, God as the "sea of essence" is "infinite and unlimited" (ἄπειρον καὶ ἀόριστον) with respect to time and nature. God is not to be understood as existing in time, or as having a nature in the sense of a definition.[19]

Gregory of Nyssa

Although he also puts this text to other theological uses, Gregory of Nyssa interprets God's identification of himself to Moses in Exod 3:14 as "I am the one who is" (ἐγώ εἰμι ὁ ὢν) to be a revelation that God's name, in the sense of God's nature, cannot be known. He holds that the name of God revealed to Moses indicates that it is the nature of God necessarily to be, and so to be "eternal and infinite in being" (κατὰ τὸ ἀΐδιόν τε καὶ ἀόριστον ἐν τῷ εἶναι), which in this context are functionally synonymous expressions. He finds the same view expressed in Isa 44:6 "I am the first and I am the last" (*Con. Eunom.* 3.6.3). In addition, it is the nature of God to be immutable: "is always the same, neither growing nor being consumed."

---

18. οἷόν τι πέλαγος οὐσίας ἄπειρον καὶ ἀόριστον, πᾶσαν ὑπερεκπῖπτον ἔννοιαν, καὶ χρόνου καὶ φύσεως.

19. Reflecting upon Exod 3:14, Jerome states that what makes God different from everything else is that God is the cause of the latter while being caused by nothing (*C. Eph.* II.3 on Eph 3:15). In addition, he writes, "I am that I am," God says; and if you compare all created things with him they have no existence (*Ep.* XLVIII. To Pammachius). Likewise in *Letter to Damasas*, he states because God is eternal God can truly be said to be an essence (XV.4). He says, "God alone who is eternal, that is to say, who has no beginning, really deserves to be called an essence. Therefore also he says to Moses from the bush, "I am that I am," and Moses says of him, "I am has sent me." Jerome does not draw the conclusion, however, that God is thereby incomprehensible.

God as the One Who Is

According to Gregory, the name revealed by God to Moses in Exod 3:14 is only a statement of the bare eternal and infinite existence of God and nothing more. What was revealed to Moses at the burning bush was "the being without a name" (τὸ ὂν ἀκατονόμαστον), by which he means the being whose nature (φύσις) is unknowable (*Con. Eunom.* 3.5.59). Gregory makes a distinction between the many names attributed to God in scripture and the nature of God, which always remains unknown.

Dependent upon Platonism, Gregory interprets the name "the one who is" as implying that God is that in which all things exist by participation. He writes, "For even if the understanding looks upon any other existing things, reason observes in absolutely none of them the self-sufficiency by which they could exist without participation in true being" (δίχα τῆς μετουσίας τοῦ ὄντος εἶναι) (*Vit. Mos.* II.25). For this reason, further drawing upon Platonism, he asserts that God can be called "truly real being" (ἀληθῶς τὸ ὄντως ὄν), which implies that God as eternal and necessary (self-sufficient) is unlike all the things that participate in his being. Similarly, based on Exod 3:14, Gregory in a quasi-pantheistic manner, using a spatial metaphor, speaks about how everything is in God insofar as God is the one who is and that on which all things depend for their being. He writes, "For who, when he takes a survey of the universe, is so simple as not to believe that there is deity in everything, penetrating it, embracing it, and seated in it? For all things depend on him who is, nor can there be anything which has not its being in him who is" (*Or. cat.* 25).[20] The fact that God is not a being but that on which all beings depend, being in all things and so forth, means that God is unlike all things and explains why God is incomprehensible.

Augustine

In his *Enarrationes in Psalmos*, Augustine interprets God's name in Exod 3:14 as implying God's eternity, immutability, and incomprehensibility. (For Augustine, God's eternity and immutability imply God's necessity.) Commenting on the phrase "your years" (Ps 102:24 [101:25]), he asserts that God's years are eternity. As eternal, God simply is, meaning that God has

---

20. μὴ ἐν παντὶ πιστεύειν εἶναι τὸ θεῖον, καὶ ἐδυόμενον καὶ ἐμπεριέχον καὶ ἐγκαθήμενον; τοῦ γὰρ ὄντος ἐξῆπται τὰ ὄντα, καὶ οὐκ ἔνεστιν εἶναί τι μὴ ἐν τῷ ὄντι τὸ εἶναι ἔχον.

The Indescribable God

no past, present, or future.[21] This conclusion leads Augustine to interpret Ps 102:24 in light of Exod 3:14. He claims the revealed name of God in Exod 3:14 means that God is Being itself (*ipsum esse*), which accounts for why God is eternal: it is God's nature to be.[22] He writes, "Behold this great 'is,' great 'is.' What is man's being to this? . . . Who can understand 'that to be' (*illud esse*)?" (*En. ps.* 101, ser II.10).[23] (It should be noted that Augustine holds that an angel spoke to Moses at the event of the burning bush, not God [*Civ. Dei* 12.2].) As Being itself, God is not a particular being that can be named in the sense of being defined.[24] Augustine points out, however, that God accommodates himself to human frailty by identifying himself by means of a temporal and relational name: "God of Abraham, Isaac and Jacob," which God reveals to Moses afterwards (see also *En. ps.* 104.4; 134.6).

Similarly, exegeting Ps 122:3 [121:3], Augustine reflects upon the meaning of "self-same" (*idipsum*), which he uses as a designation for God (*En. ps.* 121.5).[25] This inquiry is prompted by the occurrence of the phrase "*in idipsum*" in verse three: *cujus participatio ejus in idipsum* ("whose partaking is in the self-same"). He interprets "the self-same" (*idipsum*) in which Jerusalem partakes to be God, who became flesh.[26] Although he

---

21. See *Conf.* VII. 10,16; *De Trin.* VII, 5,10 for other interpretations of Exod 3:14.

22. Augustine also states that God as Being itself is true being (*esse vere*) as compared to the being of all other things; he means by this that God is necessary in contrast to the contingent beings that depend upon God as Being itself (see the phrase "supreme essence" [*summa essentia*] in *Civ. Dei* 12.2). Moreover, implied in the name "Being itself" is that God is creator, immortal, eternal, and immutable.

23. See *En. ps.* 103 ser. I.3; 127.15; 143.11 for interpretations of Exod 3:14 as expressing God's eternity and immutability.

24. Similarly, in *On Christian Doctrine*, Augustine explains that the revealed name "I am who I am" and "I am" in Exod 3:14 means that "that all other things that exist, both owe their existence entirely to him, and are good only so far as he has given it to them to be so" (1.35).

25. See *Conf.* 9.4.8–11; see also *Conf.* 7.10.16; 9.10.23–26; *Civ. Dei* 8.11; 12.2; *De. Trin.* I.8.17 for other significant references to Exod 3:14.

26. Augustine holds that the pre-existent, divine Christ spoke to Moses: "Christ himself is understood in the words I am that I am, as he is in the form of God where he has not thought it robbery to be equal to God, there he is the same" (*En. ps.* 121.5). Victorinus, a possible influence on Augustine, holds the same view (*Liber de generatione Verbi divini*, XIV). Ambrose, another influence on Augustine, interprets Exod 3:14 along the same lines: "Christ therefore is, and always is; for he, who is, always is. And Christ always is, of whom Moses says: 'He that is has sent me.' Gabriel indeed was, Raphael was, the angels were; but they who sometime have not been are by no means with equal reason said always to be. But Christ, as we read, 'was not it is, and, it is not, but, it is was in him' (2 Cor 1:19). Wherefore it is the property of God alone to be, who ever is" (*De fide* V. 25).

God as the One Who Is

claims an inability fully to understand what "self-same" (*idipsum*) means, Augustine nevertheless proposes that to be self-same is to be eternal and immutable: "that which exists always in the same way; that which is not one thing in one way and a different thing in another way."[27] In fact, according to Augustine, what changes in one way and then another (*aliter et aliter*) cannot really be said to be in the fullest sense (*non summe est*), insofar as it has no permanence. Augustine then asserts that a synonym for *idipsum* is "what is" (*quod est*); he connects God as "what is" with the revelation of God's name in Exod 3:14. Paraphrasing Exod 3:14 in accordance with this theologoumenon, he writes, "Behold the self-same, I am who am, who is, sends me to you."[28] Augustine concludes by stating that no one can understand the meaning of what is given as the name of God to Moses: "You cannot grasp it; there is so much to understand, so much to comprehend" (see *En. ps.* 130.12).

Along the same lines, Augustine brings Exod 3:14 to bear on his exegesis of Ps 134:6 "Praise the Lord, for the Lord is good" (*En. ps.* 136.6). He interprets the assertion that the Lord is good in a Platonic manner to the effect that God is the Good from which all good things originate and the Good by which they are good. Expressing his inability to understand the ineffable Good, he claims that what is meant by saying that God is good is the same as what is found in Exod 3:14: "I am who am" (*ego sum qui sum*) and "the one who is" (*Qui est*). God is not a particular thing that can be defined; rather God is ontologically before all particular things as their source. This means that God is unlike all things and so is incomprehensible in terms of them. According to Augustine, because the name revealed to Moses cannot be understood, God reveals another name that originates from God's temporal relations to human beings: God of Abraham, Isaac, and Jacob. Moreover, interpreting Ps 83:18 "You are the most high over all the earth," Augustine explains that things that are made—human beings, in particular—are as if they do not even exist when compared to God by whom they are made, who names himself appropriately "I am who am (Exod 3:14)" (*En. ps.* 82.14). The implication is that God alone can be said to exist in the fullest sense of the word and therefore is nothing like created things.

Augustine interprets Exod 3:14–15 in the same way in one of his sermons (*Ser.* 223/A.5). He argues that the name revealed to Moses "I am

27. Quod semper eodem modo est; quod non modo aliud, et modo aliud est.
28. Ecce idipsum, Ego sum qui sum, Qui est, misit me ad vos.

who am" refers to God's eternity and immutability. God is what God is because God unchangingly has always been and always will be what he is. By contrast, nothing temporal and changing can be said to exist in the truest sense in comparison to God. The name revealed to Moses in Exod 3:14 is God's "substantial name" (*nomen substantia*), or an absolute description of the eternal and immutable God. However, because God's substantial name is incomprehensible to human beings, God reveals another name in Exod 3:15: God of Abraham, Isaac, and Jacob, which is a temporal, relational name. This is said to be God's "merciful name" (*nomen misericordiae*). Augustine makes the same point about the two names of God in his *Homilies on John*: since no one can understand the meaning of the names "I am who am" and "the one who is," God reveals a comprehensible name, "I am the God of Abraham, and the God of Isaac, and the God of Jacob" (*Io. ev. tr.* 38.8; 99.5).

Exegeting Exod 3:14, Augustine asserts that defining God simply as Being ("I am") means that there is no opposite of God except non-being. What has no opposite cannot be known, since to know something is to know what it is not. He writes,

> From this, I trust, it is now made patent to spiritual minds that there cannot possibly exist any contrary to God (*nullam naturam Deo esse posse contrarium*). For if he is—and this is a word which can be spoken with propriety only of God (for that which truly is remains unchangeably; inasmuch as that which is changed has been something which now it is not, and shall be something which as yet it is not)—it follows that God has nothing contrary to himself (*nihil habet Deus contrarium*). . . . When, however, it is asked, What is contrary to that which is? The right reply to give is, that which is not."
>
> (*Fide et symb.* 4.6–7)

According to Augustine, God as creator includes within himself all being so that there can be no nature contrary to the all-inclusive God. From this it follows that God as inclusive of all cannot be conceived as a being among other beings that has a nature that could be known by way of contrast. Augustine makes the same exegetical point in *City of God*. God is what he calls the supreme essence (*summa essentia*), who is the unchangeable source of all things; this is said to be the meaning of the name "I am who am" (*ego sum, qui sum*) (Exod 3:14) (*Civ. Dei* 12.2). God creates from nothing and thereby gives being (*esse*) to what he creates, but not supreme being (*summe esse*). Rather, created things have greater or lesser degrees of being. (It should be noted again that he holds that God did not directly speak to Moses; rather an angel did on behalf of God, since God is immutable.) Augustine then draws the conclusion that God as the supreme nature (*natura*), synonymous with supreme essence, is not contrary to anything that exists, being contrary only to what does not exist. He writes, "To that nature which supremely is, and which created all else that exists, no nature is contrary save that which does not exist" (*contraria natura non est, nisi quae non est*). What is contrary to God is simply non-being. For this reason, no created thing can be like the supreme essence or nature: if nothing is unlike God then nothing is like God either. He adds, "And thus there is no being contrary to God, the supreme being, and author of all beings whatsoever" (*essentia nulla contraria est*). God as supreme essence or nature is beyond all comparisons with created essences or natures. Although he does not say so, Augustine could claim that God does not have a nature at all. This means that God is incomprehensible because God is neither like nor unlike any created thing.

John of Damascus

John of Damascus holds that, because of God's simplicity, God cannot be said to have attributes since this would make him a composite. This is why the most appropriate name for God is "the one who is" (ὁ ὤν), as revealed to Moses in Exod 3:14. He writes "The most proper of all the names given to God is 'the one who is,' as he himself said in answer to Moses on the mountain, 'Say to the sons of Israel, he that is has sent me.'" Borrowing from his predecessors, he further explains, "For he keeps all being in his own embrace, like a sea of essence infinite and boundless" (οὐσίας ἄπειρον καὶ ἀόριστον) (*O.F.* 1.9).[29] The point is that Exod 3:14 depicts God as without an essence, which is expressed by calling God by the tautologous appellation "I am the one who is." God is not a being among other beings but is that which includes within himself all beings and for this reason is eternal and necessary. This makes God incomprehensible.

---

29. See Gregory of Nazianzus, *Or.* 38.7; 45.3.

The Indescribable God

Pseudo-Dionysius

Pseudo-Dionysius explains that the divine name "I am the one who is" (ἐγώ εἰμι ὁ ὤν) indicates that God requires many names insofar as no name can describe God: "Also, as 'many named,' as when they again introduce it as saying, 'I am the one who is—the life—the light—the God—the truth.' And when the wise of God themselves celebrate him, as author of all things, under many names, from all created things" (*De div. nom.* I.6). For him, God as the one who is (ὁ ὤν) is synonymous with the Platonic-inspired description of God as being truly (ὄντως) and "superessential" (ὑπερούσιος) (*De div. nom.* V.1, 4).[30] What is implied is that God's revealed name is the disclosure that God has no essence insofar as God truly is and is superessential; as such God is eternal and necessary.

GOD AS THE ONE WHO IS IN CHRISTIAN THEOLOGY: MEDIEVAL THEOLOGIANS

Synopsis

Medieval theologians likewise interpret Exod 3:14 as meaning both that God is eternal and necessary, for which reason God is other than all things. The difference between them and their theological predecessors is that some of them use Aristotelian philosophy with its related theological vocabulary to express their views.[31] The name that God revealed to Moses, "the one who is," is said not to signify God's form, what God is, but simply to state that God exists necessarily. This is because the essence of God is inaccessible to the human intellect. Expressed differently, it could be said that as Being itself, God is outside of every genus.

---

30. Gregory Palamas holds that Exod 3:14 implies that God is "he who contains all being in himself" (*Triads* III.ii.12).

31. Peter Lombard repeats the traditional view that God's revealed name "I am who I am" denotes that God can be said to be being, or essence, insofar as God is eternal. He writes, "He himself is truly and properly said (to be) "essence" (*essentia*), whose essence knows no past or future (*Sent.* 8.1). Lombard does not, however, draw the further conclusion that, because God is eternal, God is other than all things and therefore incomprehensible.

Individual Medieval Theologians

Thomas Aquinas

Using an Aristotelian philosophical framework, Aquinas argues that the name that God gave to himself in Exod 3:14 is the most appropriate name for God for three reasons, one of which is relevant for this investigation (*ST* 1.13.11).[32] The name "the one who is" does not say anything about the form of God, what God is, but signifies simply *that* God is. He writes, "For it does not signify form, but simply Being itself."[33] He finds this to be particularly appropriate since only of God can it be said that essence is existence, insofar as God is necessary.[34]

Bonaventure

As the fifth way that God can be approached by the mind, Bonaventure says the mind fixes its sight on Being itself (*ipsum esse*), which he identifies as God (*Itin. men.* V). That God is Being itself is said to be expressed in Exod 3:14 "I am who am" (*ego sum qui sum*) (V.2). Bonaventure's explanation of what it means to call God "Being itself" is a version of neo-Platonism but expressed using Aristotelian categories. He distinguishes between particular and universal beings (*entia*) and Being itself. Particular beings are individual things, whereas universal beings are universals. Both types of

---

32. See *De potentia* 7.2: "Wherefore the name *the one who is* (Exod 3:14) is said to be most appropriate, seeing that according to Damascene it signifies the *boundless sea of substance*" and *Contra gentiles* 1.22.10: "This sublime truth Moses was taught by our Lord. When Moses asked our Lord: 'If the children of Israel say to me: what is his name? What shall I say to them?' The Lord replied: 'I am who I am.... You shall say to the children of Israel: He who is has sent me to you.' By this our Lord showed that his own proper name is he who is. Now, names have been devised to signify the natures or essences of things. It remains, then, that the divine being is God's essence or nature."

33. non enim significat formam aliquam, sed ipsum esse.

34. Aquinas assumes that God has an essence to which the human intellect does not have access. His second reason that the name 'the one who is' is appropriate of God is because of its universality (*universalitas*), by which is meant generality. In his view, since human beings do not know the essence of God, the less informative and non-specific the designations used to refer to God are, the more appropriate they are. Aquinas writes, "Therefore the less determinate the names are, and the more universal and absolute they are, the more properly they are applied to God" (Et ideo, quanto aliqua nomina sunt minus determinata, et magis communia et absoluta, tanto magis proprie dicuntur de Deo a nobis).

The Indescribable God

beings are classifiable according to genus. By contrast, Being itself is neither a particular nor a universal being, and therefore is "outside of every genus" (*extra omne genus*) (V.4). As in neo-Platonism, Being itself, which a neo-Platonist would call "the One," is ontologically before all distinctions and is the source of beings, both universal and particular. So, according to Bonaventure, when God identifies himself to Moses simply as the one who is, God is indicating that he as Being itself is outside of every genus. It follows that God is not a thing among other things and so is incomprehensible. This is why Bonaventure explains that when it looks upon Being itself, what he calls "the light itself of most high being," the mind seems to see nothing. He compares this to the times when the physical eye sees pure light and it seems to it to be seeing nothing. The unity of God, which is the emphasis of the teaching about God in the Old Testament, follows from God as Being itself, along with many other attributes.

GOD AS THE GOOD IN CHRISTIAN THEOLOGY: PROTESTANT THEOLOGIANS

Synopsis

Protestant theologians retain the traditional interpretation of Exod 3:14; this aspect of their theological heritage at least they did not reject. God's self-designation as "I am who am" or "the one who is" is interpreted to mean that God is eternal and necessary, which leads to the further conclusion that God is other than all things and incomprehensible. There is a tendency, however, for Protestant theologians to include the original biblical meaning of being faithful to God's covenantal promises with its stress on the future as another interpretation of Exod 3:14–15.

Individual Protestant Theologians

John Calvin

John Calvin translates the Hebrew אהיה אשר אהיה in Exod 3:14 as future "I will be what I will be," and interprets it as denoting "the perpetual duration of time." In his view, what God means to communicate to Moses is that he "is self-existent and therefore eternal; and thus gives being and existence to every creature."³⁵ The shortened "I am" (אֶהְיֶה) is used as a substantive in Exod 3:15. Calvin also makes it clear, however, that the revealed name of God conceals God's "incomprehensible essence," insofar as God's existence as eternal is peculiar to God alone.

Amandus Polanus

Amandus Polanus claims that the name Jehova (YHWH) has three meanings.³⁶ First, based on its occurrence in Exod 3:14, it denotes God's eternity and necessity, which further implies that God has his essence from himself and his existence through himself.³⁷ The same view of God is said to be expressed in Rev 1:4 "From him who is and who was and who is to come" and Rev 16:5 "You who are and who were." The second meaning of the name Jehova (YHWH) is the quasi-pantheistic idea that from God derives the essence of all created things.³⁸ Polanus finds confirmation of this view of God in Paul's quotation of the Stoic philosopher Epimendies, "In him we live and move and are" (Acts 17:28), and Paul's own description of God as follows, "For from him and through him and to him are all things" (Rom 11:36). Although he does not say so explicitly, Polanus would no doubt conclude that as the source of their essence God is unlike all created things and so is incomprehensible. Third, the name Jehova (YHWH) denotes God's faithfulness to his covenantal promises, which Polanus finds expressed in Exod 6:2.

Johannes Wollebius

Wollebius finds two meanings for the name Jehova (YHWH).³⁹ First, he says that Jehova denotes both that God is eternal (see Rev 1:4; Ps 102:25) and is the cause of the existence of all things (*essendi causa est aliis omnibus*) (Acts 17:28). Citing Isa 42:8 "I am YHWH, that is my name; I will not give my glory to another, nor my praise to graven images," Wollebius further concludes that God as the cause of all things is incomprehensible,

---

35. John Calvin, *Harmony of the Four Last Books of Moses*. 2 vols. (Edinburgh: Calvin Translation Society, 1852) 1.78.

36. *Syntagma theologiae Christianae*, lib. II, cap. VI.

37. Deum ex se et per se semper fuisse, esse et futurum esse: seu Deum essentiam ex se et per se subsistentem.

38. a Deo omnium rerum creaturum essentiam esse.

39. *Compendium Theologiae Christianae*, lib. I cap. I.

so that no image can be made to represent God. Second, Wollebius asserts that the name Jehova (YHWH) means God's covenantal reliability.⁴⁰

Johann Gerhard

Johann Gerhard argues that Jehovah (YHWH) as a designation for God denotes nine things, three of which are relevant to this investigation.⁴¹ The name denotes God's self-existence (*Dei* αὐθύπαρξιν, *quod per se subsistat*). Gerhard takes Exod 3:14 to mean that God can be said to be being (*esse*) because God has his being from himself and not from another.⁴² Another meaning of the name Jehovah (YHWH) is that God is supreme (eminent). God is named Jehovah (ὁ ὤν or *qui est*) in order to signify that God is supreme over all created things.⁴³ The fact that God is above and beyond all created beings is why God is described simply as being. Finally, echoing the patristic tradition, Gerhard claims that Jehovah (YHWH) denotes that God is immutable and eternal.⁴⁴ Later in his work he asserts that the term essence (οὐσία) is an appropriate name (*nomen proprium*) for God based on God's identification of himself as "I am who is" in Exod 3:14 and God's identification as "the one who is, was and will be" in Rev 1:4; 4:8.⁴⁵

Francis Turretin

Turretin claims that the name Jehova (YHWH), unlike other of God's names, is derived from the Hebrew term meaning being or existence and has no distinctive meaning beyond being the first of all (*omnium primum*) and extraordinary (*praecipuum*).⁴⁶ He argues that three inferences about the meaning of the name Jehova (YHWH) can be made from its occurrence in Isa 44:24–26, from which it can be concluded that the name only applies to God.⁴⁷ First, it denotes the necessity (eternity) and independence

---

40. In promissionibus et comminationibus divinis maximam vim habet.
41. *Loci Theologici*, locus secundus, cap. I 7–8, 18.
42. Nec ab alio nec in alio subsistentiam habeat.
43. ut significetur Deum esse ens supra et ultra omnia creata.
44. *Loci Theologici*, locus secundus, cap. I.8.
45. Ibid., locus tertius, cap. II.48.
46. *Institutio Theologiae Elencticae*, locus tertius, quaest. IV.I.
47. Ibid., Locus tertius, quaest. IV.V.

God as the One Who Is

of God.[48] He quotes Exod 3:14 and Rev 1:4 as making the same point, and claims that the ancient philosophers, and Plato especially, acknowledged this. Second, based on Isa 44:24 "I, YHWH, am the maker of all things, stretching out the heavens by myself and spreading out the earth all alone," Turretin infers that Jehova (YHWH) is the cause of all because what is first, most perfect and in a unique genus is the cause of all else. To be first, most perfect and in a unique genus means that YHWH is unlike all things that he causes to be. Third, the name Jehova (YHWH) denotes that God is immutable in the sense of being constant in his promises, according to its original, biblical meaning.

Johann Heidegger and Wilhem Baier

Johann Heidegger argues that the name revealed to Moses in Exod 3:14 means simply "that he is" (*quod quis est*) or "who is that one who is" (*qui id, quod est*), and is not a real name in the sense of revealing the nature of God. Rather, the name expresses God's ineffability resulting from God's difference from all things, which implies God's eternity and immutability.[49] Likewise, Wilhelm Baier holds the traditional view that God's revelation to Moses in Exod 3:14 denotes that God is eternal and necessary, just as Rev 1:4 "who was, is and is to come" does. For this reason God's essence is unique and not shared by any other being.[50]

CONCLUSION

Christian theologians find a *sensus plenior* in LXX Exod 3:14 that functions as a means to express the otherness of God; sometimes this is done with the aid of Platonic philosophy. The divine name is interpreted to mean that God is other than all things insofar as the revealed name is the denial of a name in the sense of definition. All that can be said about God is that God is, but nothing more than this. In fact, God does not exist in the same way that created things exist, but exists eternally and necessarily. It follows that the name of God is deliberately uninformative.

48. Deus est Ens necessarium quod per seipsum existit independenter a quovis alio αὐτοῶν.

49. *Corpus theologiae christianae*, III.XVI–XXIII.

50. *Compendium Theologiae Positivae*, I.I.II. He writes, "Seu quod Deus tale ens sit, quale aliud nullum sit, aut esse possit: ens quod non potest non esse."

5

God as the Good

CHRISTIAN THEOLOGIANS APPROPRIATE THE Platonic concept of "the Good" in order to express the biblical teaching about the otherness of God. God as the Good is unlike all the good things that participate in God's goodness and for that reason could never be described in terms of them. All things originate in the Good, but the Good is not any of those things.[1]

GOD AS GOOD IN THE OLD TESTAMENT

In the Hebrew Bible, YHWH, or God, is said to be good (טוֹב)[2] and to have goodness (טוֹב or טוֹבָה).[3] To be good and to have goodness are synonymous, referring to God's general, beneficent disposition towards Israel or human beings in general. Goodness can also refer to a beneficial act performed by YHWH on behalf of one or more human beings, or function as a collective noun denoting the good or beneficial acts that YHWH performs on behalf of Israel or human beings,[4] especially when the term

---

1. As Plato explains, "The Good may be said to be not only the author of knowledge to all things known, but of their being and essence (καὶ τὸ εἶναί τε καὶ τὴν οὐσίαν), and yet the Good is not essence (οὐσία), but far exceeds essence in dignity and power" (*Rep.* 509b).

2. See Pss 34:8; 100:5; 135:3; 145:9; Jer 33:11; Lam 3:25; Nah 1:7.

3. See Neh 9:25; Pss 25:7; 68:10; Hos 3:5.

4. Neh 9:35; Pss 23:6; 27:13; 31:19; 145:7; Isa 63:7; Jer 31:14.

is qualified by "all" (כל).[5] In some cases good or goodness is synonymous or correlated with God's lovingkindness or lovingkindnesses (חסד),[6] righteousness (צדקה),[7] and mercies (רחמים).[8] An exception to this, however, is Exod 33:19, in which, unlike its other occurrences, "goodness" (טוב) is used with a different meaning. In response to his request, "Show me your glory" (Exod 33:18), YHWH says to Moses "I myself will make all my goodness pass before you" (אני אעביר כל־טובי על־פניך) (33:19). In this context "goodness" (טוב) is a synonym for "glory" (33:18) and "face" (33:20); it refers to what God *is*, what theologians later call God's essence or nature, which is hidden from Moses and the Israelites. Assuming the equation of goodness with face and glory, YHWH tells Moses that he cannot be shown what he is: "But my face shall not be seen" (33:23). The LXX sometimes translates "good" and "goodness" by ἀγαθός[9] and ἀγαθωσύνη,[10] which creates a point of contact between the Bible and Platonism for those theologians who use the Greek Bible.[11] The LXX translates טובי in Exod 33:19, however, as "my glory," in agreement with Moses' request in Exod 33:18 "Show me your glory."[12]

In Second Temple Judaism, largely uninfluenced by Hellenism, God's goodness has a meaning consistent with its use in the Hebrew Bible: God's general, beneficent disposition towards Israel or, more exactly, the righteous in Israel. In the *Book of Watchers* God's eschatological judgment is based on his goodness. The archangel Michael explains to Enoch that on the summit of a particular mountain is the throne upon which God will sit when he descends to visit the earth in goodness (ἐπισκέψασθαι τὴν γῆν ἐπ' ἀγαθῷ) (*1 En.* 25:3). What is being described is the eschatological theophany for the purpose of judgment, or, to use the idiom, the time when God will "visit" the earth. This will be the time of salvation for the righteous. A new dimension of meaning of God's goodness in the Second Temple period is that it is

---

5. Exod 18:9; 1 Kgs 8:66.

6. Pss 23:6; 25:7; 100:5; Isa 63:7; Jer 33:11.

7. Ps 145:7; Isa 63:7.

8. Ps 145:9.

9. Exod 18:19; 1 Kgs (3 Bas) 8:66; 2 Chr (2 Par) 7:10; Pss 27:13 (LXX 26:13); 135:3 (LXX 134:3); Isa 63:7; Jer 31:14 (LXX 38:14); Lam 3:25; Hos 3:5.

10. Neh 9:25 (LXX 2 Esdras 19:25); Neh 9:35 (LXX 2 Esdras 19:35).

11. Most of the other uses are translated as χρηστός and χρηστότης.

12. So an accident of translation forestalls making an easy connection between God's goodness in the sense of his essence or nature in Exod 33:19 with the Platonic Good.

the basis of the removal of guilt, variously expressed. In *Prayer of Manasseh*, alluding to Ps 145:7 (LXX 144), Manasseh states that, according to the fullness of his goodness, God has promised release from sins to all who repent (*Pr. Man.* 8). Manasseh also confesses that, in spite of his unworthiness, in him God will manifest his goodness (ἀγαθωσύνη) (*Pr. Man.* 14). In this context, God's goodness is that attribute whereby he shows mercy to the undeserving. According to *Psalms of Solomon*, when they sin, the righteous have the confidence that, provided they confess and make restitution, God will cleanse them from their sins because of his goodness.[13] In 1QS 11.14b–15a, it is said, "In his [God's] great goodness, he atones for all my iniquities. In his righteousness he cleanses me of the impurity of men and the sin of the sons of Adam." God's "righteousness" and his "great goodness" are parallel in meaning, each denoting that attribute whereby God removes the guilt of his covenant people. In the *Thanksgiving Hymns* (*Hodayot*), the removal of guilt is sometimes attributed to God's goodness (טובה).[14] Finally, in *4 Ezra* it is said that God will be praised as merciful at the eschaton: "For in this, O Lord, your righteousness and goodness will be declared, when you are merciful to those who have no store of good works" (*4 Ezra* 8:36).

PLATONISM AND THE GOOD

A distinctive feature of all forms of Platonism is the positing of the Good (τὸ ἀγαθόν) as the ineffable first principle. In the *Republic*, Plato asserts that the Good is an idea different from all other ideas insofar as it gives truth to the objects of knowledge and power to know to the mind; it is the source of truth and knowledge, with the result that truth and knowledge are good-like (*Rep.* 6, 508e-509a).[15] The Good is both absolute object

---

13. The author writes, "And whose sins will you forgive except those who have sinned? You bless the righteous, and do not accuse them for what they have sinned. And your goodness (ἡ χρηστότης σου) is upon those who sin, when they repent" (no doubt the original Hebrew was טובך) (9:7).

14. In 1QHa 7.30 the author writes, "You purify them from offenses by the greatness of your goodness," and in 1QHa 5.22b–23a, it is said, "By your goodness alone is a man made righteous." The author of 1QHa 11.31–32 declares, "I trust in your goodness and hope in your lovingkindness; by your forgivenesses you relieve my calamities," each clause no doubt meaning that he has been the beneficiary of God's forgiveness and in 1QHa 19.9, it is stated, "In your great goodness are forgivenesses" (see 19.31).

15. "The Good may be said to be not only the author of knowledge to all things known, but of their being and essence (καὶ τὸ εἶναι τε καὶ τὴν οὐσίαν)" (*Rep.* 509b).

and subject, the self-same first principle of being and knowing. Plato also asserts that the Good is more beautiful (καλλίων) than either truth or knowledge, being the supremely beautiful; thus for Platonism in general the Good and Beautiful tend to function as synonyms. Plato stresses that the Good cannot be said to be the same as that which is caused to be by it: "The good is not essence (οὐσία), but transcends essence in dignity and power" (509b).[16] For Plato, the Good is beyond essence, which means that it transcends the ideas, the essences of all sensible things; for this reason it can be said not to be anything or even everything. Similarly, in *Phaedrus*, it is explained that the winged charioteer, representing the soul, should aim to ascend to the highest sphere, beyond the heavens (*Phdr.* 246a–250c). There it will behold "being" (τὸ ὄν) or "truly existing existence" (οὐσία ὄντως οὖσα; lit. "beingly existing essence"), "with which true knowledge is concerned, the colorless, formless, intangible essence, visible only to mind" (247c). Although not completely clear, Plato's point seems to be that the first principle, what he calls the idea of the Good in *Republic*, is beyond all essential distinctions. There is also evidence that in his esoteric teaching Plato identified the Good with the One (τὸ ἕν).[17]

Middle Platonism identifies the Good with the One, and explicitly equates the Good with God. Plutarch identifies Plato's Good (τὸ ἀγαθόν), the offspring of which is the sun, with God. In agreement with Plato, he says that "it is from the Good that things intelligible both are and are

---

16. οὐκ οὐσίας ὄντος τοῦ ἀγαθοῦ, ἀλλ' ἔτι ἐπέκεινα τῆς οὐσίας πρεσβείᾳ καὶ δυνάμει ὑπερέχοντος (*Rep.* 509b).

17. Plato was supposed to have delivered a lecture called *On the Good* in which he made the statement "Good is one" (ἀγαθόν ἐστιν ἕν) (Aristoxenus, *Elements of Harmony*). In *Eudemian Ethics*, Aristotle discloses that for Plato the highest of all things is the Good itself, the presence of which is the reason that anything else is good (1217b). He writes, "For it is said that the best of all things is the Good itself, and that the Good itself is that which has the attributes of being the first of goods and of being by its presence the cause to the other goods of their being good; and both of these attributes, it is said, belong to the idea of Good I mean both being the first of goods and being by its presence the cause to the other goods of their being good)." In further discussing Plato's doctrine of the Good, Aristotle reveals that Plato and his school hold that the Good is also the One: "On the assumption that goodness is a property of numbers and monads because the Good itself is the One (τὸ ἕν)" (1218a). Likewise, in *Metaphysics* 1.6, Aristotle explains that Plato teaches that the ideas are the cause of all things and that the One is the cause of the ideas. He writes, "Plato, then, declared himself thus on the points in question; it is evident from what has been said that he has used only two causes, that of the essence (τί ἐστιν) and the material cause or the ideas are the causes of the essence of all other things, and the One (τὸ ἕν) is the cause of the essence of the ideas" (988a).

understood" (*Mor.* 5.8.4). This is obviously a restatement of Plato's view of the idea of the Good as giving truth to the objects of knowledge and power to know to the mind. Apuleius says that Plato's first Good is true and divine (*verum et divinum*) (*DPl.* 2.II). As quoted by Eusebius, the middle Platonist Atticus, who seeks to refute Aristotle's denial of divine providence, affirms that God "is good (ἀγαθὸν εἶναι) and goodness can never have any jealousy of anything" (*Praep. ev.* 15.5). Likewise, Albinus (Alcinous) calls the first God Good, explaining that "he is Good because he benefits all things as he is able, being the cause of every good thing" (*Didask.* 10). In other words, the first God is the source of all goodness. The fact that anything exists and is good requires a cause since no particular thing is good in itself. Rather, it is good by participation in the Good. Similarly, in his *Peri Tagathon*, as quoted by Eusebius,[18] Numenius, a precursor of neo-Platonism, distinguishes between the first God and the creator God (ὁ δημιουργὸς θεός). He holds that the first God is the Good, the principle of essence (*Praep. ev.* 11.22; frag. 25.3).[19] The first God is the Good itself whereas the second God is good by imitation of the Good itself (*Praep. ev.* 11.22; frag. 25.3).[20] The first God is also called first Mind and Being itself (*Praep. ev.* 11.18; frag. 31).[21] The first God as the Good relates to the second God as creator as essence relates to generation. He writes, "And God the creator is related to the Good, of which he is an imitator, as generation is to essence, of which it is a likeness and an imitation" (*Praep. ev.* 11.22; frag. 25.3). What he has in mind is the relation between the invisible ideas and the objects of the visible, sensible world. For the first God as the Good to be the principle of essence is to be the source of the ideas, as Plato explains in *Rep.* 6, 508e–509a.

For the neo-Platonist Plotinus, who can be considered the ultimate systematizer of Platonic thought, there is a single principle or cause of all things, the transcendent One (τὸ ἕν). Among other attributes, Plotinus ascribes goodness to the One, but not in the sense that it is a being with the attribute of goodness. The One is not a being, but *beyond being*, so to call it good is simply to identify it as the Good or Goodness, not to differentiate it from its attribute of goodness. For this reason, he can refer to the One as the Good (see *Enn.* I.8.2; III.8.9, 10; V.1.5; 5.5, 10; VI.7.16). In addition,

---

18. *Praep. ev.*, 11.18, 22.
19. ἀρκεῖ τὸ ἀγαθὸν οὐσίας εἶναι ἀρχή.
20. ὁ μὲν πρῶτος θεὸς αὐτοάγαθον· ὁ δὲ τούτου μιμητὴς δημιοργὸς ἀγαθός.
21. πρῶτον νοῦν, ὅστις καλεῖται αὐτοόν.

God as the Good

Plotinus sometimes uses the term "God" (ὁ θεός) as a synonym for the One and the Good (see *Enn.* VI. 8.14–21). Likewise, for the neo-Platonic philosopher Proclus the One, which "is beyond beings" (ἐπέκεινά ἐστι τῶν ὄντων), causes beings to exist by giving unity, or identity, to individual beings (*Instit. theol.* 8). The One is also the source of the good of all beings, and for that reason is identical to the Good: "The Good itself is one, and the One is that which is primarily good" (*Instit. theol.* 13).[22] Proclus also identifies the One and the Good with God (θεός). This follows because God is the source of all things and is the Good that all things desire. He writes, "For that beyond which there is nothing, and which all things desire, is God" (*Instit. theol.* 113). He believes, however, that there can be both one God and many gods at once insofar as "every archical cause is the leader of an appropriate multitude which is similar and cognate to the cause." This is his justification for practicing traditional polytheism while maintaining a Platonic monotheism.

SYNTHESIS OF HELLENISM AND THE SCRIPTURES

The conceptual similarity between the one God of the Hebrew Bible who is called good and said to have goodness and the Platonic first principle, the One and Good, also called God, was too obvious to miss for those with a Hellenistic background. The similarities were so close that many early Christian theologians thought that the only explanation was that Greek philosophers had read and been influenced by the Hebrew Scriptures, what Clement of Alexandria calls "barbarian philosophy."[23] As indicated, the fact that the LXX, the Bible used by so many in the early church, sometimes translates טוב and טובה as ἀγαθός[24] and ἀγαθωσύνη respectively fa-

---

22. καὶ τὸ ἀγαθὸν ἕν, καὶ τὸ ἓν πρώτως ἀγαθόν.

23. Clement of Alexandria refers to Plato as "truth-loving" (φιλαληθῆ), and seeks to prove that the Greek philosophers borrowed from Moses' writings (*Strom.* 5–6). Such a historical fiction apparently was created in order to justify using Platonic concepts in the service of biblical exegesis. The saying attributed to the second-century, Neo-pythagorean philosopher Numenius "For what is Plato but an Atticizing Moses" (τί γάρ ἐστι Πλάτων ἢ Μωσῆς Ἀττικίζων) (*Tagatha* 13) was cited approvingly (Clement of Alexandria, *Strom.* 1.22; Eusebius, *Praep. ev.* 11.10). Augustine likewise has positive view of Plato (see *Civ. Dei* 8.5–6), and proposes that Greek philosophers learned from the Bible (*Doct. chr.* 2.43, 60).

24. Exod 18:19; 1 Kgs (3 Bas) 8:66; 2 Chr (2 Par) 7:10; Pss 27:13 (LXX 26:13); 135:3 (LXX 134:3); Isa 63:7; Jer 31:14 (LXX 38:14); Lam 3:25; Hos 3:5.

cilitated this identification. The God of the Bible who created all things converges with Plato's Good as the origin of all things and that by which all things are good, which is to say, exist. The identification of YHWH with the Platonic first principle provides Christian theologians with another means of expressing the otherness of God, since the Good, as Plato explains, is beyond essence in the sense of not being one good thing among other good things. As time goes on, the assertion that God is the Good, or the Good itself, becomes entrenched in Christian theology, but sometimes without an awareness of its precise meaning or its origin and conceptual background in Platonism.

The synthesis of the biblical God said to be good with the Platonic Good has its beginning with Hellenistic Judaism. Philo of Alexandria has no hesitation about interpreting the Jewish Scriptures along Platonic lines. He refers to the biblical God as "the first Good" (τὸ πρῶτον ἀγαθὸν) (*Legat.* 1.5), and "name of Goodness" (ἀγαθότητός ... ὄνομα) (*Leg.* 3.73). He also joins together the biblical view that God is good with the Platonic view that God as the Good is the cause of all good things: "For God is good, and the cause of good things" (ἀγαθὸς γὰρ καὶ ἀγαθῶν αἴτιος) (*Prelim. Studies* XXX 168).[25]

GOD AS THE GOOD IN CHRISTIAN THEOLOGY: EARLY CHURCH FATHERS

Synopsis

Early Christian theologians use the Platonic concept of the Good to express the biblical teaching of the otherness of God, although they criticize Platonists for their acceptance of idolatry, which is said to be inconsistent with their belief in the One and Good. The one God of the Bible, who is good, is without reservation identified with Platonism's One and Good. The early church fathers frequently interpret Scripture on the assumption that Platonism is not only consistent with biblical revelation but also legitimately

---

25. Combining Stoic and Platonic conceptions, Philo calls God the active cause (τὸ δραστήριον αἴτιον) and the mind (νοῦς) of the cosmos, "exceeding virtue, knowledge, the Good itself and the Beautiful itself" (κρείττων ἢ ἀρετή, καὶ κρείττων ἢ ἐπιστήμη, καὶ κρείττων ἢ αὐτὸ τὸ ἀγαθὸν καὶ αὐτὸ τὸ καλόν) (*Opif.* 8; see *Spec.* 1.18). While it is understandable why he would say that God is beyond virtue and knowledge, it is not clear how Philo can say that God as the mind of the universe is beyond the Good itself and the Beautiful itself, since for a Platonism there is nothing beyond these.

expansive of it.[26] Such scriptures include Exod 3:14, "I am who I am," 1 Cor 2:9, "what no eye has seen," and Ps 134:6, "Praise the Lord, for the Lord is good." Likewise, early Christian theologians adopt the Platonic view that everything that exists is good and exists insofar as it participates in Goodness. They differentiate God as the Good from the good things that participate in the Good by a qualifying the former in different ways: God is variously called the Good itself, first Good, archetypal Good, supreme Goodness, highest Good, good Good, simple Good, super-unknown and surpassing Goodness and super-good Goodness, in order to distinguish the original Good from its derivative goods. The metaphor of the fountain of good is used: God is the source from which all goodness flows. The simplicity of God is sometimes used to explain why God is good essentially: God does not have good as an attribute but God as incomposite is his own goodness. Not surprisingly, in addition to the Good, God is sometimes called the Truth and Light, as well as the Beautiful. The idea that God is the Good in which all things participate sometimes creeps towards a Stoic-like pantheism that God is the good in everything.

The fact that God is the Good in which all good things participate means that God cannot be described as one good thing among other good things. God as the Good cannot be said to be like any or even all the things that participate in God's goodness, for which reason God is said to be other than all things, the ineffable Good. This is what is meant when it is said that God is beyond good or transcends the all. The same thing is meant by calling God, as the Good, unlimited or infinite, by asserting that God is superessential or super-Good and by saying that God as the Good is in all things or that all things are in God.

Individual Early Church Fathers

Clement of Alexandria

Clement identifies God with the Good in a such way that suggests a Platonic influence: "For there is one Good, the Father" (ὅτι εἷς ἀγαθός, ὁ Πατήρ) (*Strom.* 5.10) and "But nothing is better than the Good (τὸ ἀγαθόν). The Good, then, does good. And God is admitted to be good.

---

26. Origen writes, "We, then, on hearing these words ['the first good can by no means be described in words, etc.'], admit that they are well said, for it is God who revealed to men these as well as all other noble expressions" (*Con. Cels.* 6.3).

The Indescribable God

God therefore does good. And the Good, in virtue of its being good, does nothing else than do good" (*Paed.* I.8). Similarly, he calls God the eternal "Lord and Good": "For God did not make a beginning of being Lord and Good (κύριος καὶ ἀγαθός), being always what he is" (*Strom.* 5.14). He also refers to God as Father and Good (θεὸς ὄντως καὶ πατὴρ ἀγαθός) (*Strom.* 6.12). Allegorizing the story of the Binding of Isaac along Platonic lines, Clement explains Abraham's three-day journey to Mount Moriah as the soul's journey to the transcendent good.[27] The first stage of the journey represented by the first day is existence within the visible world, the world of generation, in which a person perceives individual good things by means of the physical senses. The second stage of the journey, represented by the second day of Abraham's journey, is what Clement calls "the soul's best desire," which seems to be identical with "the region of God" (ἡ χώρα τοῦ θεοῦ), also identified with Plato's "region of ideas" (ἡ χώρα τῶν ἰδεῶν) (*Strom.* 5.11). (Allegedly Plato's theory of ideas derives from Moses: "having learned from Moses.") Although it is not completely clear, it seems that at this stage the soul comes to understand the ideas that transcend all the particular sensible goods identified as such in the world of generation: "sole pure and incorporeal applications of the intellect" (*Strom.* 5.11).[28] He explains further that "it was a place that contained all things universally" (*Strom.* 5.11).[29] As abstractions, the ideas are universals. This is said to be the experience that Paul describes in 1 Cor 13:12 "Now we see as through a glass, but then face to face."[30] On the third stage of the journey, it is said that "the mind perceives spiritual things, the eyes of the understanding being opened."[31] Although again it is unclear, this seems to describe the mind's movement from the contemplation of the ideas to the idea of the Good. Clement writes, "And do not quit the sphere of existences, until, rising up to the things which transcend it, he apprehends by the mind itself that which is good (ὅ ἐστιν ἀγαθόν)" (*Strom.* 5.11). The Good transcends the ideas, and cannot be described in terms of them.

27. Clement's allegory is loosely modeled on Plato's Allegory of the Cave (*Rep.* 7).
28. κατὰ μόνας ἐκείνας τὰς ἀκραιφνεῖς, καὶ ἀσωμάτους τῆς διανοίας ἐπιβολάς.
29. ὡς τῶν ἁπάτων, καὶ τῶν ὅλων περιεκτικόν.
30. Clement gives Paul's statement in 1 Cor 13:12 a Platonic interpretation as statement of the contrast between perception and the mind's knowledge of the ideas (*Strom.* 5.11).
31. Clement connects the three-day journey to the three days that Jesus spent in the tomb: "by the Teacher who rose on the third day."

Along the same lines, Clement quotes the Stoic philosopher Menander's statement ἅπαντα δ' ἀγαθὸν εἶναι τὸν θεόν approvingly and interprets it to mean that God is not a particular good but is rather the Good in all things (ἐν πᾶσι τὸν θεὸν ἀγαθόν) (*Strom.* 5.14). This is said to explain why Jesus says that God alone is Good (Mark 10:18) (*Paedag.* 1.8). Drawing upon the portrayal of Jesus as high priest in Hebrews, Clement further explains that the "enlightened ones" ("gnostics"), a term used to refer to the souls that have chosen virtue, progress until they "come to the Good itself (ἐπ' αὐτὸ ἀφίκωνται τὸ ἀγαθόν), to the Father's vestibule, so to speak, close to the great high priest" (*Strom.* 7.7). In this context, the Good itself is a synonym for God who dwells in the invisible, intelligible world. Since God is not a particular good, Clement is led to call God "the ineffable goodness" (ἡ ἄρρητος ἀγαθότης), meaning that, as the Good, God is incomprehensible, being beyond all sensible and intelligible things (*Strom.* 6.17).

Origen

Like Clement of Alexandria, Origen is receptive to the Platonic view of the ineffable first Good: "The first Good cannot be described in words" (ῥητὸν οὐδαμῶς ἐστι τὸ πρῶτον ἀγαθόν) (*Con. Cels.* 6.3). He believes this insight was revealed by God to the ancient sages: "It is God who revealed to men these as well as all other noble expressions" (*Con. Cels.* 6.3). Nevertheless, he holds that those who have correct ideas of God may still be liable to punishment because this truth is held in unrighteousness, as Paul explains in Rom 1:18: "who suppress the truth in unrighteousness." This is because they still participate in idolatrous activities and therefore do not worship God in a manner consistent with their theological beliefs (*Con. Cels.* 6.3–5).

Gregory of Nazianzus

Gregory of Nazianzus refers to God as "the supreme Goodness" (ἡ ἄκρα ἀγαθότης) (*Or.* 2.17), "the fountain of the beautiful" (ἡ πηγὴ τοῦ καλοῦ) and the Beautiful on high (τὸ καλὸν ἐνταῦθα), the vision of which human beings will receive in the afterlife as a reward (*Or.* 7.17).[32] For him the terms

---

32. In his exegetical reflections on Gen 1:1 "In the beginning God created the heaven and the earth," Basil of Caesarea refers to God the creator as the bountiful goodness

τὸ ἀγαθόν and τὸ καλόν are synonyms, as they are for Platonists generally. He also asserts that God is the One "who is in all this universe, and again is beyond the universe; who is all the good, and beyond all the good" (*Or.* 2.76).[33] In other words, he conceives God not only as the Good that is in all good things by participation, but also as being beyond all good things, so that God is not simply a collective name for all the good. The source of all good things is not like any of the things that are good because of it, but is unlike all things and so is incomprehensible.

Gregory of Nyssa

Gregory of Nyssa adopts a Platonic vocabulary in order to express his view of God. Like the Arian Eunomius, he holds that God as ingenerate and the source of all existence has goodness by nature: "goodness is inseparable from the idea of the ungenerated nature" (*Con. Eunom.* 1.1.518).[34] This explains why he holds that "the divine, then, is never void of good" (οὐκοῦν οὐδέποτε κενὸν ἀγαθοῦ τὸ θεῖον). Rather the nature of God is "perfection in all good" (ἐν παντὶ ἀγαθῷ τελειότης) (*Con. Eunom.* 3.7.21).[35] Gregory explains further that God, the uncreated nature (ἡ ἄκτιστος φύσις), is Good in himself and not by participation: "It does not possess the good by acquisition, or participate only in the beauty of some beauty that lies above it: in its own nature it is Good, and is conceived as such and is a fountain of good" (*Con. Eunom.* 1.1.276).[36] In this context the terms τὸ ἀγαθόν and τὸ καλόν are synonyms.[37] The difference

(ἡ ἄφθονος ἀγαθότης), thereby synthesizing biblical teaching with Platonism (*Hex.* I.2).

33. ὃς ἐν τῷ παντὶ τῷδε, καὶ τοῦ παντός ἐστιν ἔξω· ὃς καλόν ἐστιν ἅπαν, καὶ ἄνω παντὸς καλοῦ.

34. εἰ οὖν ἐν τῇ ἀγεννήτῳ οὐσίᾳ ἡ ἀγαθότης νοεῖται.

35. Eunomius is similarly Platonic in his interpretation of God's goodness. As quoted by Gregory, he interprets Jesus' statement that no one is good but God (Mark 10:18) in a fuller, Platonic sense to mean that God is "the cause of his own goodness and of all goodness." Moreover, his view is that, since God is the cause of all things, which is to say all good, God can be called the one who is (τὸ ὄν), possibly deriving from Exod 3:14 (*Con. Eunom.* 3.9.1; see 3.9.23). It follows, according to Eunomius, that the Son does not have communion with that goodness (τῆς τοῦ ἀγαθοῦ κοινωνίας), since God alone is Good (3.9.20; 11.2). Rather, the Son is called the angel of the one who is.

36. ἅτε οὐκ ἐπίκτητον ἔχουσα τὸ ἀγαθὸν οὐδὲ κατὰ μετοχὴν ὑπερκειμένου τινὸς καλοῦ τὸ καλὸν ἐν ἑαυτῇ δεχομένη, ἀλλ᾽ αὐτὸ ὅπερ ἐστὶ τῇ φύσει ἀγαθὸν οὖσα καὶ ἀγαθὸν νοουμένη καὶ ἀγαθοῦ πηγή.

37. Plato seems to identify these two in *Rep* 6; 508e-509a: "Do you think that the

between God as the Good (and the Beautiful) and any created good thing is that the former is good by nature, whereas the latter is good by participation in God, who is the fountain of all good, or existence. This is what he means when he calls God "the archetypal Good" (τὸ ἀρχέτυπον ἀγαθὸν) (*Con. Eunom.* 1.1.531). Thus, while it is true that in Scripture in addition to God human beings are called "good," the use of a common term conceals a profound difference of meaning: God as the "fountain of goodness" (πηγὴ τῆς ἀγαθότητος) is good by nature and is named for it, whereas any human being said to be good is good by participation in God the Good. He writes, "From these considerations it must obviously be allowed that the idea of participation is one thing, and that of essence another" (*Con. Eunom.* 3.10.49).[38] Another way to express this is to say that God is good essentially (ἀγαθὸν οὖσαν) because, as simple, God is identical to his own goodness and does not possess it as an attribute, unlike good things (*Con. Eunom.* 1.1.235–36).

Identifying God as the Good requires that God not be understood in terms of the things that are good only by participation. As the source of all good, God is completely unlimited in goodness (ἀόριστος πάντως ἐν τῷ ἀγαθῷ), which means that God is not a particular good that can be said to be like another particular good (*Con. Eunom.* 1.1.169). Along the same lines, Gregory writes, "The first Good is in its nature infinite" (*Con. Eunom.* 1.1.291).[39] God is the first Good because God is the infinite, or unlimited, source of all good. He explains why there is no limit to God as Goodness: "The unlimited, in fact, is not such owing to any relation whatever, but, considered in itself, escapes limitation" (*Con. Eunom.* 1.1.236).[40] What he means is that God as unlimited Goodness is not known as such by being compared to something else, since this would be a limitation on God. Rather, God as unlimited can only be considered in himself, which means that God is different from all things. Commenting on Paul's statement in 1 Cor 2:9, "what no eye has seen," Gregory says that what no eye has seen nor ear heard is God himself as the Good, from which it follows that "for the Good that is above hearing and eye and heart must be that Good that

---

possession of all other things is of any value if we do not possess the Good? or the knowledge of all other things if we have no knowledge of Beauty and Goodness?"

38. Οὐκοῦν φανερῶς ἐκ τούτων ὁμολογεῖται ὅτι ἄλλος ὁ τῆς κοινότητος καὶ ἄλλος ὁ τῆς οὐσίας ἐστὶ λόγος.

39. ἄπειρον τῇ φύσει τὸ πρῶτον ἀγαθόν.

40. τὸ δὲ ἀόριστον οὐ τῇ πρὸς ἕτερον σχέσει τοιοῦτόν ἐστιν, ἀλλ' αὐτὸ καθ' ἑαυτὸ νοούμενον ἐκφεύγει τὸν ὅρον.

transcends the all" (*Anim. et res.* 56.152; see *Vit. Mos.* II.239, 242).⁴¹ God as the Good is unlike all things that participate in God's goodness. Gregory also refers to God as that nature of the Good (ἐκείνης τῶν ἀγαθῶν φύσεως) (*In cant.* 8.245–46) and, again inspired by 1 Cor 2:9, as the ineffable nature of the Good (τῆς φύσεως τῶν ἀφράστων ἀγαθῶν) (*In cant.* 8.247).⁴²

Augustine

Foundational to the theology of Augustine is the Platonic concept of God as the Good. Under the influence of Platonism, Augustine identifies God the Father, Son, and Holy Spirit, as the sole simple and unchanging Good (*bonum*), through which all other goods (*bona*), not simple and not unchangeable, have been created (*Civ. Dei* 11.10). Likewise, along Platonic lines, he identifies God as "the Good itself" (*ipsum bonum*), which makes all other things good and desirable, what he also calls "the good Good" (*bonum bonum*). He writes, "So God is to be loved, not this and that good, but the Good itself . . . the good Good" (*De Trin.* VIII. 4). Synonymous with God as the Good itself is God as the "simple Good" (*simplex bonum*), the "highest Good" (*summum bonum*) (*De Trin.* VIII.5; see III.1, 8; XI.8; XIII.11) and the "highest and unchangeable Good" (*summum atque incommutabile bonum*) (*Doct. chr.* 1.38). He further explains, "This thing is good and that thing is good, but take away this and that, and regard Good itself if you can, so will you see God, not good by a good that is other than himself, but the Good of all good" (*De Trin.* VIII.4; see *Doct. chr.* 1.35). Similarly, he states that God is "the supreme Good, from which all is good" (*a quo est omne bonum*) (15.3 [5]). What he means is that God is inseparable from his goodness and is the Good from which all things derive their goodness, which is to say, in which all good things participate. If one were to abstract from all the changeable contents of things that are identified as good, so that only the Good remains, then one has perceived or discerned God, for God is not a good thing among other things, but the unchangeable Good

---

41. τὸ γὰρ ἀγαθὸν τὸ ὑπὲρ ἀκοὴν καὶ ὀφθαλμὸν καὶ' καρδίαν, αὐτὸ ἂν εἴη τὸ τοῦ παντὸς ὑπερκείμενον.

42. Christologically, he argues against Eunomius that the Son cannot be called good if (God) the Father alone is good, "having goodness not as a thing acquired, but in his nature" (ἀγαθὸς οὐκ ἐπίκτητον ἔχων ἀλλ' ἐν τῇ φύσει τὴν ἀγαθότητα), and the Son "does not share the Good essence of the Father" (ὁ τῆς ἀγαθῆς οὐσίας ἀμέτοχος), which would mean that the Son would be the opposite of "Good" (*Con. Eunom.* 3.9.6–7).

itself. Doing so, however, leaves nothing distinctive, identifiable as a particular thing. As the unchanging Good by which all things are good, God is different from all things and so is incomprehensible.[43]

Augustine finds his view of God as the Good taught in Scripture. In his exegesis of Ps 134:6 "Praise the Lord, for the Lord is good," he interprets the assertion that the Lord is good in a Platonic manner to the effect that God is the Good from which all good things originate and the Good by which they are good (*En. ps.* 136.6).[44] Expressing his inability to understand the ineffable Good, he claims nonetheless that what is meant by saying that God is good is the same as what is found in Exod 3:14: "I am who am" (*ego sum qui sum*) and "the one who is" (*Qui est*). God is not a particular being that can be defined, but ontologically is before all beings as their source, for which reason God cannot be said to have a real name. In other words, God is the Good itself and not a particular good thing.[45]

Pseudo-Dionysius

(Pseudo-)Dionysius the Areopagite brings together the biblical God and the Platonic Good; for him the terms "God" and "the Good" are convertible. The Good is also identical to the Beautiful (*De div. nom.* 4.7–10), the One (4.31) and Being (5). He sometimes calls the Good superessential (ὑπερούσιον) and super-Good (ὑπεράγαθον) in order to communicate

---

43. Augustine also refers to God as the Truth (*veritas*), which functions as a synonym for the Good. He differentiates between the true things that are created and the Truth by which they were created; by the latter, he means God (*De Trin.* VII.1). He then lists what God is not: in short, God is nothing like anything in creation. Rather, quoting Wis 9:15, he affirms that "God is Truth" (*deus veritas est*) and then says, "For it is written that 'God is Light' (1 John 1:5); not in such way as these eyes see, but in such way as the heart sees, when it is said, he is truth (*veritas*)" (*De Trin.* VII.3). God as Truth and God as Light are conceptually closely associated: by an inner illumination, God as Light enables the heart to understand that God is Truth. For him, God is not one truth among other truths, but the Truth that makes other truths true. As such God is other than all true things.

44. Augustine also connects his understanding of God as the Good with Acts 17:27–28: God as the Good is that in which "we live and move and have our being" (Acts 17:28), thereby blending together Stoicism and Platonism (*De Trin.* VIII. 5).

45. Augustine asserts that, although unknown and unknowable, God still allows human beings to worship him. He writes, "And yet God, although nothing worthy of his greatness can be said of him, has condescended to accept the worship of men's mouths, and has desired us through the medium of our own words to rejoice in his praise" (*Doct. chr.* 1.6). So God allows himself to be named *deus*, even though this two-syllable word "conveys no true knowledge of his nature."

that the Good is not one good thing among other good things but is the source of all that exists and is good (see *Mys. th.* 1.1). The Good cannot be named or defined in the same way that particular things or goods can be. This is why he states, "It is not possible either to express or to conceive what the One, the unknown, the superessential, the Good itself is" (τὸ ἕν, τὸ ἄγνωστον, τὸ ὑπερούσιον, αὐτὸ τ'ἀγαθόν) (1.5). The Good is said to be "above word" and for that reason to be "unutterable by word" (ἄρρητόν τε λόγῳ παντὶ τὸ ὑπὲρ λόγον ἀγαθόν) in the sense that what God is is inexpressible in language (1.1). He even calls the Good the super-unknown and surpassing Goodness (ἡ ὑπεραγνώστος καὶ ὑπερφανὴς ἀγαθότης) (1.5) and the super-good Goodness (ἡ ὑπεράγαθος ἀγαθότης) (2.4), implying that the Good transcends all particular manifestations of itself in the visible, sensible world. Even to predicate "the Good" of God is inaccurate, being only a linguistic expedient. To call God the Good and then describe the Good as superessential, super-Good, and so forth is really to affirm that nothing can be affirmed of God: "a desire of understanding and saying something concerning that inexpressible nature" (περὶ τῆς ἀρρήτου φύσεως ἐκείνης) (13.3). The term "inexpressible nature" is an oxymoron since natures by definition are expressible.

John of Damascus

John of Damascus reiterates the Platonic view that God is the Good and that the goodness of all things originates with God. Influenced by Pseudo-Dionysius, he calls God "super-Good" (ὑπεράγαθος), meaning that God is beyond all good things and so incomprehensible (*O.F.* 1.8). Also influenced by Pseudo-Dionysius, he identifies God with being Good. He writes, "Or as the holy Dionysius says, 'He that is Good.'[46] For one cannot say of God that he has being in the first place and goodness in the second" (*O.F.* 1.9). For him, God's goodness is not a name or attribute at all, but is synonymous with the incomprehensible God: "Through his unspeakable goodness (δι' ἄφατον . . . ἀγαθότητα), then, it pleased him to be called by names that we could understand" (*O.F.* 1.12). This is an expression of God's simplicity. As he writes later, "For goodness is concomitant with essence," by which is meant that God does not have goodness as an attribute, unlike the attributes of contingent and changeable beings. God is essentially Goodness. He adds that "God is in all things" and "all things are dependent on

---

46. *De div. nom.* c. 2, 3, 4

God as the Good

that which is, and nothing can be unless it is in that which is" (*O.F.* 1.13).⁴⁷ These two assertions function to communicate that God is not one thing among other things, but is that whereby all things exist.

GOD AS THE GOOD IN CHRISTIAN THEOLOGY: MEDIEVAL THEOLOGIANS

Synopsis

Mediaeval theologians continue to interpret God as the Good from which all good things derive their goodness; sometimes Truth is used as a synonym for the Good. God as the Good is other than all good things, and for that reason is incomprehensible. On the assumption of divine simplicity, it is asserted that God is not distinct from his goodness, or, in other words, that God does not have goodness as an attribute. Rather God is his own goodness, or is Goodness itself. This is what makes God's goodness other than the goodness of things that participate in divine goodness and derive from it, and why God is called the first Good, sole Good or true Good. Jesus' statement in Mark 10:18 "No one is good except God alone" is interpreted as supporting this conclusion. From this it follows that nothing is like God even though it has its origin in God's goodness. God transcends all the things that are good by his own goodness, which implies that God is other than all things. Some medieval theologians use Aristotelian categories to express and modify this Platonic doctrine, which tends to make it much more complicated. In particular, God as Goodness itself is connected to God as first final cause and first efficient cause. God as the Good is so much part of the theological tradition that it is not abandoned even though Platonism is no longer the dominant philosophical influence on Christian theology.

Individual Medieval Theologians

Anselm

In the first chapter of the *Monologium*, Anselm asserts that the many things sought and experienced as good by all human beings in various degrees

---

47. ἐν πᾶσι γάρ ἐστιν ὁ θεός· τοῦ γὰρ ὄντος ἐξῆπται τὰ ὄντα· καὶ οὐκ ἔστιν εἶναί τι, εἰ μὴ ἐν τῷ ὄντι τὸ εἶναι ἔχει.

are good by participation in the Good.⁴⁸ Were it not the case, this great diversity of experiences would have nothing in common and so could not be classified as the same thing, namely as good. Anselm writes,

> This must be, then, a good through itself, since ever other good is through it. It follows, therefore, that all other goods are good through another than that which they themselves are, and this other alone is good through itself. Hence, this alone is supremely Good, which is alone good through itself. For it is supreme, in that it so surpasses other beings that it is neither equaled nor excelled. But that which is supremely Good is also supremely great. There is, therefore, something (*aliquid*) that is supremely Good, and supremely great, that is, the highest of all existing beings.⁴⁹
>
> *Monol.* 1

In Platonic fashion, he concludes that this something that is supremely Good (*summe bonum*) is God, who is intrinsically Good, "alone Good through itself" (*solum est per se bonum*), in contrast to other beings, which are good "through another being than that which they themselves are" (*per aliud quam quod ipsa sunt*), which is to say by participation in the Good. The reason that God is called supremely Good is because nothing that is good by participation in God could exceed God in goodness. Anselm adds that being supremely Good implies being supremely great; peerlessness with respect to goodness is the basis of God's greatness.

In *Proslogium*, Anselm draws the further conclusion that as supremely Good (and great) God is unlike all the good things made good through participation in it. He writes, "For, if individual goods are delectable, conceive in earnestness how delectable is that good which contains the pleasantness of all goods; and not such as we have experienced in created objects, but as different as the creator from the creature (et non qualem in rebus creatis sumus experti, sed tanto differentem, quanto differt creator a creatura). For, if the created life is good, how good is the creative life" (*Monol.* 24). In other words, God as the Good is unlike all good things and so cannot be understood in terms of them, which makes God incomprehensible. Like Augustine, Anselm makes a similar argument about truth: because all things said to be true or have truth, there must be one Truth in which they

---

48. Translation from Anselm, *Works of St. Anselm*. Translated by Sidney Norton Deane (Chicago: Open Court, 1903).

49. See *Prosl.* 5, 9, 10, 22, 23, 24, 25.

all participate, for otherwise they would not be recognized as true. This Truth is God, the source of all that is true or has being (*Dialogue on Truth*).

Boethius

In his *De Hebdomadibus*, Boethius argues Platonically that God is the Good (*bonum*) from which all other good things derive. God is also known as the first Good (*primum bonum*), sole Good (*solum bonum*) and true Good (*vere bonum*).[50] For this reason God as the Good is absolutely unlike all the things that participate in him and so is incomprehensible. Unlike some of his predecessors, Boethius holds that created things are good by substance (*substantia*), or essentially, by which he means by virtue of existing, as opposed to being good by participation (*participatione*). In this work he investigates the question of how everything can be good by substance, not by participation, but at the same time not be God, who is the first Good.

Central to Boethius's argument is the premise that, since God is simple, God's existence is not separate from God's goodness, unlike all composite things, whose existence is not identical to their goodness. This means that only God is necessary and all other things that are substantially good exist and are good because God has willed it. For this reason, Boethius distinguishes between God as the first Good (*primum bonum*), or Being itself, and secondary goods that derive their being and goodness from God. He writes, "For the prime Good is essentially good in virtue of being; the secondary good is in its turn good because it derives from the good whose being itself is good. But the being itself of all things derives from the prime Good, which is such that of it being and goodness are rightly predicated as identical. Their being itself is good; for thereby it resides in him" (*De Hebd.* 122–27). Whatever derives from the first Good is good substantially, not by participation, but these secondary goods are nonetheless not the same as the first Good. Speaking of the things that derive from the first Good, he writes, "Their substance, therefore, is good, and yet it is not like that from which it comes" (*De Hebd.* 133–34).[51] He adds, "And yet that which springs from the substantial Good is not like its source, which produces it" (*De Hebd.* 144–46).[52] Thus God as the Good is incomprehensible because God is different from all the good things that originate from God.

50. Also known as *Quomodo Substantiae*.
51. Ideiirco ipsum esse bonum est nec est simile ei a quo est.
52. Ideirco et esse eorum bonum est et non est simile substantiali bono id quod ab

The Indescribable God

Thomas Aquinas

Aquinas maintains the traditional Platonic view that God is the Good, but provides a conceptual framework for it that is more compatible with his Aristotelianism. For Aquinas, like his predecessors, the implication of God as the Good is that God is unlike all created good things. He argues in *Summa contra gentiles* that God is his own goodness (*sua bonitas*), which he also expresses by saying that God is Goodness itself (*ipsa bonitas*) (*SCG* 1.38.1–2). This conclusion rests on two premises: first that to be in act is to be good and, second, that God is not only a being in act but is his very act of being.[53] The latter means that, for God, essence is existence, or that God is a necessary being. If to be is to be good, insofar as what is good is what is in act, and if God is his very act of being in the sense that God's essence is existence, then it follows that God is Goodness itself (*SCG* 1.38.1–2). By contrast, all other things insofar as they are in act and therefore good are good only by participation in God. He explains that God is good essentially (*per essentiam suam bonum*) because God is the first Good and functions as a final cause of all things: "But the good has the nature of an end. We must, therefore, reach some first Good, that is not by participation good through an order toward some other good, but is good through its own essence. This is God" (*SCG* 1.38.4). Scriptural support for his position is found in Mark 10:18 "One is good, God." It follows that God as essentially good, or as Goodness itself, is unlike all things that are good by participation.

In addition, on the assumption of the correlation of perfection and goodness, Aquinas reasons that since God is absolutely perfect, God's goodness comprehends all goodness, from which it follows that God is "the Good of every good" (*omnis boni bonum*) (*SCG* 1.40.2). In other words, God as absolutely perfect is the source of the goodness of all created things that are not absolutely perfect. Synonymous with the assertion that God is the Good of every good is that everything else is good by participation in God. He writes, "That which is said to be of a certain sort by participation is said to be such only so far as it has a certain likeness to that which is said to be such by essence" (*SCG* 1.40.3).[54] Aquinas stresses, however, that it is

eo fluxit.

53. Deus non solum est ens actu, sed est ipsum suum esse.

54. Aquinas also asserts that God is the highest Good (*summum bonum*), which he explains as meaning that God is the "universal Good" (*bonum universale*) that "stands higher than any particular good" (SCG 1.41.1–3). As the highest Good, God is unlike all created things because God is good essentially (*per suam essentiam*).

only insofar as God is the first final cause that God imparts a likeness of his goodness to the created things that participate in God's goodness. He writes, "It is the last end, then, from which all things receive the nature of good" (SCG 1.40.3). He thereby avoids the quasi-pantheistic emanationism of neo-Platonism, according to which the Good overflows itself and permeates all things making them good thereby. From this it follows that created things only have "a certain likeness of divine goodness" (*aliquam similitudinem divinae bonitatis*), not a univocal identity (SCG 1.40.3). In spite of their participation in divine goodness, created things are fundamentally different from God.

In his *Summa theologiae*, Aquinas argues from God as first efficient cause to God as Good, rather than God as first final cause.[55] He first asks whether God is good, and concludes that "To be good belongs pre-eminently to God" (ST 1.6.1).[56] Since God is the first efficient cause and since God's creation, the effect of God's efficient causation, is good and therefore desirable (insofar as it seeks after its own perfection and obtains it), it follows that God must have goodness, for the effect (*effectus*) necessarily has a likeness to its agent (*agens*). He writes, "The perfection and form of an effect consist in a certain likeness to the agent, since every agent makes its like; and hence the agent itself is desirable and has the nature of good. For the very thing which is desirable in it is the participation of its likeness."

Aquinas next answers in the affirmative the question of whether God is the *supreme* Good (ST 1.6.2). He claims that God is the supreme Good absolutely (*summum bonum simpliciter*), which means that God alone is the supreme Good and therefore does not belong to a genus or order of things, to which other things also belong (see SCG 1.41). This is because God is the source of all goodness as its efficient cause, the cause of the fact that actual and therefore perfect things are desirable: "All desired perfections flow from him as from the first cause." He qualifies this statement, however, by saying that all desired perfections, or good things, flow from God, not as a univocal agent, but "but as from an agent which does not agree with its effects either in species or genus." In other words, the goodness of things results from God as efficient cause and does not represent

---

55. Aquinas holds that being and goodness are the same and that the distinction between them is only in thought (*ST* Ia. Q. 5). What is good is what is desirable, and what is desirable is what is perfect. What is perfect is fully actual, which is to say that it is, since being makes things actual (*esse enim est actualitas omnis rei*). So it follows that being and goodness are identical.

56. Bonum esse praecipue Deo convenit.

the actual presence of the divine goodness in them; rather the goodness of things is found in God eminently. God as the eminent and non-univocal cause of goodness implies that God's goodness is more excellent than the goodness of his effect or creation, which is why God is the supreme Good absolutely. It also implies that God as the Good is unlike all good things and for that reason is incomprehensible.

CONCLUSION

The concept of God as the Good, a conceptual tool originating in Platonism, is used by Christian theologians to express the otherness of God. This is facilitated by the fact that in the Hebrew Bible God is called good and said to have goodness. God as the Good is other than all good things that derive from the Good. The concept of God as the Good persists into the medieval period, even among theologians who are more Aristotelian in orientation.

6

God as Infinite

CHRISTIAN THEOLOGIANS HAVE CONSISTENTLY asserted the infinity of God, by which is meant that God is unlimited. In some cases, the assertion that God is infinite expresses that God is other than all finite things and is thereby incomprehensible.

SCRIPTURAL BASIS OF GOD'S INFINITY

God is never directly said to be infinite in the Christian Scriptures; the Greek terms ἄπειρος or ἀόριστος used by early Christian theologians to describe God as infinite, or the Hebrew and Aramaic equivalents of these, do not occur in the Bible. What is appealed to as evidence is inferential in import. The putative scriptural support for God's infinity is threefold. First, it is said to be justified by passages in which God is said to be greater than human beings can know.[1] Second, God's infinity is an extrapolation from statements that God is beyond the limits of time and space.[2] The strategy

---

1. There are three occasions in Scripture where God is *unsearchably* great (Ps 145:3; Job 5:9; 9:10). There are other passages that state that God cannot be understood by human beings because what is to be known is so vast (Job 11:7–9; 11:7–9; 1 Chr 29:11; Sir 43:28–32). Finally, God's knowledge is said to be inscrutable to human beings (Job 15:8; 26:14; Isa 40:13, 28; Jer 23:18; Rom 11:33–35; 1 Cor 2:16).

2. Time: Isa 44:6; Ps 90:2, 4; 102:25–27; 2 Pet 3:8; Rev 22:13); space: 1 Kgs 8:27; 2 Chr 2:6; 6:18; Ps. 139:7–10; Isa 66:1; Jer 23:24; Acts 17:24–28; Eph 1:23.

of this type of argument is to prove the whole from the part: from being unlimited in one respect the conclusion is generalized so that God is unlimited in every respect.[3] Third, statements affirming that nothing is too difficult for God are interpreted as implying that God is unlimited, or infinite, in power.[4] On the basis of these three types of assertions about God, Christian theologians have attributed infinity to God.

HELLENISTIC ORIGIN OF CONCEPT OF INFINITY

The concept of the infinity of God has its origin in Greek thought, which Christian theologians appropriate because they believe that the term succinctly expresses biblical content. The concept of the infinite in Greek philosophy is used with two meanings. On the one hand, the term infinite is used to qualify God's type of being. Aristotle holds as axiomatic that whatever can be said to exist that is neither predicable of a subject nor present in a subject is a substance, even God, the unmoved mover.[5] Nevertheless, among substances God is unique: unlike all other substances, God as the unmoved mover is infinite, for God causes infinite motion (*Phys.* 8.10; *Meta.* 12.7). He reasons that God produces motion through infinite time and an infinite effect requires an infinite cause.[6]

On the other hand, the term "infinite" is used more generally to mean not being finite in the sense of not being limited or determinate, being one type of thing as opposed to another type of thing. Anaximander asserts that the first principle (ἀρχή), to use Aristotle's terminology, is not water, contrary to Thales' view, but what he calls the ἄπειρον, translatable as "the infinite" in the sense of the unlimited or indeterminate. Aetius reports, "Anaximander . . . says that the first principle of things is the infinite; for from this all things come, and all things perish and return to this" (*Aet.* 1.3).

---

3. Although not usually acknowledged, this type of argument requires an appeal to a rationalistic dictum to the effect that it is impossible to be both infinite in one respect and finite in another.

4. Gen 18:13–14; Jer 32:27; Job 42:1–2; Mark 10:27; Luke 1:37.

5. Aristotle writes, "Substance, in the truest and primary and most definite sense of the word, is that which is neither predicable of a subject nor present in a subject; for instance, the individual man or horse" (*Categ.* 5 2a11–13).

6. In Aristotelian theology, the uniqueness of God as an infinite substance also requires that God have no matter and be immovable. The former follows from being infinite, since there can be no infinite magnitude (μέγεθος). The latter follows from being the unmoved mover.

The first principle is not any of the elements—earth, water, air, or fire—but that which is ontologically before all the elements (and everything else), the substrate of existence, from which the elements emerge and that which they ultimately are. Moreover, Anaximander identifies the ἄπειρον as God, as Aristotle explains: "They identify it with the divine, for it is 'deathless and imperishable' as Anaximander says, with the majority of the physicists" (*Phys.* 203b). Since it is "deathless and imperishable," the ἄπειρον must be God, on the assumption that whatever is immortal is divine. As God, the ἄπειρον cannot be thought of as insentient matter; rather it is conscious and has will, so that, as Aristotle says, it "steers all," by which he means it gives direction to the unfolding of all things, which it itself is (*Phys.* 203b). It does so while encompassing all, which seems to mean that the ἄπειρον surrounds the world and contains it. Along the same lines, the neo-Platonist Plotinus attributes infinity to the One: "We must therefore take the One as infinite not in measureless extension or numerable quantity but in fathomless depths of power" (*Enn.*VI.9.6; see V.5.11). Being no thing, but the source of all things, the One is unlimited in power of production and for this reason is infinite. He also attributes infinity to the One on account of its simplicity; the possibility of limit or determination presupposes plurality, since a limit is a predicate.[7] He writes, "It is infinite also by right of being a pure unity" (*Enn.* V.5.11).[8]

GOD AS INFINITE IN CHRISTIAN THEOLOGY

Synopsis

Although they do not always distinguish them, Christian theologians posit two ways in which God is infinite in the sense of being unlimited, one positive and one negative, corresponding to the two different meanings in Greek philosophy. On the one hand, making use of the theological method of *via eminentiae*, some theologians hold that God is that substratum to

---

7. Philo of Alexandria interprets the menorah in the holy place as symbolizing heaven, which is said to be bounded by God. The fact that no measurements are supplied for the menorah, unlike the other articles in the holy place, is explained as the result of impossibility of measuring God, in the sense of being able to define God. He writes, "As, therefore, 'the existent One' (τὸ ὄν) is incomprehensible (ἀπερίληπτον), so also that which is bounded by him is not measured by any measures which come with the range of our intellect" (*Her.* 229).

8. καὶ τὸ ἄπειρον τούτῳ τῷ μὴ πλέον ἑνὸς εἶναι.

The Indescribable God

which *infinite* communicable attributes belong.[9] Under the influence of the Aristotelian tradition, they hold that God is a substance, or a being, and use the term infinite adjectivally to modify the attributes of that substance, thereby differentiating God from all other substances. God has an infinite instantiation of attributes that are instantiated finitely in created things. In other words, the infinite is an extension of the finite: infinite according to substance.[10] Sometimes God's infinity is also specified as being actual infinity, as opposed to potential infinity.[11] On this interpretation, God's infinity has a positive meaning, insofar as something is affirmed of God.[12]

On the other hand, of interest for this investigation is the second, less common use of the term infinite with the meaning of not being finite, being

---

9. God as the underlying substratum of the attributes provides the basis of their unity. The Lutheran theologian Isaak Dorner seeks to avoid the conclusion that God is without all definitiveness and yet still refers to God as infinite (*System of Christian Doctrine.* 2 vols. [Edinburgh: T. & T. Clark, 1888] 1.237–48). He writes, "By the fact that God is something defined, a logical, further, a moral limitation is of course placed upon His Idea. He is not at the same time the opposite of what He is, nor can He be. Were he absolutely without definiteness, His would be no stable idea, but an absolutely mutable one; He would be in relation to all distinctions absolutely indifferent" (ibid., 237–38). Dorner holds to what could be called a finite infinite, insofar as God has an Idea (Begriff), by which is meant that God is something as distinct from what is not God, although what God is has no limits. He states paradoxically, "God has no limits, although He has preciseness (ὅρους) in Himself" (ibid., 237). It is not clear how God could have an Idea (Begriff) and be infinite.

10. God's infinity is often said to be according to substance (*secundum substantiam*), as opposed to quantity and quality. God's infinity is also said to be *in actu* (*entelecheia*) as opposed to *in potentia* (*dunamei*), since the latter implies that God has matter, for only what has matter can change. For this reason God is said to be infinite *simpliciter* (ἁπλῶς) as opposed to infinite on account of something (κατά τι) (*secundum quid infinitum*) in the way that a body is infinite on account of its unlimited capacity to receive forms. God is infinite simply, by himself (*per se* and not *per aliud*) (see Amandus Polanus, *Syntagma theologiae Christianae*, lib. II, cap. X).

11. The actual infinite is a complete whole without the possibility of more (*tot ut non plura*), whereas the potential infinite is an incomplete whole with the possibility of more (*non tot quin plura*), or, in other words, an incomplete collection of finite things to which more finite things can be added.

12. The best-known defender of univocal predication is John Duns Scotus, who holds Aristotle's view that the science of metaphysics studies being as being (*ens inquantum ens*), which includes a study of infinite being. He holds that the transcendental "being" is univocally attributable to God and to created things. (Being is the simplest of all transcendental concepts and for that reason cannot be defined.) The difference between them is that God is a different type of being, namely, a being that has unlimitedness as its intrinsic mode of existing.

God as Infinite

an application of the *via negativa*.¹³ The negative formulation of God's infinity functions as a means of expressing the otherness of God. On this apophatic use of the term, infinity attributed to God has no positive meaning, not even denoting God as the supreme or greatest substance or being.¹⁴ Even though it is a noun, the word "God" is said to be unlike other nouns since it does not signify anything.¹⁵ In other words, God as infinite is not to be conceived as a substance with attributes at all, even a substance with infinite attributes. To be infinite is to be other than all things, which, as things, are by definition finite. It is not to be a thing among other things.¹⁶

---

13. Johann Gerhard defines infinity negatively, as opposed to privatively as follows: "Something negatively infinite is that which lacks terminus and limitation in such a way that it cannot and should not be bound and limited . . . which simply has no end . . . neither beginning nor end" (Non-finitum negative est, quod ita caret termino et limitatione, ut finiri et limitari nec debeat nec possit . . . quod simpliciter non habet finem . . . nec principium nec finem habet) (*Loci theologici* II sect. VII 162). Later, however, Gerhard denies that infinity is purely a negative attribute; rather he claims that infinity includes something affirmative, namely that God is supreme perfection by virtue of being "a being existing from himself and through himself, completely independent of another, hence not finite in the property of his essence" (ens a se ipso et per se ipsum existens ab alio prorsus independens et proinde essentiae proprietate nequaquam finitum) (*Loci Theologici* II sect. VII). Likewise, Hodge takes exception to the views of Hamilton and Mansel, who hold that infinity is a negative concept, a denial that God is something, and not an affirmation. Extrapolating from the alleged meaningfulness of the statement that space is infinite, Hodge argues that to affirm that God is infinite is equally meaningful. He writes, "When, therefore, we say that God is infinite, we mean something; we express a great and positive truth" (*Systematic Theology*. 2 vols. [New York: Scribner, Armstrong, and Co., 1873], I.382.)

14. On this interpretation, the statement that God is infinite should not be taken as a *de facto* affirmation, as if being infinite were something positive (see Pannenberg, *Systematic Theology*, vol. 1 [Grand Rapids: Eerdmans, 1991], 397-98).

15. Because of God's simplicity, Augustine is reluctant to call God a substance, since to be a substance implies a distinction between the subject and its defining predicates (*De Trin.* VII.10; see V.3). He prefers the term essence (*essentia*): the implication is that for God to be (*esse*) is to be what he is or to be his essence (*essentia*), which is true only of God. When discoursing on the Trinity, Augustine is nevertheless willing to use the term "substance" since there is none better. He writes, "God is a sort of substance: for that which is no substance, is nothing at all. To be a substance then is to be something" (Deus est quedam substantia; nam quod nulla substantia est, nihil omnino est. Substantia ergo, aliquid esse est) (*En. ps.* 69.5). There is no third option in Latin to substance or non-existence. So Augustine agrees to call God a "*sort of* substance" (*quedam substantia*) because he does not want to deny that God exists, all the while recognizing that God is not a substance in the same way that a created, finite thing is a substance.

16. Schleiermacher explains, "For infinite does not mean that which has no end, but that which is in contrast to the finite, by which is meant that which is co-determined

The Indescribable God

What it means for God to be infinite in the negative sense of the term of not being finite and so other than all things is explained by Christian theologians variously by saying that God is indeterminate, indefinite, without a circumscribed form, without a definite limitation and without distinctiveness. What is denied, in other words, is that God can be limited in any respect in the sense of being definable as one thing rather than another. For this reason God is incomprehensible. Another way of expressing this is to say that God has no opposite, since God is neither like nor unlike any finite thing, or that God cannot be enclosed by any boundary. God as infinite can have no relation to anything by which God can be limited, determined, and defined; this is also expressed as God's separation from all things. Similarly, in order to explain why God as infinite cannot be compared to anything, Christian theologians use the spatial metaphor that God is that which contains all things but is contained by nothing. Correlates or near synonyms of infinity include being immense, invisible, and ineffable.

God as infinite in the negative sense is not to be conceived as the opposite of the finite, as if the infinite and finite were two extremes of a continuum, like hot or cold or light and dark. Rather the confession of God's infinity is the denial that God can be conceived as a definable thing. In addition, God's infinity is said to be implied by God's simplicity, since to be finite requires that a distinction be made between a thing and its predicates. It is also implied by the concept of God as creator insofar as, unlike a created thing that is limited by definition, being one thing and not something, God as creative source is unlimited. Sometimes it is said that God has an infinite essence or nature, but at other times it is said that God as infinite has no essence or nature. In fact these statements mean virtually the same thing since an infinite nature is really no nature at all. The same thing is meant by calling God superessential, above all things, and above essence. Scriptures cited that are said to imply that God is infinite in the negative sense are Exod 3:14, "I am the one who is," John 1:18, "No one has seen God at any time," 1 Tim 6:16, "dwells in unapproachable light," Phil 2:9, "name above every name," and Ps 145:3, "His greatness is unsearchable."

---

by other things (*durch anderes mitbestimmten entgegengesetzte*)" (*The Christian Faith* [Philadelphia: Fortress, 1976], 228–32). Likewise Pannenberg writes, "Strictly, the infinite is not that which is without end but that which stands opposed to the finite, to what is defined by something else" (*Systematic Theology*, 1.397).

Individual Christian Theologians on God as Infinite

Irenaeus

Although he sometimes uses the adjective "infinite" to qualify a divine attribute (*Adv. haer.* 4.20.5; 4.36.6), Irenaeus also understands God to be infinite in a more fundamental way, as expressing that God is not an object that can be defined, but is unlike all definable things and so is incomprehensible. He chides his Gnostic opponents for seeking to inquire into God by their various means ("numbers, syllables, and letters"), as if God were comprehensible (*Adv. haer.* 2.25.1); he claims that they seek to go beyond God himself (*Adv. haer.* 2.25.4). In this context, he asserts that a human being is "infinitely inferior to God" (*in infinitum minor Deo*), which implies the converse, that God is infinitely superior (*Adv. haer.* 2.25.3). For God to be infinitely superior to human beings is what Irenaeus means when he calls God "indeterminate" (*indeterminabilis*), which he also expresses by saying that no one is "able to conceive of any other above the Father himself" (*super ipsum alium excogites Patrem*) (*Adv. haer.* 2.25.4). For God to be indeterminate means that God cannot be classified as one thing in distinction to other things, which is why it is impossible to conceive of a being that is greater than God. This is also the meaning of the statement that God "cannot be surpassed" (*non enim transibilis est*): nothing can be conceived that would be greater than God because God cannot be conceived in order to be surpassable (*Adv. haer.* 2.25.4). For this reason, Irenaeus writes that a human being "cannot have experience or form a conception of all things like God" (*omnium experientiam et cogitationem habere posit, ut Deus*) (*Adv. haer.* 2.25.3). It is not that God is the greatest, but rather that God is beyond measurement. In summary, as Irenaeus uses the concept in this passage, for God to be infinite is to be the negation of all finite, created things, which leads to the conclusion that God is incomprehensible. For Irenaeus, the infinity of God is implied by the fact that God is the creator of all things. He writes, "Nor is God from things made, but things made are from God. For all things originate from one and the same God" (*Adv. haer.* 2.25.1). As creator, God is nothing like any created thing, but is the origin of them all. Dependent on *Shepherd of Hermes*, he asserts further that God as creator, while "containing all things, alone is uncontained" (*Demonstr.* 3).[17]

---

17. καὶ πάντα χωρῶν, μόνος δὲ ἀχώρητος (Herm., *Mand.* 1.1). See *Adv. haer.* 1.15.5, "the Father, who cannot be contained, but contains all things"; 2.1.1–5 "He is the only God, the only Lord, the only Creator, the only Father, alone containing all things,

The Indescribable God

To contain all things is to be the source and support of all things; not to be contained implies that God is nothing like the things contained.

Clement of Alexandria

Clement asserts that God is infinite (ἄπειρον), by which he means "being without dimensions, and not having a limit" (*Strom.* 5.12). The phrases "to be without dimensions" (κατὰ τὸ ἀδιάστατον) and "not to have a limit" (μὴ ἔχον πέρας) should be taken as coordinate in meaning and therefore interpretive of each other. Together they refer to the fact that God cannot be described as having defining attributes insofar as God is not one thing among other things. Clement also makes a connection between the fact that no parts (μέρη) can be attributed to God, or, in other words, that God as one is indivisible (ἀδιαίρετον), and being infinite. The reasoning behind this connection is that what is one in the sense of being simple cannot have attributes since this would require the plurality of subject and predicate. It follows that what cannot have attributes is infinite in the sense of being unlimited and indefinable.

Hilary of Poitiers

Hilary of Poitiers describes God as infinite or having infinity (*De Trin.* 1.4, 7, 8, 11, 13; 2.1, 5; 3.24; 4.4, 36; 8.43; 9.72; 10.16; 11.4, 47; 12.21, 24, 32, 34, 37). In some of these passages, he uses the term infinite in the negative sense of not being finite, or indeterminate, and so indefinable. On the basis of God's infinity, Hilary condemns the practice of idolatry insofar as idolaters seek to confine "the Lord of the universe and Father of infinity (*infinitatis parens*) within these narrow prisons of metal or stone or wood" (1.4). In this context, being infinite functions as the equivalent of not being a definable thing, especially one that can be sensibly depicted. Somewhat later, having discussed God's infinity in the positive sense with respect to duration (eternity) (Exod 3:14), power (omnipotence) (Isa 40:12), and spatiality (omnipresence) (Isa 66:1), Hilary then makes an obscure statement about God's unqualified infinity: "Nothing else was worthy of God than to be beyond the intelligence of things in such a way that to the extent in

---

and himself commanding all things into existence"; 4.19.3 "And that his greatness is not defective, but contains all things, and extends even to us"; 4.20.2 "He who contains all things, and is himself contained by no one."

God as Infinite

which the infinite mind stretches itself towards the limit (*modum*) of even a presumed opinion, that to the same extent the infinity of limitless eternity exceeds all infinity of a nature that tries to reach it" (*De Trin.* 1.6; see 1.13). His use of the term infinite in this passage has the negative meaning of not being finite in the sense of being unlimited or indeterminate.[18] For God to be beyond the intelligence of things (*ultra intelligentias rerum esse*) means that God cannot be understood as a thing, which is to say, limited or determinate and therefore definable. According to Hilary, the human mind, which he also calls infinite, cannot reach a limit of the infinite God because there is no such limit; the implication is that the human mind cannot define God.[19] The result is that God is incomprehensible to human beings.[20]

Along the same lines, Hilary uses the term infinite (*infinitus*) to refer to God's absolute difference from all created things (*De Trin.* 2.6–7).[21] He describes God the Father as the "source of the all" (*origo omnium*) because everything owes its existence to God (*Pater est, ex quo omne quod est*) (2.6). As such, God the Father, in contrast to everything else, is "self-existent" (*ejus esse in sese est*), which is further explained as not drawing his being from without but possessing it from himself and in himself: "He does not draw his being from without, but maintains it from himself and in himself."[22] All things have their being from elsewhere, namely from God. It is in this context that Hilary introduces the term infinite to refer to the fact that God is indeterminate, not identifiable as anything. Using a spatial

---

18. He makes the same point *De Trin.* 4.2, but without using the term infinite: "That which is ineffable surpasses the bounds and limits of any kind of a description" (Quod enim inerrabile est, significantiae alicujus finem et modum non habet). In this case then ineffable and infinite are synonyms for Hilary in some contexts. Likewise in *De Trin.* 8.48 Hilary refers to God as "indefinite" (*indefinitus*), which is synonymous with infinite in this sense.

19. See *De Trin.* 1.8 "His is a greatness too vast for comprehension, but not for faith" (quantus et intelligi non potest, et potest credi) and 1.13 "And in such wise that the utmost efforts of the earthly mind to comprehend him are baffled by that infinite eternity and omnipotence" (ut dum infinitas aeternae in eo est potestatis. omnen terrenae mentis amplexum potestas aeternae infinitatis excedat). Hilary means the same thing when he affirms, "Imperfect beings cannot conceive the perfect" (*non enim concipiunt imperfecta perfectum*) (*De Trin.* 3.24).

20. Following this reflection is an interpretation of Ps 139:7–10 as expressing God's spatial infinity (omnipresence).

21. Hilary refers to God's "infinity of immense eternity" (*De Trin.* 1.7; see 1.11, 13; 2.1) and refers to God's "uncircumscribable immensity" (1.7). He also associates infinity with incompositeness (8.43).

22. Non aliunde quod est sumens, sed id quod est, ex se atque in se obtinens.

metaphor, he defines God's infinity as meaning that God "is not in anything, but all things are in him."[23] Not to be in anything expresses the idea that God is independent of all things, whereas for all things to be in God means that God is the source of all things and so is not a thing.[24] Hilary explicates God's infinity in this negative sense in relation to space and time: "He is eternally outside of space, for he is not contained; eternally before time, for time is from him."[25] In other words, God is both non-spatial and non-temporal, since God is not a being among other beings; to be such is to be unlike all things, which are spatial and temporal. Hilary then explains that for God to be infinite is for God's nature not to be confined (*non natura claudetur*) (*De Trin.* 2.6). To be confined in this context means to be limited and determinate. He again calls God infinite, but this time in association with the attributes of being ineffable (*ineffabilis*) and invisible (*invisibilis*); these three terms express what he calls God the Father's "unfathomable nature" (*inperspicabilis natura*): "This is a true statement of the mystery of that unfathomable nature which is expressed by the name 'Father': God invisible, ineffable, infinite" (*De Trin.* 2.6). To have an unfathomable nature is the result of being "invisible, ineffable, infinite." In particular, God has an unfathomable nature because God as infinite has no limits. One could even argue that an unfathomable nature is no nature. Hilary concludes, "Let us confess by our silence that words cannot describe him; let sense admit that it is foiled in the attempt to apprehend, and reason in the effort to define" (*De Trin.* 2.6).

Later in *De Trinitate*, Hilary affirms that the infinite God is not anything in particular and so is incomprehensible. He writes, "I ask whether . . . the infinite God can also be presented to view under the likeness of a circumscribed form?" (*De Trin.* 8.48).[26] By circumscribed form (*forma*

---

23. non ipse in aliquo, sed intra eum omnia.

24. Hilary interprets the name of God in Exod 3:14 as an expression of the infinity of God: "For such an indication of God's infinity (*infinitatis*) the words 'I am that I am' were clearly adequate" (*De Trin.* 1.6). In this context, what he means by infinity is God's eternity, which is a function of God's necessary existence: "For no property of God which the mind can grasp is more characteristic of him than existence, since existence, in the absolute sense, cannot be predicated of that which shall come to an end, or of that which has had a beginning, and he who now joins continuity of being with the possession of perfect felicity could not in the past, nor can in the future, be non-existent; for whatsoever is divine can neither be originated nor destroyed" (*De Trin.* 1.5).

25. semper extra locum, quia non continetur, semper ante aevum, quia tempus ab eo est.

26. per formae circumscriptae imaginem coimaginari posit ad speciem.

circumscripta) he means a limitation or determination expressed in language. A synonym for infinite in this passage is indefinite and a synonym for circumscribed form is definite limitation (*definita moderatio*): "Nor will a definite limitation represent that which is indefinite."[27] Without elaborating, Hilary argues that God as infinite and indefinite is not identifiable as anything, since there is no "circumscribed form" or "definite limitation" applicable to God. The result is that God cannot be said to be anything and so is incomprehensible.

Gregory of Nazianzus

Alluding to the identification of God as in Exod 3:14 as "the one who is" (ὁ ὤν), Gregory of Nazianzus compares God to "some great sea of essence, infinite and unlimited, transcending all intelligibility, of time and nature (*Or.* 38.7; see *Or.* 45.3).[28] Moreover, he adds that God is not a being but "comprehending in himself the whole, contains all being."[29] For Gregory, God is not a being with a nature existing among other beings with natures. Rather, God is that in which all beings with natures exist. This he expresses by means of the metaphor of the sea, which is vast and contains all essences, or types of things, within itself. As such, unlike all the things in it, God as the sea of essence is "infinite and unlimited" (ἄπειρον καὶ ἀόριστον) with respect to time and nature. God is not to be thought of as existing in time or as having a nature, being one thing as distinct from another.

Gregory of Nyssa

Gregory of Nyssa defines the term "infinite" (ἄπειρος and ἀόριστος) as meaning "boundless" or "without limit": "Infinity is free from limitation altogether" (*Abl.* 52).[30] Although he sometimes uses the term "infinite" to qualify certain attributes of God, he also refers generally to God as infinite, in the negative sense.[31] For him God as infinite means that God is unlike

27. nec indefiniti species definita moderatio.
28. οἷόν τι πέλαγος οὐσίας ἄπειρον καὶ ἀόριστον, πᾶσαν ὑπερεκπῖπτον ἔννοιαν, καὶ χρόνου καὶ φύσεως.
29. ὅλον γὰρ ἐν ἑαυτῷ συλλαβὼν ἔχει τὸ εἶναι.
30. ἐκφεύγει τὸν ὅρον ἡ ἀπειρία.
31. See "the infinitude of the divine life" (τὸ ἀόριστον τῆς θείας ζωῆς) (*Con. Eunom.* 1.1.359; see 2.1.469-70) and "the infinity of the divine power" (τῷ ἀπείρῳ

The Indescribable God

all finite things and so is incomprehensible. According to Gregory, God as infinite is unlike all created things insofar as God is not subject to any limit (ὅρον or πέρας) or any measure (μέρος), unlike a finite creature that is what it is by virtue of its limits or measures.[32] This is also expressed by saying that God is not circumscribed (περιγεγραμμένος) in the sense of being definable as something.[33] In an important passage, he refers to God as "the infinite nature" (ἡ ἀόριστος φύσις), impossible to comprehend not only by human beings but also by angels (*Con. Eunom.* 2.1.67). The reason for this is that, unlike created things, God as uncreated is without limits and so is without definition. He writes, "For wide and insurmountable is the interval that divides and fences off the uncreated nature from the created essence.[34] The latter is limited, the former not.[35] The latter is confined within its own boundaries according to the pleasure of its maker. The former is bounded only by infinity.[36] The latter stretches itself out within certain degrees of extension, limited by time and space: the former transcends all notion of degree, baffling curiosity from every point of view"[37] (*Con. Eunom.* 2.1.69–70). The statements that God as uncreated has no "limits," is "bounded only by infinity," and "transcends all notion of degree" describe how God is indeterminate and so cannot be defined as anything and so distinguished from other things. It is not simply that God is not limited by time and space, but by any limit or measure whatsoever. It

---

τῆς θεϊκῆς δυνάμενως) (3.6.68). Gregory interprets God's eternity as expressed in Isa 40:6–8 as God's infinity (3.6.3–8). He calls God "him who is infinite, illimitable, and without end" (τὸ ἀόριστον καὶ ἄπειρον καὶ οὐδενὶ τέλει) (2.1.446), and contrasts God's "pure and infinite nature" (ἡ ἀόριστος τε καὶ ἀκήρατος φύσις) with the "small and perishable" (nature) (ἡ μικρὰ καὶ ἐπίκηρος) (*OSR* 46.44).

32. See *Con. Eunom.* 1.1.170; 2.1.470; 3.2.20–21; 3.6.71; 3.7.33.

33. See *Con. Eunom.* 3.7.73: "Thus it is idle to try to circumscribe the infinite by 'beginning' and 'ending'— for what is circumscribed cannot be infinite" (μάταιον ἄρα τὸ ἄπειρον ἀρχῇ καὶ τελευτῇ περιγράφειν· τὸ γὰρ περιγεγραμμένον ἄπειρον εἶναι οὐ δύναται). Gregory also refers to God's nature by the less exact phrase "the superior nature of the most high" (καὶ τῆς ὑπερεχούσης φύσεως τοῦ ὕψους) (*Con. Eunom.* 2.1.418).

34. πολὺ γὰρ τὸ μέσον καὶ ἀδιεξίτητον, ᾧ πρὸς τὴν κτιστὴν οὐσίαν ἡ ἄκτιστος φύσις διατετείχισται.

35. αὕτη πεπεράτωται, ἐκείνη πέρας οὐκ ἔχει.

36. αὕτη τοῖς ἰδίοις μέτροις κατὰ τὸ ἀρέσαν τῇ σοφίᾳ τοῦ πεποιηκότος ἐμπεριείληπται, τῆς δὲ μέτρον ἡ ἀπειρία ἐστίν.

37. ἐκείνη ὑπερεκπίπτει πᾶσαν διαστήματος ἔννοιαν, καθ' ὅπερ ἄν τις ἐπιβάλλῃ τοῦ νοῦν κατ' ἐκεῖνο τὴν πολυπραγμοσύνην ἐκφεύγουσα.

God as Infinite

follows that human beings cannot comprehend the divine nature, so that no speculation about God can be tolerated: "For, however far speculation may proceed, when it comes to the uncertain and ungraspable (τὸ ἀμαχανόν τε καὶ ἀκατάληπτον) it must stop" (*Con. Eunom.* 2.1.71, 72). In fact, it could even be said that God does not have a nature at all. Likewise, Gregory states that for God to have an infinite nature is to have an "unspeakable and ungraspable nature" (τὴν ἄφραστόν τε καὶ ἀπερίληπτον φύσιν) (*Con. Eunom.* 3.5.55). Again it would seem that to be infinite is not to have a nature, since it is arguable that every nature is finite. To say that God has an *infinite* nature is to say that God is unlike all created things, which are finite. The word "nature" is used presumably because there is no other word that could be used. This explains why it is impossible for a human being to comprehend God.

In his *Life of Moses*, Gregory explains that paradoxically what makes the nature of God distinctive is that it has no distinctiveness: "Yet the distinctive of the Divine is to transcend all distinctions" (*Vit. Mos.* II.234).[38] Another way of expressing this is to say that the divine nature is infinite (ἀόριστον), which is then explained by means of the spatial metaphor of being that which can be "enclosed by no boundary" (οὐδενὶ περουνδαρ-ψιειγόμενον πέρατι) (*Vit. Mos.* II.236). This is impossible since what would encompass God would be greater than God, but nothing could be greater than God: "No consideration will be given to something enclosing the infinite nature" (*Vit. Mos.* II.236–38).[39] For this reason God cannot be said to be anything, since to do so would mean that God is limited insofar as God would *not* be what is outside of that limit. It follows that God as infinite differs from all things by being the negation of a thing, which is finite by definition. It is arguable that the use of the term infinite nature of God is really the denial that God has a nature. Gregory also explains that the human desire for God as the good is unlimited since God is "unlimited and infinite" (τὸ ἄπειρόν τε καὶ ἀόριστον) and there is no limit to the good (οὐδὲ τινα τοῦ ἀγαθοῦ ὅρον) (*Vit. Mos.* II.242).[40]

Gregory criticizes anyone who seeks to grasp God by means of language, since to do so is not to recognize that God is infinite and so

---

38. ἴδιον δὲ γνώρισμα τῆς θείας φύσεώς ἐστι τὸ παντὸς ὑπερκεῖσθαι γνωρίσματος.

39. οὐκ ἄρα περίληψίς τις τῆς ἀορίστου φύσεως νομισθήσεται.

40. See *In cant.* 8 "The soul progresses . . . towards the infinite" (πρὸς τὸν ἀόριστον).

The Indescribable God

transcends all things (*In eccl.* 7.411).[41] According to him, God's nature cannot be grasped because "it lacks space, time, measure and anything else we can apprehend" (*In eccl.* 7.414).[42] What he means to say is that God is indeterminate, unlike a created thing, and so cannot be described as if he were a created thing. Unlike all created things, God has no limits, or characteristics, that define him as one thing and not another. Gregory interprets Ps 145:3 (LXX 144:3) "His greatness is without limit" apophatically to mean that the divine nature cannot be grasped because it is unlimited (οὐκ ἔστι πέρας) (*In eccl.* 7.415). An unlimited nature is really no nature.

In contrast to the Arian Eunomius, Gregory insists that nothing can be truly and univocally predicated of God because this would function to limit and define, but God is without such limits and definition (*Con. Eunom.* 3.1.110). He writes about the Samaritans (John 4:20), whom he compares to Eunomius and his supporters, "But not knowing that the infinity of God exceeds all the significance and comprehension that names can furnish" (*Con. Eunom.* 3.1.110).[43] Likewise, he asserts that no term (προσηγορία) can express the unspeakable and infinite nature (ἡ ἄφραστός τε καὶ ἀόριστος φύσις) (*Con. Eunom.* 3.5.54). God's nature is infinite in the sense of being limitless and for that reason cannot be expressed in language, since language functions to limit or determine and so define. He could also have said that God as infinite has no nature. For this reason, he rejects Eunomius' method of identifying the essence of God as being ingenerate and then differentiating God's essence from that of the Son.[44] Gregory's view is that no name, or descriptor, signifying an essence can be attributed to God because God's nature is infinite, which is to say, unlimited and indefinable. He cites scriptural passages in which God's name is said not to be known or that God is not knowable to prove that the nature of God is infinite in this sense (Exod 3:13–14; 6:3; John 1:18; 1 Tim 6:16).

Gregory argues that it is not even possible to give the name "Godness" (ἡ θεότης) to God, because Godness is a name and no name can be attributed to the divine nature (ἡ θεία φύσις) since it is infinite (ἀόριστος). To give a name, or attribute, to God, even to say that God has Godness, is to

---

41. ὁ δὲ λόγῳ διαλαμβάνειν ἐπιχειρῶν τὸ ἀόριστον οὐκέτι δίδωσι τὸ ὑπὲρ πᾶν εἶναι ἐκεῖνο.

42. οὐ τόπον, οὐ χρόνον, οὐ μέτρον, οὐκ ἄλλο τι τοιοῦτον οὐδέν.

43. ἀγνοοῦντες δέ, ὅτι πάσης τῆς ἐξ ὀνομάτων σημασίας καὶ περιλήψεως ὑπερπίπτει τοῦ θεοῦ τὸ ἀόριστον.

44. Eunomius's strategy is to define God as ingenerate and then conclude that the generated son cannot therefore have the same essence as God the Father.

limit (ὁρίζειν) what cannot be limited. He explains, "That therefore which is without limit is surely not limited even by name. In order then to mark the constancy of our conception of infinity in the case of the divine nature, we say that the Deity is above every name: and 'Godness' is a name" (*Abl.* 3, 1.52–53). Gregory further explains that to be infinite is to be "above every name" (ὑπὲρ πᾶν ὄνομα), which is an allusion to an apophatic interpretation of Phil 2:9 "name above every name."

Gregory compares God to the sea and the power of human language to scooping a mere handful of water from the sea. Drawing upon Platonism, he identifies God as infinite as the first Good: "The first Good is in its nature infinite" (ἄπειρον τῇ φύσει τὸ πρῶτον ἀγαθόν) (*Con. Eunom.* 1.1.291). The first Good is the unlimited and indeterminate source of all finite goods and so is indescribable in terms of what emerges from it. Gregory asserts that there is no limit to God as Goodness. He writes, "The unlimited, in fact, is not such owing to any relation whatever, but, considered in itself, escapes limitation" (*Con. Eunom.* 1.1.236).[45] What he means is that God as infinite Goodness is not known as such by being related, or compared, to something else, since this would be a limitation on God. Rather, God is considered in himself, which makes God different from all things and therefore incomprehensible.[46] Similarly, he writes, "The Good ... transcends creation and thought" (*In eccl.* 7.412).[47] Gregory makes the same point in *Life of Moses*. He argues that God as the Good has no limit to his nature, unlike other things, which are limited by their opposites (τῇ ἑαυτοῦ φύσει ὅρον οὐκ ἔχει) (*Vit. Mos.* I.5–6). Since God as the Good, the source of all things, has no opposite, God cannot be said to be of one nature and not of another; for this reason, any form of dualism is ruled out.[48] He could just as easily have said that God has no nature.

---

45. τὸ δὲ ἀόριστον οὐ τῇ πρὸς ἕτερον σχέσει τοιοῦτόν ἐστιν, ἀλλ' αὐτὸ καθ' ἑαυτὸ νοούμενον ἐκφεύγει τὸν ὅρον.

46. On this basis he claims that his Arian opponents cannot make distinctions between the Father, Son, and Holy Spirit, since that would require comparing infinites to one another and would also deny the simplicity of God.

47. τὸ ἀγαθὸν ... ἄνω ὂν τῆς κτίσεως ἄνω ἐστὶ τῆς καταλήψεως.

48. Because the Beautiful (τὸ καλόν), synonymous with the Good, has no limit (πέρας), Gregory argues that the desire for the Beautiful can never be satisfied (*Vit. Mos.* II. 239).

The Indescribable God

Ambrose

Ambrose criticizes the Arian view of the generation of the Son on the grounds that it wrongly uses the analogy of human procreation to explain it (*De Fide* 1.63). He says that the use of this analogy is misguided because "we cannot compass the greatness of immense Godhead 'of whose greatness there is no end' (Ps 145:3) . . . in our straitened speech." The assertion that God's divinity is "immense" (*immensus*) interprets the statement in Ps 145:3 that God's greatness is without end (*cujus magnitudinis non est finis*), so that by immense Ambrose means too great ever to be understood. According to him, human language cannot express what is inexpressible, because language functions to limit, but God has no limits. It is clear that, for Ambrose, immensity is synonymous with infinity, being a functional equivalent.

Pseudo-Dionysius

Pseudo-Dionysius uses the term "infinite" in combination with other terms to express what he calls God's superessentiality, by which is meant that God is beyond all definition. He describes God as infinite greatness: "This greatness is infinite (ἄπειρον), and without measure and without number." God's infinite greatness is also described as ungraspable (ἀπερίληπτος): "And this is the preeminence as regards the absolute and surpassing flood of the ungraspable greatness." Since God, being indeterminate, is beyond all limits, God exceeds all definition and so cannot be grasped (*De div. nom.* IX.2). Likewise, God is described as "limiting every infinitude, and surpassing every limit, and by none contained or comprehended" (*De div. nom.* XIII.1).[49] Although somewhat obscure, the point seems to be that nothing limits God and so allows God to be defined *as* something. God is said to surpass every limit, which means that God cannot be said to be one thing and not another. This is why it is said that God is not contained or comprehended by anything. In other words, God cannot be understood as belonging to a higher classification and so as being an instantiation of it. For God to limit every infinitude (καπᾶσαν ἀπειρίαν ὁρίζειν) seems to mean to be beyond the type of infinity that understands God as a substratum with infinite attributes.

---

49. καὶ πᾶσαν μὲν ἀπειρίαν ὁρίζον, παντὸς δὲ πέρατος ὑπερηπλωμένον καὶ ὑπὸ μηδενὸς χωρούμενον ἢ καταλαμβανόν.

God as Infinite

The reason that God is infinite is that God is not a being among beings, but the source of all beings. Pseudo-Dionysius asserts that God is not a being relatively (πῶς ἐστιν ὤν), as one being among other beings, but is being simply and infinitely (ἁπλῶς καὶ ἀπεριορίστως). He explains this by means of a spatial metaphor: the whole is *in* God (ἐν ἑαυτῷ) (*De div. nom.* V.4). In this context, he refers to God as having "super-simplified infinity" (ὑπερηπλωμένη ἀπειρία), by which he means that God as simple, or incomposite, is not a being, but the One, unlimited source of all beings. God is described as "the essentiating progression and goodness, both penetrating all, and filling all things with its own being" (*De div. nom.* V.9).[50] What is meant is that God is not a thing, but that whereby all things exist and are what they are, through God's figurative overflow of himself ("essentiating progression and goodness"). He uses the metaphor of God's being in everything and filling everything to express the idea that God is not a thing. Pseudo-Dionysius also calls God the pre-existing, the beginning (ἀρχή) and end (τελευτή) of all things, the infinitude of all infinitude (ἀπειρία πάσης ἀπειρίας). By beginning is meant cause (αἴτιος), and by end "for whom" (τοῦ ἕνεκα), the goal; to be the infinitude of all infinitude is a superlative way of expressing God's infinity. God is further described as limit of all (πέρας πάντων) (*De div. nom.* V.10). The point is that, since God is not a being but the source of all, God is not limited in the sense of being one thing and not another; rather God as indeterminate can be said to be that which limits the all, or causes it to be what it is.[51]

Maximus the Confessor

Maximus uses the term infinite (ἄπειρος) to refer to the fact that, different from all things, God is not definable and for that reason is incomprehensible. He writes "[God] is unlimited, unmoved and infinite" (*Cent. gnost.* 1.2). The terms unlimited (ἀόριστος) and infinite (ἄπειρος) seem to be synonyms, whereas the term "unmoved" (ἀκίνητος) refers to God's immutability. The meaning of the terms "unlimited" and "infinite" is provided in

---

50. τῆς οὐσιοποιοῦ προόδου καὶ ἀγαθότητος ἀρξαμένη καὶ διὰ πάντων φοιτῶσα καὶ πάντα ἐξ ἑαυτῆς τοῦ εἶναι πληροῦσα.

51. Anselm's definition of God as "that than which nothing greater can be conceived" (*aliquid quo nihil maius cogitari possit*) is another way of expressing the infinity of God. On this quasi-definition, God is not said to be the greatest being, but unlimited or infinite in greatness.

The Indescribable God

the explanation that follows: "He is infinitely beyond all essence, potentiality, and actuality."[52] First, to be unlimited and infinite means to be beyond all essence. In other words, God has no essence in the sense of determination, or definition. Second, drawing upon Aristotelianism, Maximus asserts that God also has no potentiality (which explains the attribute of being "unmoved"); this follows from the fact that God has no essence, since to have an essence includes potentiality: what a thing may become because of what it is. Finally, God has no actuality because only an essence can be something (the term ἐνεργεία seems to mean "actuality" in the Aristotelian sense). Maximus asserts that God is "infinitely infinite," which for him removes God from every category of relation: "Being infinitely infinite, above every relation" (*Cent. gnost.* 1.7).[53] The denial of relation to God implies that God cannot be compared to or contrasted with anything, and so is imcomprehensible. In his work *Mystagogy*, Maximus says that God as infinite means that God has no quantity or parts, is without dimension and that there is no way that one can understand God's infinity according to essence (κατ' οὐσίαν) (*Myst.* 5). In other words, to be infinite is to be without definition.

John of Damascus

John of Damascus connects God's infinity with God's incorporeity and with the fact that God's essence is ungraspable. Infinity is a means of expressing God's "separation from all things" (ἐκ τῆς ἁπάντων ἀφαιρέσεως), the fact that God is "above all things" (ὑπὲρ πάντα τὰ ὄντα) and "above essence" (ὑπὲρ οὐσίαν) (*O.F.* 1.4). In other words, it expresses that God cannot be conceived as a thing that can be related to other things. He writes, "The divine therefore is infinite and ungraspable (ἄπειρον ... καὶ ἀκατάληπτον) and all that is graspable about him is his infinity and nongraspability" (*O.F.* 1.4).[54] For him, the terms "infinite" and "ungraspable" are co-ordinate in meaning, together referring to God's incomprehensibility resulting from God's lack of definition.

---

52. ὡς πάσης οὐσίας καὶ δυνάμεως καὶ ἐνεργείας ὑπερέκεινα ἀπείρως ὤν.

53. καθόλου πάσης σχέσεως ὑπάρχων ἀπειράκις ἀπείρως ἀνώτερος.

54. John Scotus Eriugena argues that even God cannot know himself because this would compromise his infinity, since the infinite is without definition and therefore "incomprehensibilis quippe in aliquo et sibi et omni intellectui" (*Periphyseon*, 589B; see 589A–C).

Paul Tillich

In the modern period, Paul Tillich uses the term "infinite" in order to assert that God cannot be limited in the sense of being one thing rather than another thing. According to him, for God to be infinite is the semantic equivalent of being the depth and ground of being, Being-itself or the power of being, expressions that are characteristic of Tillich's theological vocabulary. He writes that God "is the power of being in everything and above everything, the infinite power of being"[55] and "Everything finite participates in Being-itself and in its infinity."[56] Similarly, he asserts, "The name of this infinite and inexhaustible depth and ground of all being is God. That depth is what the word God means. And if that word has not much meaning for you, translate it, and speak of the depths of your life, of the source of your being, of your ultimate concern. . . . Perhaps, in order to do so, you must forget everything traditional that you have learned about God, perhaps even that word itself."[57] For God to be infinite is to be the "inexhaustible depth and ground of all being" and, as applied to the individual human being, "depths of your life, of the source of your being." Being infinite means that God is not a being, but rather that which makes all being possible, including human being. For this reason God is a human being's "ultimate concern." For Tillich it is advisable that human beings dispense with the anthropomorphic understanding of God as a being since God as infinite is not a being that can be comprehended.

John Macquarrie

John Macquarrie gives an existential interpretation to the second meaning of infinity. He argues that infinity is to be understood existentially, as opposed to "metaphysically," as the contrast between limited and fragile human being and Being itself, which human beings cannot measure.[58] He writes, "The word 'infinite,' when spoken of God, points to the contrast between our particular beings as 'beings-there' (*Dasein*) and Being itself as

---

55. Paul Tillich, *Systematic Theology*, vol. 1 (Chicago: University of Chicago Press, 1951), 236.

56. Ibid., 237.

57. Tillich, *The Shaking of the Foundation* (London: SCM, 1949), 63–64.

58. Macquarrie, *Principles of Christian Theology*. 2nd ed. (New York: Scribner's Sons, 1977), 204–5.

that which makes any being there possible."[59] For him, God is not a particular being ("being-there") that could be described and defined. Whether the distinction between existential and metaphysical is as precise as he thinks, however, is debatable.

CONCLUSION

In some instances, the term "infinite" is used to describe the otherness of God: God is not finite. Only a finite thing can be understood as something, a thing among other things. In this use of the term, infinite does not have the positive meaning of an infinite instantiation of communicable attributes but is the denial that God can be conceived as a thing to which attributes belong.

---

59. Ibid., 205.

7

God as Invisible

IN THE HISTORY OF Christian theology, there have been two meanings for the assertion that God is invisible. First, God's invisibility has meant that God is incorporeal, not a possible sensible object. This term is a convenient way of expressing the view that God cannot be visibly represented, and is used polemically against idolatry. Second, of significance for this investigation, the concept of God's invisibility is extended to mean that God is incomprehensible.[1] In other words, God is not a possible intelligible object.

---

1. Four times in the New Testament God is said to be invisible (ἀόρατος). In two of these it is clear that the intention is to assert that God is incorporeal, not a possible sensible object. First, Paul refers to how the invisible things of God (τὰ ἀόρατα) are known from the sensible world (Rom 1:20). What he means when he refers to the "invisible things" of God is that, contrary to the assumption of idolatry, God is incorporeal and so a visible representation of God is impossible. What can be known about God is only an inference from sensible experience. The apparent contradiction of speaking about "seeing" "the invisible things" of God is resolved by understanding "seeing" as a seeing with the mind, or understanding. Second, the author of Hebrews says that Moses "by faith left Egypt, not fearing the wrath of the king; for he endured, as if he saw the one who is invisible" (11:27). Since the intention is to admonish his readers to have a faith like that of Moses, the meaning of "invisible" in this passage is God's incorporeity: the fact that Moses could not see God with his eyes explains why he needed faith to leave Egypt. In the other two references to God's invisibility the exact meaning of the term is not provided. In the hymn that Paul quotes in Colossians, Christ, God's beloved son, is said to be the image of the "invisible God" (τοῦ θεοῦ τοῦ ἀοράτου) (Col 1:15), and in 1 Tim 1:17 Paul describes God as "the King . . . invisible" (ὁ βασιλεῦς . . . ἀόρατος). In both cases, it is not certain what is meant by the term "invisible."

The Indescribable God

In this second sense, God's invisibility becomes a means to express the otherness of God.

THE USE OF THE TERM INVISIBLE IN HELLENISM

Plato makes the distinction between the visible (ὁρατός) and intelligible (νοητός) realms (see *Rep.* 6.509d; 7.524c; *Phdo.* 79d–83c). The former is marked by *becoming* whereas the latter, the realm of the ideas and souls, is marked by *permanence* (see *Rep.* 6. 484b; 6.485a–b; 6. 500b). In middle Platonism, God, as belonging to the intelligible realm, is sometimes said to be invisible (Apuleius, *De Platone*, I, 5; Maximus of Tyre, *Dissertations* 1; see Plutarch, *Moralia*, 5.3.2; 8.4). As used in Platonism, invisible refers to God's incorporeity, although, since God as the idea of the Good is said to be beyond essence, God's invisibility indirectly implies that God is incomprehensible insofar as God is indefinable in principle.

The Greek term "invisible" (ἀόρατος) is used by Hellenistic Jews both before and after the time of the New Testament to express God's incomprehensibility and by implication God's otherness, although sometimes there is not clear distinction made between that and its meaning as incorporeal.[2] In *Sib. Or.* 3.11–12, God is said to be invisible, and this attribute is associated with being ineffable: "ineffable, dwelling in the sky, self-begotten and invisible" (ἀόρατος). Ineffability is a function of being incomprehensible, so that the association of invisibility with ineffability may imply that to be invisible is to be incomprehensible. Likewise, Philo of Alexandria uses the term "invisible" (ἀόρατος) to express God's incomprehensibility. He affirms that God, the existing one (τὸ ὄν), is not apprehended by human beings, neither perceived by the physical senses nor by the mind (οὔτ' αἴσθησιν . . . οὔτε νοῦν) (*Mut.* 7). God is neither a possible sensible object nor an intelligible object. In the same passage he interprets the dark cloud that Moses approached (Exod 20:21) as figuratively expressing "the invisible and incorporeal essence" (τὴν ἀόρατον καὶ ἀσώματον οὐσίαν) (*Mut.* 7). By calling God's essence incorporeal (ἀσώματος) Philo means that God does not have a body and so is not a possible sensible object. By calling God's essence invisible (ἀόρατος), given the context, Philo means that God is incomprehensible. So in this passage ἀόρατος is not a synonym for ἀσώματος and the phrase "invisible and incorporeal" is not a

---

2. The term ἀόρατος does not occur in the LXX in reference to God, although 2 Macc 9:5 does refer to an "invisible blow" (ἀοράτῳ πληγῇ) caused by God.

hendiadys. Likewise, Philo writes in another work, "For he [God] has not shown his nature (φύσις) to any one; but keeps it invisible to every kind of creature" (*Leg. all.* 3.206). For God's nature to be invisible (ἀόρατος) is for it not to be made known to created beings. Along the same lines, Philo equates the fact that God or God's essence (οὐσία) is grasped by no one (ἀκατάληπτος) with the fact that God is invisible (*Post.* 15–16).

GOD AS INVISIBLE IN CHRISTIAN THEOLOGY

Synopsis

Early Christian theologians take over the idea that God is invisible in the sense of being incomprehensible, not a possible intelligible object. In so doing, they use the idea of the invisibility of God as a means of expressing the otherness of God. The invisibility of God becomes part of an apophatic theology, although over time it tends to become a less important divine attribute and even omitted altogether. In the modern period, however, the assertion of God's invisibility as a means of expressing God's otherness is revived somewhat in dialectical theology and theologies antithetical to what Heidegger calls onto-theology. There are two nuances of meaning of the statement that God is invisible in the sense of being incomprehensible. In some cases it is not clear which nuance is intended and in other cases both are affirmed by the same Christian theologian. On either interpretation, however, God's otherness is established.

Sometimes it is said that for God to be invisible is to be incomprehensible in the sense of being unknowable in terms of human experience, for which reason God can be said to be other than all things. Invisibility is said to be a function of God's supremacy or depth, each of which expresses the fact that God is beyond human comprehension. Sometimes God's invisibility in this sense is directly or indirectly causally connected with the fact that God's essence or nature is inaccessible to created beings, expressed in different ways. Other, mostly negative attributes within the semantic field of invisibility include: unapproachable, ineffable, ungraspable, incomprehensible, inconceivable, immense, inaccessible, sublime, and hidden. A distinction is sometimes made between what God does, God's visible providence, energies or effects, which can be known by human beings, and God as invisible. On this basis, it is conceded that a partial and indirect knowledge of the invisible God is possible, which is presupposed by Jesus' statement in Matt 5:8, "Blessed are the poor in spirit for they shall see God." Whatever is predicated of God, however, is not what God is, because God is invisible, but what God does, which alone is visible, or knowable, to human beings. In addition, it is sometimes said that the Word of God, or the Son, can make the invisible God known to human beings.

At other times for God to be invisible is to be incomprehensible in the sense of being indefinable in principle. In other words, being invisible means not being a determinate thing that can be differentiated from other determinate things. Only God can be said to be invisible because only God in principle is not a possible intelligible object. God as invisible in this sense is causally associated with God's formlessness, being uncircumscribable and being without a circumscribed form, all of which mean that God is not one type of thing that can be differentiated from other types of things and so be defined. This is also what is meant by saying that God as invisible is beyond all and is superessential. Similarly, it is said that God as invisible has infinite depth, implying indefinability. Likewise, associated with being invisible and interpretive of it are the terms "indeterminate," "infinite," and "boundless." Each of these reinforces that for God to be invisible is to be other than all things insofar as God is not a thing among other things that can be defined. God as invisible is metaphorically said to be uncontained and to be that in which all determinate things are or are contained. This functions to separate God from all created things.

Scriptural passages used to support the view that God is invisible in the sense of being incomprehensible include: John 1:18, "No one has seen God at any time. The only-begotten God, who is in the bosom of the Father, he has declared him"; Rom 1:20, "His invisible attributes"; 1 Tim 6:16, "dwells in unapproachable light, whom no man has seen or can see"; Heb 11:27, "Him who is unseen"; Exod 20:21, "the thick cloud where God was"; Ps 89:6, "Who is he among the clouds that shall be compared unto the Lord?"; and Eccl 5:2, "For God is in heaven above, and you upon earth beneath." Also the prohibition against idolatry is interpreted as expressive of God's invisibility.

Individual Christian Theologians on God as Invisible

Irenaeus

Irenaeus uses the term "invisibility" with the meaning of being incomprehensible in the sense of being unknowable in terms of human experience. Contesting the Gnostic claim that the angels are ignorant of the supreme God (*primus deus*), he concedes that God may be invisible to them on account of his supremacy (*propter eminentiam*), but hastens to add that they could have inferred his existence from his providence (*providentia*), by which is meant what God has done (*Adv. haer.* 2.6.1).[3] What is implied is that God's invisibility is a function of God's supremacy: God is so great as to be incomprehensible in terms of human experience. Similarly, Irenaeus explains, "Because to created things the Father of all is invisible and unapproachable, therefore those who are to draw near to God must have their access to the Father through the Son" (*Demonstr.* 47; see 5, 6). The original Greek of "invisible and unapproachable" was probably ἀόρατος καὶ ἀπρόσιτος.[4] The meaning of this phrase is that God the Father is incomprehensible to human beings. This means that each term is synonymous with the other: not to be visible and not to be approachable mean to be incomprehensible.

Irenaeus qualifies his view of God's invisibility: although human beings are by nature incapable of knowing God, he holds that God can make God known to them (*Adv. haer.* 4.6.4). He interprets John 1:18, "No one has seen God at any time," to mean that, although God the Father is invisible in the sense of being incomprehensible, the Son makes God the Father known to human beings. He writes, "For he, the Son who is in his bosom, declares to all the Father who is invisible" (*Adv. haer.* 3.11.6).[5] The same

---

3. The second-century Gnostics referred to the invisibility and incomprehensibility of Buthos, see Irenaeus, *Adv. haer.* I 1.1, 3; 5.1; 14.5. 19.1–2; II 6.1; III 16.6; IV 20.5; Clement of Alexandria. *Strom.* 4.13; Tertullian, *Adv. Valen.* 7.

4. See Athanasius, *Ar.* 1.63 "And God is invisible and inaccessible to originated things" (καὶ ἔστιν ὁ θεὸς ἀόρατος καὶ ἀπρόσιτος τοῖς γεννητοῖς).

5. According to Irenaeus, the Word reveals to human beings the invisible God the Father in two ways. First, different from his Gnostic opponents, Irenaeus claims that the Word reveals God the Father through creation (*Adv. haer.* 4.6.6). In this sense it seems that the Word is being identified as reason inherent in human beings that make possible inference from effect to cause, from creation to God its creator. Second, the Word becomes incarnate and reveals God the Father through proclamation: "But by the law and the prophets did the Word preach both himself and the Father alike" (*Adv. haer.* 4.6.6).

The Indescribable God

interpretation of John 1:18 occurs elsewhere in his work. Irenaeus states that God is invisible and indescribable to human beings until the Word reveals God to them: "[God] is invisible and indescribable to all things which have been made by him, but he is by no means unknown: for all things learn through his Word that there is one God the Father, who contains all things, and who grants existence to all, as is written in the Gospel: 'No man has seen God at any time, except the only-begotten Son, who is in the bosom of the Father; he has declared [him]'" (*Adv. haer.* 4.20.6). Likewise he writes, "It is manifest that the Father is indeed invisible, of whom also the Lord said, 'No one has seen God at any time.' But his Word, as he himself willed it, and for the benefit of those who beheld, did show the Father's brightness, and explained his purposes" (*Adv. haer.* 4.20.11).[6] According to Irenaeus, the Word is the instrument of God's self-revelation; the history of this self-revelation culminates in the incarnation (see *Adv. haer.* 4.20.4; 4.24.2).

In spite of the Word's revelation of God the Father to human beings, Irenaeus explains that the Word nonetheless preserves the invisibility of the Father, by which he means that God the Father is not fully revealed, but always remains partially unknown: "For whom he made such great dispensations, revealing God indeed to men, but presenting man to God, and preserving at the same time the invisibility of the Father, lest man should at any time become a despiser of God, and that he should always possess something towards which he might advance" (*Adv. haer.* 4.20.7).[7] Irenaeus reconciles Exod 33:20 "No one shall see God and live" with Matt 5:8 "Blessed are the poor in spirit for they shall see God" by saying that, whereas no one shall see God with respect to "his greatness and his wonderful glory, for the Father is incomprehensible," human beings are allowed to know God "in regard to his love, and kindness, and as to his infinite power." The distinction is between what God is in himself and God's effects or acts that are known to human beings. It is God who makes possible this partial revelation: "For man does not see God by his own powers; but when

---

6. Manifestum est, quoniam Pater quidem invisibilis, de quo et Dominus dixit: 'Deum nemo vidit unquam.' Verbum autem ejus, quemadmodum volebat ipse et ad utilitatem videntium, claritatem monstrabat Patris, et dispositiones exponebat.

7. Propet quos fecit tantas dispositions, hominibus quidem ostendens Deum, Deo autem exhibens hominem: et invisibilitatem quidem Patris custodiens, ne quando homo fieret contemptor Dei, et ut semper haberet ad quod proficeret.

he pleases he is seen by men, by whom he wills, and when he wills, and as he wills" (*Adv. haer.* 4.20.5).[8]

Irenaeus also uses the term "invisible" to mean incomprehensible in the sense of being indefinable in principle. He asserts that God the Father is both invisible and indeterminate: "And his Word knows that his Father is, as far as regards us, invisible and indeterminate" (*Adv. haer.* 4.6.3). The pairing of "invisible" (invisibilis) with "indeterminate" (indeterminiabilis) should be taken to imply that these two terms are roughly synonymous, in which case for God to be invisible is not to be definable, since what is indeterminate is not knowable *as* anything. This is confirmed by his further statement that God the Father cannot be declared (*inenarrabilis*) (*Adv. haer.* 4.6.3). Invisibility in this context seems to refer to the fact that God is not a determinate thing that can ever be defined.

Clement of Alexandria

Clement interprets the statement in John 1:18 as expressing the idea that for God to be invisible is to be incomprehensible in the sense of being indefinable in principle. He writes, "And John the apostle says: 'No man has seen God at any time. The only-begotten God, who is in the bosom of the Father, he has declared him'—calling the bosom of God invisible and ineffable. Hence some have called it depth, as containing and embosoming all things, inaccessible and boundless" (*Strom.* 5.12).[9] Although complicated, it seems that for Clement, the "bosom" (κόλπος) of God is an anthropomorphic expression describing God as invisible (ἀόρατος) and ineffable (ἄρρητος), which are complementary terms. The bosom of God as God's invisibility and ineffability is also referred to as "depth" (βάθυν); the use of this spatial metaphor implies that God is *too* deep to be comprehended. God is also described "as containing and embosoming all things," alluding to John 1:18 "the bosom of the Father" (*Strom.* 5.12). In other words, God is the source of all things but not one of the things that originate from the source. So it follows that God cannot be compared to any of the things that he "contains" or "embosoms." This is why Clement refers to God as

---

8. In support of the possibility of God's partial self-revelation, Irenaeus cites Luke 18:27 as a proof text: "For those things that are impossible with men, are possible with God." He also sometimes speaks of an eschatological seeing of God that will result in immortality (see *Adv. haer.* 4.28.3).

9. περιειληφότα, καὶ ἐγκολπισάμενον τὰ πάντα, ἀνέφικτόν τε καὶ ἀπέραντον.

"inaccessible and boundless" (ἀνέφικτόν τε καὶ ἀπέραντον). To be boundless is to be unlimited and indefinable insofar as God is not a determinate thing comparable to other things. The reason that God is too deep to be comprehended is that, since God is boundless, there is no limit to God's depth, which explains God's inaccessibility. In addition, Clement interprets the statement in Exod 20:21 that Moses entered into the dark cloud where God was as symbolizing that God is "invisible and ineffable" (ἀόρτος ... καὶ ἄρρητος) (*Strom.* 5.12). These two terms are intended to interpret each other, in which case to be invisible means to be inexpressible (*Strom.* 5.12).

In another passage, Clement again uses the term invisible to mean incomprehensible in the sense of being indefinable in principle. He interprets the adjective invisible (ἀόρατος) as synonymous with "uncircumscribed" (ἀπερίλημτος and ἀπερίγραφος), which for him means not being identifiable as something (*Strom.* 5.11).[10] For God to be invisible is not to be a determinate thing. According to Clement, Moses expresses symbolically the fact that God is invisible and uncircumscribed by not placing an image of God in the tabernacle. He writes, "And since the gnostic Moses does not circumscribe within space him that cannot be circumscribed (τὸ ἀπερίλημτον), he set up no image in the temple to be worshipped; showing that God was invisible, and incapable of being circumscribed" (ἀόρατον καὶ ἀπερίγραφον) (*Strom.* 5.11). Along the same lines, Clement believes that Greek philosophers, especially the "truth-loving" Plato, understood what the apocryphal work cited by him as *The Preaching of Peter* affirms: "That there is one God, who made the beginning of all things, and holds the power of the end; and is the invisible one (ὁ ἀόρατος), who sees all things; incapable of being contained, who contains all things (ἀχώρατος, ὃς τὰ πάντα χωρεῖ); needing nothing, whom all things need, and by whom they are, ungraspable (ἀκατάληπτος), everlasting, unmade," etc. (*Strom.* 6.5). Being invisible and being ungraspable are closely associated and may even function as synonyms. In addition, invisibility is associated with the fact that God is "uncontained but contains all things," which is a spatial metaphor intended to portray God both as the cause of all things and at the same as being indefinable in principle. The container is not a determinate thing that could be defined, unlike the things that are contained by it.

---

10. See *Strom.* 5.6, 14.

God as Invisible

Tertullian

Tertullian sometimes uses the term "invisible" to mean incorporeal.[11] In one passage, however, he uses it to mean that God is incomprehensible in the sense of being unknowable in terms of human experience. He writes, "He is invisible, though seen, unknowable though present through his grace, inconceivable though perceived by the sense of man" (*Apol.* 1.17). Tertullian's view is that, while partially knowable to human beings, God is too great ever to be fully knowable, which he expresses by asserting that God is invisible (*invisibilis*), unknowable (*incomprehensibilis*), and inconceivable (*inaestimabilis*); these terms are intended to be roughly synonymous. He also refers to God as "immense" (*immensus*), in the sense of being too great to be knowable, from which it follows that God can only be known to God: "But that which is immense is known to itself alone" (*quod vero inmensum est, soli sibi notum est*) (*Apol.* 1.17). The term immense is another synonym for invisible, which serves to express God's inaccessibility to human comprehension.

Athanasius

Although for him it also has the meaning of incorporeal, Athanasius uses the term "invisible" with the meaning of incomprehensible in the sense of being unknowable in terms of human experience.[12] He affirms that God by nature is invisible and ungraspable (ἀόρατος καὶ ἀκατάληπτος τὴν φύσιν), and then insists that God is nothing like any created thing: "having his essence beyond all created existence" (ἐπέκεινα πάσης γενητῆς

---

11. See *Adv. Marc.* 2.27; *Adv. Prax.* 14-16, 24. According to Tertullian, God the Father becomes visible only indirectly through the works of the incarnate Son: "He only becomes visible in the Son from his mighty works (*ex virtutibus*), and not in the manifestation of his person" (*Adv. Prax.* 24). It is for this reason that Jesus reproves Philip for asking to see the Father (John 14:8-9). Tertullian holds the somewhat idiosyncratic position that the Son, because he was derived from the Father, is visible and for this reason was the object of the Old Testament theophanies (*Adv. Prax.* 14-15). He pits the version of Exod 33:13 found in the LXX "that I may know and see you" (*ut cognoscenter videam te*) against Exod 33:20 "You cannot see my face, for no one can see me and live." He concludes that both passages cannot be true unless, contrary to the Monarchians, such as Praxeas, one makes a distinction between the person of the Father, who is invisible, and the person of the Son, who is visible; God as one person cannot be both visible and invisible at the same time.

12. In his *Thalia*, Arius, whom Athanasius opposes, affirmed the invisibility of God even to the Son (see Athanasius, *Ar.* 1.6; *De syn.* 15).

οὐσίας ὑπάρχων) (*Adv. gen.* 35:1–3).[13] For him, the terms "invisible" and "ungraspable" function as synonyms. The reason that God is invisible and ungraspable is that what God is, or God's essence, is beyond the capacity of created beings to comprehend. It follows that human beings cannot truly know God and so may "miss the way to the knowledge of him" (*Adv. gen.* 35.1). For this reason God provides evidence of his existence as "maker and artificer" from the order displayed in creation, which exists insofar as God created the cosmos through his Word (*Adv. gen.* 35.1–3). Influenced by Rom 1:18–20, he writes, "For God did not take his stand upon his invisible nature . . . and leave himself utterly unknown to men; but as I said above, he so ordered creation that although he is by nature invisible he may yet be known by his works" (*Adv. gen.* 35.2). According to Athanasius, God can be said to be invisible because God's nature, what God is, is inaccessible to human beings. He cites Rom 1:20 and Acts 14:15 because he believes that these texts confirm his view that God is invisible in this sense (35.3).[14] For this reason God has provided evidence of his existence and nature indirectly through what was made. In another work, Athanasius affirms that the essence (οὐσία) of God is "invisible and ungraspable" (ἀόρατος καὶ ἀκατάληπτος), two terms that again are functional synonyms (*Decr.* 22.1). Along the same lines, he says that "God is invisible and inaccessible to created things (ἀόρατος καὶ ἀπρόσιτος τοῖς γενητοῖς), and especially to men upon earth" (*Ar.* 1.63). These two terms are likewise synonyms, so that to be invisible is to be inaccessible. For God to be inaccessible implies that God is incomprehensible to human beings, not a possible intelligible object. For this reason God the Father uses his Word to mediate his beneficence to human beings.

---

13. "He is by nature invisible and incomprehensible, having his essence beyond all created existence" (*Adv. gen.* 35.1).

14. Rom 1:20: "For the invisible things of him since the creation of the world are clearly seen, being understood by the things that are made"; Acts 14:15: "We also are men of like passions with you, and bring you good tidings, to turn from these vain things unto a living God, who made the heaven and the earth and the sea, and all that in them is, who in the generations gone by suffered all nations to walk in their own ways. And yet he left not himself without witness, in that he did good, and gave you from heaven rains and fruitful seasons, filling your hearts with food and gladness."

Hilary of Poitiers

Hilary of Poitiers uses the term "invisible" of God to mean incomprehensible, in the sense of being indefinable in principle. In an important passage, he associates the attributes of being ineffable (*ineffabilis*) and infinite (*infinitus*) with being invisible, three complementary terms for him. These are then associated with God's "unfathomable nature." He writes, "This is a true statement of the mystery of that unfathomable nature which is expressed by the Name 'Father': God invisible, ineffable, infinite" (*De Trin.* 2.6).[15] According to Hilary, God the Father has an "unfathomable nature" (*inperspicabilis natura*), by which he means that God is unknowable to human beings. The three attributes that express the fact of God's "unfathomable nature" are "invisible, ineffable, infinite." To say that God is ineffable is to say that God is indescribable, which is explained by the fact that God's unfathomable nature is infinite. For God to be infinite in this context is to be unlimited and so indefinable insofar as, according to Hilary's spatial metaphor, all things are in God, as in a container. He writes, "God is infinite, for he is not in anything, but all things are in him" (*De Trin.* 2.6).[16] For God not to be *in* anything but for all things to be in God implies that God is not a determinate thing, unlike the things that are in him. The association of being ineffable and infinite with being invisible, all of which together express God's "unfathomable nature," suggests that being invisible means that God is not a definable thing. It follows that God's nature is unfathomable in principle in the sense that it has no limits; Hilary could just as easily say that God has no nature. Hilary maintains that his position that God alone is invisible in this sense is supported by 1 Tim 6:16 "whom no man has seen nor can see" and John 1:18 "No one has seen God at any time" (*De Trin.* 4.8).[17] A few sentences later Hilary twice joins together the divine attributes of being not understandable (*incomprehensibilis*) and invisible (*invisibilis*) (along with "eternal" in the first instance and "immortal" in the second) (*De Trin.* 2.7).

---

15. A nature unapproachable, invisible, inviolable, ineffable, and infinite, endued with omniscience and omnipotence, instinct with love, moving in all and permeating all, immanent and transcendent, sentient in all sentient existence (*De Trin.* 11.4).

16. infinitus, quia non ipse in aliquot, sed intra eum omnia.

17. He objects to the Arians, who deny invisibility and other divine attributes to the son: "They are raising up this word alone as a barrier to cut off the son from his share in these attributes" (*De Trin.* 4.9).

The Indescribable God

Hilary again equates invisibility with infinity in order to express that God is incomprehensible in the sense of being indefinable in principle. He sets out to reconcile John 14:9 "He who has seen me has seen the Father also" with Col 1:15 "image of the invisible God" (*De Trin.* 8.48).[18] What is of interest for this investigation is that Hilary assumes that to be visible is to be finite in the sense of being identifiable as something and, conversely, to be invisible is to be infinite in the sense of not being identifiable as something. For him visible and finite are negative correlates of invisible and infinite. He writes, "I ask whether he is the visible likeness of the invisible God, and whether the infinite God can also be presented to view under the likeness of a circumscribed form (*per formae circumscriptae imaginem coimaginari posit ad speciem*)?" A "circumscribed form" (*forma circumscripta*) denotes a type of thing, the definition of which differentiates it from other types of things. So God as infinite and invisible is not classifiable according to a "circumscribed form," and so is not definable as anything. Finally, in another passage, Hilary attributes invisibility to God the Father, and then remarks that to human beings it is inconceivable that a being could exist as invisible: "If you say that he is invisible, a being that does not visibly exist cannot be sure of its own existence" (*De Trin.* 2.7).[19] What Hilary seems to mean is not so much that God is incorporeal but that God is indefinable. It is inconceivable to human beings that anything could exist as indefinable. This explains why in this passage being invisible is associated with being not understandable (*incomprehensibilis*),[20] and why he remarks "I am well aware that no words are adequate to describe his attributes."

Basil of Caesarea

According to Gregory of Nyssa, Basil of Caesarea teaches that God's "unapproachable and sublime nature" (τῆς ἀπροσπελάστου καὶ ὑψηλῆς φύσεως) is invisible; he means by "invisible" incomprehensible in the sense of being unknowable in terms of human experience (*Con. Eunom.* 2.1.138). Basil says that human reasoning (ἀνθρωπίνη διάνοια) is not "keen-sighted enough to see clearly what is invisible" (ὀξυωποῦσα ὡς ἐναργῶς ἰδεῖν τὸ ἀόρατον) (*Con. Eunom.* 2.1.138). He means that God

18. Hilary also quotes or alludes to Col 1:15 a few more times in discussing the status of the son: "image of the *invisible* God" (*De Trin.* 3.7; 11.4, 5; 12.24).

19. Si quod invisibilis est, caret se ipso quidquid non exstat ad visum.

20. See also *De Trin.* 2.11, 25, 31; 3.3.

is invisible, not to the physical eyes, but to the human mind. On the assumption that this summary is accurate, Basil uses the term "invisible" as to express God's incomprehensibility in terms of human experience.

Gregory of Nyssa

Gregory of Nyssa associates the attributes of invisibility, incorporeity, intangibility, and formlessness, which seem to be mutually implicative (*Con. Eunom.* 3.10.6).[21] If so, then invisibility is synonymous with formlessness (ἀνείδεον), the affirmation that God is not to be identified as any type of thing. In other words, God as invisible means that God is incomprehensible in the sense of being indefinable in principle.

Gregory also uses the term "invisible" to mean incomprehensible in the sense of being unknowable in terms of human experience. He interprets the statement that God is invisible in Heb 11:27 in an apophatic manner to mean that knowledge of the essence of God is impossible. He writes, "For so speaks the apostle of the believer, that 'he endured as seeing him who is invisible.' Vain, therefore, is he who maintains that it is possible to take knowledge of the divine essence" (τὴν θείαν οὐσίαν) (*Con. Eunom.* 2.1.93). He also cites Ps 89:6 "Who is he among the clouds that shall be compared unto the Lord?" and Eccl 5:2 "For God is in heaven above, and you upon earth beneath" as confirmation of his view that God as invisible means that God's essence exceeds the comprehension of human beings (*Con. Eunom.* 2.1.94). Along the same lines, Gregory mentions together the negative divine attributes of being intangible, immutable, and invisible and contrasts these with their opposites, which are characteristics of human beings (*Con. Eunom.* 3.10.17).[22] Again his point is that for God to be invisible is to be incomprehensible. According to Gregory, the nature of God only becomes visible indirectly through God's energies, by which is meant God's effects in the world: "For being by nature invisible, he becomes visible only in his energies, and only when he is contemplated in the things that are external to him" (*In beat.* 6).[23] To prove this point he quotes 1 Tim 6:16 "whom no one has seen or can see," which is applied to the nature of God.

21. τῶν δὲ τοιούτων οὐδὲν περὶ τὸν ἀόρατόν τε καὶ ἀσώματον καὶ ἀναφῆ καὶ ἀνείδεον καθορᾶται.

22. ὁ ἀναφής τε καὶ ἀμετάθετος καὶ ἀόρατος.

23. ὁ γὰρ τῇ φύσει ἀόρατος, ὀρατὸς ταῖς ἐνεργείαις γίνε, ἔν τισι τοῖς περὶ αὐτὸν καθορώμενος.

The Indescribable God

Gregory interprets Exod 20:21 "the thick cloud where God was" as expressing God's invisibility in the sense of being unknowable in terms of human experience. He identifies the term "bed" in Cant. 3:1 "I sought him on my bed at night" as having the allegorical meaning of a more perfect participation in the Good, and he interprets "night" as the time of darkness, which he identifies with the darkness into which Moses entered on Mount Sinai (Exod 20:21) (*In cant.* 6; 6.181). The night, or time of darkness, is allegorically interpreted to mean "the contemplation of what is invisible" (τῶν ἀοράτων ἡ θεωρία), by which is meant God. The bride, symbolizing the soul, enters into the invisible realm and is embraced by the divine night; like Moses, the soul paradoxically sees God hidden in the darkness. Later in the same text, Gregory explains that the soul first moves from the darkness to light insofar as a person in conversion abandons false, deceptive ideas about God in favor of correct ones. However, the soul can move higher still, from light to what is called "the divine darkness" (ὁ θεῖος γνόφος), to an understanding of God's invisible nature (ἡ ἀόρατος φύσις). He explains that the cloud overshadowing Mount Sinai in Exod 20:21 is symbolic of the "overshadowing of all appearance," allowing a person to become aware of "the hiddenness" of God. To overshadow all appearance (τὸ φαινόμενον) is to transcend all comprehensibility, and the hiddenness (τὸ κρύφιον) of God means God's inaccessibility to human understanding. Gregory continues, "The soul forsakes everything without, that is, appearance and graspability; the only thing left for her contemplation is the invisible and ungraspable in which God is (τὸ ἀόρατόν τε καὶ ἀκατάληπτον, ἐν ᾧ ἐστιν ὁ θεός) (*In cant.* 11.323). In this passage the terms "invisible and ungraspable" are synonyms, and stand in antithetical parallelism to "appearance and graspability" (τὸ φαινόμενον καὶ τε καταλαμβάνον). The former characterizes God: "in which God is." Gregory also states that God, represented by the bridegroom in Song of Songs, bestows upon the soul, represented by the bride, a perception of his presence, but a distinct apprehension of God escapes the soul because of God's invisible nature that lies hidden (τῷ ἀοράτῳ τῆς φύσεως ἐγκρυπτόμενος) (*In cant.* 11.324). To have an invisible nature is to be ungraspable by human understanding, which is why it is described as hidden.

The same interpretation of Exod 20:21 occurs not surprisingly in his *Life of Moses*. Gregory refers to the darkness into which Moses entered by the phrase "the invisible darkness" (ὁ ἀόρατος γνόφος) (*Vit. Mos.* II.164). It was while in the darkness that Moses was instructed in the ineffable teaching of God (ἐν τῇ ἀπορρήτῳ τοῦ θεοῦ διδασκαλίᾳ), which is the teaching that God is unknowable in terms of human experience (*Vit. Mos.* I.56). Later, when again considering the theophany in Exod 20:21, Gregory uses the synonymous term "unseen" (ἀθέατος), rather than "invisible" (ἀόρατος), and pairs it with "ungraspable" to describe the realm in which the mind "sees" God: "until it gains access . . . to the unseen and ungraspable God (*Vit. Mos.* II.163).[24] To see God is to understand that God is incomprehensible. Scriptural support for this view is found in John 1:18 "No one has seen God."

John Chrysostom

In his *On the Incomprehensible Nature of God*, Chrysostom uses the term "invisibility" to mean being incomprehensible in the sense of being unknowable in terms of human experience. For God to be invisible means that the essence of God is not known or knowable to human beings. He asks, "Do you profess to know accurately the essence of the invisible God?" (*De incomp.* 2.50).[25] He includes invisibility among several other divine attributes: "Let us call upon him, then, as the ineffable God who is inconceivable, invisible, ungraspable, who transcends the power of human speech" (*De incomp.* 3.5).[26] God as invisible is functionally equivalent to being ineffable; likewise God is different from all things insofar as God transcends the power of human speech.

Pseudo-Dionysius

Pseudo-Dionysius uses the term "invisible" of God to mean being incomprehensible in the sense of being indefinable in principle. He writes, "And enters into the altogether impalpable and invisible, being wholly of the one who is beyond all" (*Mys. th.* I.3). For God to be "beyond all" (ὁ πάντων ἐπέκεινα) is not to be a determinate thing. Because God is beyond all, God is impalpable and invisible, which is to say indefinable. In *Ep.* 5, he identifies the divine darkness (ὁ θεῖος γνόφος), an allusion to LXX Exod 20:21,

---

24. ἕως ἂν διαδύῃ . . . πρὸς τὸ ἀθέατόν τε καὶ ἀκατάληπτον κἀκεῖ τὸν θεὸν ἴδῃ.

25. καὶ τοῦ ἀοράτου θεοῦ μετὰ ἀκριβείας ἐπαγγέλλῃ τὴν οὐσίαν εἰδέναι;

26. καλῶμεν τοίνυν αὐτὸν τὸν ἀνέκφραστον, τὸν ἀπερινόητον θεόν, τὸν ἀόρατον, τὸν ἀκατάληπτον, τὸν νικῶντα γλώττης δύναμιν ἀνθρωπίνης.

The Indescribable God

"And Moses entered into the darkness," with the unapproachable light in which God dwells, an allusion to 1 Tim 6:16, "dwells in unapproachable light, whom no man has seen or can see." God is said paradoxically both to be darkness and to dwell in unapproachable light. Pseudo-Dionysius states that God as darkness is invisible[27] "on account of the surpassing brightness."[28] He adds that God is unapproachable "because of the superessential stream of light" (δι' ὑπερβολὴν ὑπερουσίου φωτοχυσίας) emanating from God. The light is called superessential because God is beyond essence insofar as God is not a determinate thing among other things; this is what it means for God to be invisible.

Gregory Palamas

Gregory Palamas uses the term "invisible" (ἀόρατος) to refer to the fact that God is incomprehensible in the sense of being unknowable in terms of human experience. According to his theory of human cognition, knowledge comes through union with its object by means of contact, either sensible or intellectual contact. Applying this theory to the vision of God's uncreated light, one of the energies of God, he concludes that there must be an intellectual, or better, spiritual union by means of which there is contact between a human being and the illuminations (πρὸς τὰς ἐλλάμψεις), which he compares to the rays of the sun (*Triads* III.ii.14). Gregory insists, however, that there is no contact with the divine essence: "But the divine essence is in itself beyond all contact" (ἡ δὲ οὐσία τοῦ θεοῦ ἀνέπαφος καθ' ἑαυτὴν). If there is no contact with it, it follows that there can be no union with or knowledge of the essence of God. He makes the same point by affirming that the essence of God is invisible: "But the essence of God is completely invisible" (ἡ δὲ οὐσία τοῦ θεοῦ ἀόρατός ἐστι παντάπασι), in contrast to the unoriginate and endless rays, by which is meant the illuminations. The latter is not to be identified with the former but is its energy: "There is therefore an eternal light other than the essence of God; it is not itself an essence—far from it—but is an energy of that superessential" (ἐνέργεια τῆς ὑπερουσιότητος ἐκείνης).

---

27. Possibly alluding to 1 Tim 1:17, "the King eternal, immortal, *invisible*"
28. καὶ ἀοράτῳ γε ὄντι διὰ τὴν ὑπερέχουσαν φανότητα.

Karl Barth

In the modern period, Karl Barth includes the invisibility of God as an expression of the hiddenness of God, along with God's incomprehensibility and ineffability (*CD* 2/1:179–204). He writes, "God is known by God and by God alone" (*CD* 2/1:179) and "God is invisible. He is invisible to the physical eye of man; he is also invisible to the so-called spiritual. He is not identical to any of the objects which can become the content of the images of our external or internal perception" (*CD* 2/1:190). Clearly, by the hiddenness of God he means that God is incomprehensible in the sense of being unknowable in terms of human experience. Barth distinguishes his position, however, from the "older theology," by claiming that the latter, in spite of its claim, does not actually consider God to be hidden, i.e., incomprehensible, invisible, and ineffable. He writes, "We must not, therefore, base the hiddenness of God on the inapprehensibility of the infinite, the absolute, that which exists in and of itself, etc. For all this in itself and as such . . . is the product of human reason in spite of and in its supposed inapprehensibility" (*CD* 2/1:188). He explains that to know an object is to possess it, so that the one who claims to know God even as "inapprehensible" claims a unity between the possessor and the possessed (i.e., God), which is a form of idolatry: "Between God and man, as between God and the creature in general, there consists an irrevocable otherness. Because this is so, because the mystery of unity underlying all our other apprehension does not exist here, we cannot conceive God of ourselves" (*CD* 2/1:189). As Barth repeatedly states, because human beings have no innate capacity to know God, God can only be known by faith in his revelation in Jesus Christ: "God reveals Himself to us and therefore makes Himself object to us" (*CD* 2/1:182). God is both the *terminus a quo* and *terminus ad quem* of the knowledge of himself. He explains further, "But we ourselves have no capacity for fellowship with God. Between God and us there stands the hiddenness of God, in which He is far from us and foreign to us except as He has of himself ordained and created fellowship between Himself and us—and this does not happen in the actualising of our capacity, but in the miracle of His good pleasure" (*CD* 2/1:182). The capacity to know God is given by revelation, and is not natural to human beings. In this section Barth seems to imply that the hiddenness of God is not epistemological but soteriological insofar as this hiddenness is viewed as judgment (*CD* 2/1:191–92). At any rate, why Barth thinks that theologians who claim that God is incomprehensible are somehow knowing God and therefore do not know the true God, the knowledge of whom only comes by revelation, is not clear. In fact, it is arguable that there could be no revelation unless human beings have some innate pre-understanding of God. However, this is anathema to Barth, who rejects all general, or natural, revelation.

Jean Luc Marion

In very recent times, Jean Luc Marion makes use of the term "invisible" to express the incomprehensibility of God in the sense of being unknowable in terms of human experience. He does so with his own unique and sometimes opaque vocabulary, originating in his phenomenological analysis. He distinguishes between the idol and the icon, which are "two modes of apprehension of the divine invisibility."[29] Unlike the idol, the icon is not seized by our gaze, but gazes upon us all the while remaining invisible. He writes, "Whereas the idol results from the gaze that aims at it, the icon summons the sight in letting the visible . . . be saturated little by little with the invisible."[30] An object becomes an idol when, insofar as it is gazed upon (*regarder*), it assumes the function of representing the divine for the one gazing. The icon is also gazed upon but, unlike the idol, it never loses its invisibility, by which is meant that the divine is never fully revealed by the icon but remains hidden behind it, as it were. Marion interprets Col 1:15, "*eikon* of the invisible God," as meaning that God always remains invisible in spite of the fact that Christ is the visible *eikon* of God. This is because God is "unenvisageable," by which is meant incomprehensible by nature and therefore inaccessible to human intentionality. By contrast, the idol functions metaphorically like a mirror merely reflecting back the gaze (*regarde*) to the one who gazes; there is no awareness, however, that the gaze sees merely its own reflection, rather than God who is "invisible," which is to say, not a possible object of human intentionality.

Marion also uses the concept of infinity in conjunction with that of invisibility to explain the difference between an idol and an icon. He writes, "The icon summons the gaze to surpass itself by never freezing on a visible,

---

29. Jean-Luc Marion, *God Without Being* (Chicago: University of Chicago Press, 1991), 9; Jean-Luc Marion, *Dieu sans l'être*. 2nd ed. (Paris: Press Universitaires de France, 2002), 18: "deux modes d'appréhension du divin dans la visibilité."

30. Marion, *God Without Being*, 17; Marion, *Dieu sans l'être*, 28 "Tandis que l'idole résulte du regarde qui la vise, l'icône convoque la vue, en laissant le visible . . . peu à peu se saturer d'invisble."

God as Invisible

since the visible only presents itself here in view of the invisible. The gaze can never rest or settle if it looks at an icon; it always must rebound upon the visible in order to go back in it up the infinite stream of the invisible. In this sense, the icon makes visible only by giving rise to an infinite gaze."[31] Infinite is used in this context to mean inexhaustible and incomprehensible, so that an infinite gaze is one that never identifies God, who is invisible, or incomprehensible, with anything that is visible, or comprehensible. According to Marion, concepts can be either idolatrous or iconic depending on whether the human gaze is "frozen" or not.[32] A theological formulation is an idol ("frozen") when it limits the divine to the scope of the human gaze. In other words, idolatrous theological formulations are those that purport to define God according to the predicates of Being, or human conceptual categories, such as *causa sui*, *prima causa* or moral god; this is referred to as onto-theology, a term that derives from Heidegger. By contrast, an iconic formulation preserves the invisibility, or infinite depth, of God. He writes, "The only concept that can serve as an intelligible medium for the icon is one that lets itself be measured by the excessiveness of the invisible that enters into visibility through infinite depth."[33] He contrasts the act of using a concept in order to "determine an essence" with using it to "determine an intention." In his judgment, a concept should function only to determine the intention of the invisible that manifests itself in the visible. He writes, "It is not a question of using a concept to determine an essence but of using it to determine an intention—that of the invisible advancing into the visible and inscribing itself therein by the very reference it imposes from this visible to the invisible."[34] In other words, God uses human concepts in order to reveal who he is, but these concepts are never adequate to their object—they never "determine an essence." Rather they determine an intention in the sense that they function to point to the invisible, or unknowable, God. He further explains, "I am attempting to bring out the absolute freedom of

---

31. Marion, *God Without Being*, 18; Marion, *Dieu sans l'être*, 29.

32. Marion, *God Without Being*, 22–24; Marion, *Dieu sans l'être*, 35–37.

33. Marion, *God Without Being*, 23; Marion, *Dieu sans l'être*, 35–36 "Ne peut server de support—intelligible— à l'icône qu'un concept qui admette de se laisser mesurer à la démesure de l'invisible qui entre en visibilité par la profondeur infinie, donc qui lui-même dise ou promette de dire cette profondeur infinie." See also "distance of infinite depth" and (ibid., 23) "indeterminable by concept" (ibid., 23).

34. Marion, *God Without Being*, 23; Marion, *Dieu sans l'être*, 36 "Il ne s'agit pas de determiner par concept une essence, mais une intention—celle de l'invisible s'avançant dans le visible, et s'yinscrivant par le revoi meme qu'il impose de ce visible à l'invisible"

The Indescribable God

God with regard to all determinations, including, first of all, the basic condition that renders all other conditions possible and even necessary—for us, humans, the fact of Being."[35] God can never be described univocally by using conceptual categories derived from human experience ("the fact of Being").

CONCLUSION

The otherness of God is sometimes expressed by asserting that God is invisible. To be invisible is not to be a possible intelligible object for the human understanding, which thereby makes God incomprehensible. There are two senses in which God as invisible is said to be incomprehensible. First, God is incomprehensible in the sense of being unknowable in terms of human experience. In other words, God is beyond human capacity to understand. Second, God as invisible is incomprehensible in the sense of being indefinable in principle. God is not a determinate thing that can be comprehended. Both uses of the term invisible express the otherness of God.

---

35. Marion, *God Without Being*, xx.

8

Other Possibilities of Expressing the Otherness of God

IN THEIR THEOLOGICAL METHOD, Christian theologians make use of Greek philosophical concepts in order to give expression to the biblical teaching about the otherness of God, being anticipated in this by Hellenistic Jewish exegetes. With some exceptions, it is agreed that Plato, Aristotle, and other Greek philosophers provide the church with a valuable service by making available useful conceptual tools by which to articulate biblical content more clearly. Using this same rationale, Christian theologians could effect a synthesis of biblical teaching about the otherness of God with philosophical traditions other than those inherited from Greek philosophy. Three possibilities will be considered from Chinese and Indian philosophy. In each case, a point of contact with biblical revelation provides a conceptual bridge to move from one to the other.

THE TAO

The central philosophical concept of Taoism is the Tao (Way), also called the one, which in many ways is the functional equivalent of the apophatic God in Christian theological tradition. There are numerous parallels between what is said, or better, *not* said about the Tao and Christian depictions of the otherness of the God. For this reason it would be possible to

The Indescribable God

borrow Taoist concepts in order to expand and clarify biblical teaching about the otherness of God.

The Tao is a creative principle, "the originator of heaven and earth" (*Tao te Ching* 1.3). Also in agreement with biblical teaching, the Tao is indefinable and incomprehensible: "The Tao that can be trodden is not the enduring and unchanging Tao. The name that can be named is not the enduring and unchanging name" (*Tao te Ching* 1.1). By naming is meant delineating the nature of something, defining a thing by comparing and contrasting it with other things. However, it is impossible to delineate the nature of the Tao since it is before all such delineations. Implicit is the assertion that the Tao is beyond all linguistic distinctions. Any named "Tao" is no Tao at all, since the Tao is other than all the things that originate from it. The Tao is also described as a thing "undefined and complete," meaning that, although it encompasses all things, it is indistinct, not being identifiable as one or more of those things (*Tao te Ching* 25.1). The result is that one cannot say what the Tao is, for to define it one would have to identify it as something, which the Tao is not, since ontologically it is before all things. The Tao is called "still" and "formless," which is a way of describing its lack of characteristics or specificity, for to be still and formless is to be undetectable by the mind (*Tao te Ching* 25.1). The author explains that, since he does not know its name, for want of a better term he will call it the Tao. Thus the name Tao itself is only an artifice, an intellectual construct, created for practical purposes, because naming implies differentiating and the Tao is undifferentiated. The Tao can also be given the makeshift name "the great" (*Tao te Ching* 25.2). Being great, it is also described as becoming remote or receding, which means that it eludes detection and definition. Or it may describe how things come into being and then pass out of being, returning to the Tao. The coming into being of a thing is becoming remote from the Tao in the sense that the thing is a determinate thing whereas the Tao is not; but when it ceases to be, the thing returns to the Tao insofar as it loses its ontological determinateness.

The Tao is said to be empty, which means that it is devoid of all predicates insofar as to be something it would have to be differentiated from other things (*Tao te Ching* 4.1). This is impossible, however, since everything comes from it and the Tao cannot be like anything that comes from it. Emptiness is the absence of all positive attributes: the Tao is not a thing. In other words, emptiness is a way of describing the nature of the Tao by saying nothing about it: it is other and incomprehensible. The Tao is compared

Other Possibilities of Expressing the Otherness of God

to the emptiness of a vessel, inasmuch as the Tao is not a thing but is what causes things to be, just like the vessel would not be a vessel without its emptiness. Without empty space a pot or cup would be merely a lump of clay, so likewise without the emptiness of the Tao no-thing would exist (see *Tao te Ching* 11). It is recommended that "in our employment of it we must be on our guard against all fullness," which means that a human being must not speak about the Tao as if it were a thing among other things, rather than the "emptiness" that makes all things what they are. Similarly, it is affirmed of the Tao: "How deep and unfathomable it is." The Tao is opaque to human understanding and cannot really be said to exist in the same way that its differentiations can be said to exist. The author adds, "I know not whose son it is. It might appear to have been before God." He means that, although he does not know its origin, the Tao appears to precede God ontologically, so that Tao is the cause of God. The God he is referring to is the God of human conception and creation, the God who is the subject of discourse, what Christian theologians might refer to as the energies or effects of God.

In the discourse known as "The Great Supreme" in the *Chuang tsu*, the Tao is described as having "its inner reality and its evidences" (*Chuang tsu* 4.3). The former is what the Tao is, which is inaccessible to human comprehension, whereas the latter denotes all the things that come from the Tao and give evidence of this inner reality. It is explained that the Tao "is devoid of action and of form," by which is meant that the Tao has no identifying attributes. It is further said that the Tao "may be transmitted, but cannot be received; it may be obtained, but cannot be seen" (*Chuang tsu* 4.3). What is being described is the Tao's incomprehensibility and ineffability; the Tao may be transmitted or obtained, in the sense of understanding what the Tao does, which provides evidence of the Tao, but this is not the same as seeing or receiving the Tao in the sense of comprehending the Tao. The Tao is further said to be "based in itself, rooted in itself," which precludes access to it.

The parallels between the Tao and the biblical God are so close that it would be natural and even inevitable in some cultural contexts that Taoist concepts would be borrowed in order to express the otherness of the biblical God. In this case, the stress would be on God as the indefinable source of all things. A point of contact between the concept of the Tao and biblical tradition that would facilitate the identification of the two is the use of the term "way" (דרך) (Exod 33:13; Ps 77:13) or "ways" (דרכים) (Isa 55:8–9) in the latter to describe what YHWH is, or YHWH's essence or nature. YHWH's way and ways are inaccessible to human beings, which expresses

YHWH's otherness. It would be a natural step to move from the way and ways of YHWH to YHWH as the Way (Tao), in the same way that YHWH as good becomes the good in early Christian theology. God is the Way, the incomprehensible and ineffable source of all things.

BRAHMAN

In the *Upanishads*, Brahma, the Vedic god of creation, becomes Brahman, the source and support of all things, shorn of all mythological and idolatrous elements. There are conceptual parallels between the concept of Brahman in the Upanishads and the biblical God, YHWH. If they had access to the *Upanishads*, Christian theologians may conceivably have drawn upon Vedantic reflections about Brahman in order to express the otherness of God more fully. It would be no theological stretch to refer to YHWH in terms used of Brahman. However, just as with Greek philosophy, Christian theologians could reject certain parts of Indian philosophy without rejecting the whole. In particular, they would be adverse to the monistic identification of Brahman with Atman in the *Upanishads*: "You are that" (*tat tvam asi*), as well as the tolerance shown to popular idolatry.[1]

In *Kena-Upanishad* 1.5–9, the gods that the unenlightened person worships are contrasted unfavorably with Brahman, just as in the biblical tradition YHWH is said to be absolutely unlike the other gods. Different from the anthropomorphic gods of the unenlightened, Brahman does not think, see, hear or breathe. Rather Brahman is conceived as different from all the multiplicity of things, even human beings; it is inexpressible by speech, being incomprehensible. Yet Brahman is said to be the source and support of all things, expressed poetically as that by which speech is possible, that by which the mind thinks, that by which the eyes and ears function and that which enables breathing. In the same text, it is said paradoxically that Brahman is known only by the one who knows that Brahman is unknown: "It is known to him to whom it is unknown; he to whom it is known does not know it. It is unknown to those who know, and known to those who know not" (*Kena-Upanishad* 2.3).

The reason that Brahman is unknown is that as the first principle of all things it is beyond all human experience: "that which is without sound,

---

1. Origen refuses to identify the God of the Old Testament with pagan high gods, such as Jupiter. He holds that behind all idols are demons masquerading as gods (*Con. Cels.* 5.46). See Lactantius, *D.I.* 2.1; 3.10.

Other Possibilities of Expressing the Otherness of God

without touch, without form, without decay, without taste, eternal, without smell, without beginning, without end, beyond the great, and unchangeable" (*Katha-Upanishad* 3.15). Brahman is beyond any predicate, even a predicate that one would attribute to a god; the result is that nothing can be said univocally about Brahman. That which is ontologically before all things cannot be understood in terms of the things that come after it and depend upon it. Similarly, in *Mundaka Upanishad* 1.1.6–7, Brahman is described as "that which cannot be seen, nor seized, which has no family and no caste, no eyes nor ears, no hands nor feet, the eternal, the omnipresent (all-pervading), infinitesimal, that which is imperishable, that which the wise regard as the source of all beings." Brahman is not like anything in ordinary experience ("no family and no caste, no eyes nor ears, no hands nor feet"), and therefore cannot be seen or seized in the sense of being comprehended. Brahman is not a god in the traditional, polytheistic sense; rather, Brahman is eternal, omnipresent, infinitesimal—in the sense of not being easily recognized—and imperishable. As imperishable, the source of all things, Brahman creates the world from itself analogously to the way that a hair grows from a head and a spider spins a web. These similes communicate that Brahman is the supporting source of all things without being a thing among other things.

Given the obvious parallels between the Bible and the Upanishads, it would not be surprising to find Christian theologians borrowing from the *Upanishads* in order to explicate more clearly their position on the otherness of God, in the same way that Greek philosophical concepts were appropriated at a much earlier period. A point of contact between Brahman in the *Upanishads* and the Bible would be the rejection of idolatry as absurd. Both the Hebrew Bible and the *Upanishads* agree that a visible representation of the one God is impossible. In the Hebrew Bible, however, it is never fully explained why idolatry, which is always connected with polytheistic beliefs, is wrong. The absurdity of fetishism, the attribution of supernatural powers or presence to a manufactured object, is exposed by the prophets (Isa 2:8; 17:8; Jer 1:16; Hab 2:18–19; Hos 14:3), but why a more enlightened, non-fetish idolatry is not possible is not explicitly provided. The depiction of Brahman in the *Upanishads* therefore would provide Christian theologians with a fuller explanation of the absurdity of idolatry: God as other than all things cannot be depicted as something sensible.[2] From this initial

---

2. Of course, unlike the Old Testament, the *Upanishads* are tolerant of polytheism and its attendant idolatry, viewing it as unenlightened rather than reprehensible. What

point of contact, more parallels could be established between Brahman and YHWH.

EMPTINESS IN MAHAYANA BUDDHISM

Christian theologians could appropriate the Mahayana Buddhist teaching about emptiness (*sunyata*) in order to refine the biblical teaching about the otherness of God. In Mahayana Buddhism all things, or dharmas, are said to be empty, or devoid, of "marks" (*lakana*), or attributes of true existence. In other words, everything is empty or devoid of own-being (*svabhana*) (sometimes translated as "self-nature") insofar as they are impermanent.[3] The *Heart Sutra* asserts, "All dharmas are marked with emptiness. They do not appear or disappear, are not tainted or pure, do not increase or decrease." Only that which has own-being can receive attributes and therefore be the true subject of predicates; only it has true individuality, or self-identity.

---

a worshipper erroneously thinks is a distinct god or goddess is actually a manifestation of Brahman (*Brhadaranyaka Upanishad* 4.6). Christian theologians would not be sympathetic to this tolerance, but, as Athanasius does, responding to a similar view in the Greco-Roman world, reject any accommodation to idolatry (*Adv. gen.* 2.19). The so-called gods in Jewish and Chrstian understanding are actually demons.

3. The Buddha's teaching of the Chain of Causation or Dependent Origination is the presupposition of the Mahayana concept of emptiness (*sunyata*). In the Pali canon, the Chain of Causation or Dependent Origination is applied in particular to human beings to explain how they are what they are in the present and how they can escape from samsara in the future; the goal of this sort of anthropological analysis is to provide insight into the ultimate empty nature of any conception of the self, which is the presupposition of the cessation of craving. What is applied primarily to the individual in the Pali canon, however, is applied to all dharmas in the Mahayana sutras. Whatever dharmas that exist in the phenomenal world (or samsara) are what they are only by virtue of being conditioned by (or dependent on) other dharmas. In the *Avatamsaka Sutra* (*Flower Garland Sutra*), the conditioned nature of all dharmas is compared to the Jewel Net of Indra, which is a net extending in all directions infinitely. The net has a multifaceted jewel at each vertex that is reflected in all the other jewels; in addition the reflections are also reflected in each jewel. This reflectivity gives the collection of jewels its brilliance. The point is that all the jewels are co-dependent for their quality of brilliance, just as all dharmas are co-dependent on all other dharmas for their existence and identities. The assumption is that only that which is permanent has own-being and for that reason can be said to exist in a real sense; only that which is unconditioned can be permanent. All dharmas are without own-being (*asvabhana*), because nothing exists in a state of permanence and independence. They have come into being as conditioned (or caused) and will in turn condition other things to come into being. This is the more profound truth of the Buddha's teaching about the Chain of Causation or Dependent Origination.

Other Possibilities of Expressing the Otherness of God

Dharmas, however, as already indicated, lack own-being, and so nothing can be affirmed nor denied about them, since they are not true subjects.

In Mahayana Buddhist texts, there is a subtle back and forth movement between speaking of the emptiness of all dharmas and speaking about emptiness as the unconditioned and permanent, what Western philosophers would call the first principle or Absolute and what Christian theologians would call God. In other words, the Mahayanist is not simply claiming that all dharmas lack own-being, or true existence, because of their conditioned and impermanent nature, but also that emptiness itself, which characterizes all dharmas, is that which is independent and unconditioned and so truly exists. For example, the *Prajnaparamita Sutra in 8000 Lines* states opaquely, "And being empty, such are also inexhaustible of emptiness. And what is emptiness is also immeasurableness" (*Prajnaparamita Sutra* 18). When it is said that the own-being of dharmas is empty what is also meant is that all dharmas are manifestations of emptiness as first principle.[4] Since they are all empty (*sunya*), dharmas are all the same (*sama*) by virtue of being empty. In other words, they are all manifestations of the same emptiness, the unconditioned and permanent source of all conditioned and impermanent dharmas. That which supports dharmas is appropriately called emptiness, since nothing can be affirmed or denied of it. In other words, emptiness is no dharma, but the "cause" of all dharmas.[5]

It would be useful for Christian theologians in certain socio-linguistic contexts to make use of the concept of emptiness in their attempt to explicate the biblical teaching of the otherness of God. In spite of all the obvious differences between them, a point of contact between Mahayana Buddhism and the Bible is the latter's assertions about the nature of God's existence as compared to created beings. In the Bible, God is distinguished from all beings because of the former's permanence; for this reason God is unlike all types of beings and so is incomprehensible. First, other gods are said to be nothing like YHWH. YHWH declares through the prophet Isaiah, "I am he" (אני הוא), and then states in parallelism, "Before me there was no god formed, and after me there will be none" (43:10). For YHWH to say "I am he" is to say he alone is God and there are no other true gods (see Deut 32:39). Whatever their nature, the other gods are nothing like

---

4. This is not far from Augustine's view that there is nothing contrary to God as being (*Fide et symb.* 4.6–7; *Civ. Dei* 12.2). He could easily have said that God is emptiness.

5. In the Pali Canon, nirvana is described as "not-born, not-brought-to-being, not-made, not-conditioned," which explains why nirvana is sometimes used in Mahayana Buddhism as a synonym for emptiness (*Udana* VIII. 3).

The Indescribable God

YHWH. There has never been, nor can there ever be, a rival god because only YHWH is permanent: there is no god before YHWH and any so-called god that arises after YHWH could not be a true rival to YHWH since such a being would not have permanence. The same thing is meant by the declaration "I, I, am YHWH" (43:11). Second, when compared to God, human beings are said not truly to exist by comparison. This is expressed poetically by comparing them to short-lived grass and flowers: "All flesh is grass, and all its loveliness is like the flower of the field. The grass withers, the flower fades . . ." (Isa 40:6b–7a; cf. Job 14:2; Ps 103:15; Jas 1:10–11; 1 Pet 1:24–25). In Israel's climate, the luxuriant growth of pasture lands dies back during the hot, dry summer. This becomes a metaphor of impermanence, applied in particular to "all flesh," by which is meant all human beings. Likewise, James compares human beings to a mist (ἀτμίς), which "appears for a little while and then vanishes away" (Jas 4:14). The inconstancy and impermanence of a mist is an appropriate metaphor for human existence as compared to that of God. Put into Mahayanist terms, unlike God, all beings are empty of own-being (*svabhana*) insofar as they are impermanent. By extension, God could be called emptiness first, because God is other than all things, being nothing like any being, a god or a human being, and second, because God is the source of all emptiness, or dharmas. God is the emptiness of all things or the permanent and unconditioned source of all impermanent and conditioned beings, or dharmas.